Plain English Please

PLAIN
ENGLISH
PLEASE

Gregory Cowan

Elisabeth McPherson

CLARK COLLEGE

WITH THE ASSISTANCE OF

Glenn Leggett

GRINNELL COLLEGE

RANDOM HOUSE NEW YORK

The authors are grateful to the following publishers for permission to quote from the works listed:

DOUBLEDAY & COMPANY, INC.: Peter L. Berger, *Invitation to Sociology: A Humanistic Perspective,* copyright © 1963 by Peter L. Berger.

HARPER & ROW, Publishers: E. B. White, *Here is New York,* copyright 1949 by The Curtis Publishing Company.

HOLT, RINEHART AND WINSTON, INC.: Richard D. Altick, *Preface to Critical Reading,* 4th Edition, copyright © 1960 by Holt, Rinehart and Winston, Inc.

HOUGHTON MIFFLIN COMPANY: Norman L. Munn, *Psychology: The Fundamentals of Human Adjustment,* 1946.

THE MACMILLAN COMPANY: Ashley Montagu, *The Natural Superiority of Women,* copyright 1953 by The Macmillan Company.

MC GRAW-HILL BOOK COMPANY: Konrad Bates Krauskopf, *Fundamentals of Physical Science,* 2nd Edition, copyright 1948, McGraw-Hill Book Company.

DAVID MC KAY COMPANY, INC.: Vance Packard, *The Hidden Persuaders,* 1957.

THE NEW REPUBLIC: "T.R.B. from Washington," October 24, 1964.

OXFORD UNIVERSITY PRESS, INC.: Samuel Eliot Morison and Henry Steele Commager, *The Growth of the American Republic,* 1942.

PRENTICE-HALL, INC.: Martin Bernstein, *An Introduction to Music,* 2nd Edition, © 1951, Prentice-Hall, Inc.

SATURDAY REVIEW: John Ciardi, "Manner of Speaking," December 12, 1964; James K. Feibleman, "What Happens in College," October 20, 1962.

THIS WEEK MAGAZINE: "See America Now," April 11, 1965, copyright 1965 by the United Newspapers Magazine Corporation.

THE WORLD BOOK ENCYCLOPEDIA: "Boll Weevil," Vol. 2, copyright © 1965 by Field Enterprises Educational Corporation.

THE WORLD PUBLISHING COMPANY: Charlton Laird, *The Miracle of Language,* copyright 1953 by Charlton Laird.

ACKNOWLEDGMENTS

The authors wish to thank all the members of the Clark English Department, who have been generous with criticisms and suggestions, and particularly Richard Hawkins, who gave us a great deal of help in the early stages of the book. Further, had it not been for the forbearance of our families, who amiably assumed more than their share of homework, and the friendship of Barbara Relyea of Washington State University, who gave up several perfectly good vacations to help with the manuscript, the book could not have been written.

Table of Contents

CHAPTER **IV**

What Do You Mean? Explaining   65

CHAPTER **V**

Telling What Happened: Objective Reports   111

Appendixes

Appendixes

Plain English Please

I

A Note to the Student Who Will Use This Book

We might as well begin by facing the facts: you would not be starting this book unless it can be fairly said that you are "not very good in English," by which we mean that you are not very good at writing, and perhaps not highly skilled in reading either.

There may be many reasons why your writing is below college standard. Probably you didn't like English. Maybe you didn't see any sense to all that grammar and thought you would never need it; you may even be inclined to blame your high school teachers and think that if they had only "made" you work a little harder, you would have been better off. But very likely these teachers put all the pressure on you that they had time for or that you were willing to accept. It is also very likely that nothing or nobody could have made you learn to write well when you were more interested in watching television or playing ball or going out on dates. Certainly nothing can help you improve your writing now unless you really want to improve.

Well, why should you want to improve? You have been speaking English for years, writing it for almost as long, and probably you think you can write and talk well enough. When you ask for a hamburger, you get a hamburger. When you say, "Fill it up with regular," you never get kerosene. And last summer during your vacation, if you managed to get off a postcard, your message, "Having a wonderful time; wish you were here," was clear enough. So why are the unsympathetic college authorities making you take English again? Are they all sadistic monomaniacs, bent on your total frustration? As a matter of fact, they have sound reasons for requiring more English, quite apart from any sadism or monomania. Before this course is over we hope you will be convinced that the reasons are good. We hope you will discover that you want to do more than just "get along."

To succeed in college you will need to do more reading and writing than you are used to doing. In many courses you will be expected to own a textbook or two and to read fifty pages or so between class meetings. And not only will you have to remember snatches and grabs of what you have read, you will have to understand and be able to discuss the main points. Further, if you want a good grade, you will have to see how the main points of each assignment fit into the whole idea of the course. You will have to show that you see these relationships by writing clear, orderly explanations on your tests and in your papers.

In other words, you don't need English simply for English class, for it is not an end in itself, even though you may have run across some people who thought it was. English is a tool that you will need in your other classes. Fortunately, your other classes will help you to improve in English. When you read an assignment in biology or history, the main value for you will come from your increased understanding of biological detail, of the sweep of history and the clash and strife of political forces. And if you read well, you will get some extra value. You will be learning to improve your writing by a kind of transfer process or osmosis. What you read will show you how other writers express themselves, and your reading will suggest to you ways of organizing your own ideas, arranging your sentences, and presenting your ideas clearly and forcefully.

What we are saying is that reading well will help you write well. The two skills are so intertwined that almost no one who reads well writes badly. So if you want to read well, the answer is to read—and read and read and read. It does make some difference what you read, for some books and articles will be more valuable to you than others. But it is better to read anything than nothing. It is the habit of reading that you need.

Just as the habit of reading is the only route to reading improvement, so nothing but the habit of writing will teach you to write well. Of the two, writing well takes much the greater effort. When you write, you must find your own ideas, choose the best words to express those ideas, develop a sensible order, and work out your own examples. As if this weren't enough, your efforts to write down your ideas may also be hampered by your worry over spelling and punctuation, the problems of "correctness" that may have given you trouble in high school. It is true that ideas, words, order, examples, spelling, and punctuation all enter into good writing. And all of them must be dealt with. But by far the most important of these things is finding your own ideas and presenting them so other people can understand you. This must be your first concern. All the other problems of writing are secondary.

This book hasn't any spelling rules in it, though most good writers agree that conventional spelling is important. You will not spend your time studying punctuation rules, though unless you use commas and periods in the usual places you are likely to confuse your readers. There will be no exercises in sentence structure just for the sake of sentence structure, and no time will be spent getting you to say "lie" instead of "lay" or "lend" instead of "loan." The English courses you have already taken have dealt with these rules and conventions. We have no intention of warming up these high school leftovers in the hopes that the stew or hash we make of them this time will be more to your taste. If as you write you are worried about spelling, use a dictionary. If you are worried about punctuating a sentence you have written, consult a handbook. If you are uncertain about the "correctness" of something you have written, look up what you want to know in a current dictionary of correct usage. And if you can't understand the explanations in these books, or can't find what you are looking for, ask your teacher for help. Problems of spelling, punctuation, and "correctness" should concern you only after you have written something, not before. These are problems of revision, not problems of writing.

Even though your knowledge of spelling, punctuation, and usage is a little shaky, there are a few simple things you can do that will automatically improve your papers. Your poorest writing will be more acceptable if you follow these suggestions, and your cleverest writing, no matter how brilliant, will be unacceptable if you do not.

Before you begin to write any paper, you must know what the assignment is. Once you know, follow it exactly, even if you get it from your teacher. Perhaps you think you could make up a more fascinating topic, or even a more profitable one, but stay with the assignment anyway. In such matters most teachers are narrow-minded enough to prefer their own originality to yours.

If the directions have been given in class, and you don't understand them, ask questions, as many as you need to ask in order to make the assignment clear to you. This suggestion does not mean that your hand should be constantly waving so you can ask silly or unjustified questions. No teacher grows fond of the student who daydreams or does his algebra while the English assignment is being given and then asks eagerly, "What did you say we were supposed to do?" Get into the habit of listening, and listen not only with your whole mind but with a pencil in your hand. Notes taken during class will be very useful if your memory fails you when you face the assignment in the evening.

If the directions are written, and very often they will be, read them slowly and carefully. Five minutes spent finding out what you are supposed to do is worth fifty minutes of doing it wrong. Yet sometimes even a slow and careful reading will not make written directions clear to you. When that happens, drop around during office hours and ask your instructor for an explanation. The student who is willing to take a little time to get an assignment straight is so rare that your teacher will probably spend more time helping you than he can easily spare.

Follow directions: write the kind of paper you are asked to write and also make it the length you are asked. If you have been told to write a two-page paper, a ten-page paper is likely to tempt a busy instructor to lower your grade. But don't knock yourself out counting words. If the assignment is a three-hundred word paper, most teachers will allow fifty words more or fifty words less without feeling betrayed.

Find out how your instructor wants the paper set up. Some of his requirements may seem trivial to you, or even silly, but he may set such store by them that if you ignore them, the writing on which you have spent so many hours of sweat and agony may simply be tossed into his basket of *F* papers.

There are some things about preparing papers, however, that may seem so obvious that your instructor may not even mention them. Be sure that you

1. write on one side of the paper only;
2. do all your in-class work in ink and your home assignments in ink or on a typewriter;
3. write on every other line.

There are good reasons for all these requirements. The rumor that most English teachers hold stock in a paper mill is entirely unfounded. Teachers are not trying to increase paper sales, but they are concerned with making their own jobs easier, and it will be to your advantage to cooperate with them. Papers written on both sides are confusing to read. Single-spaced writing (or typing) is not only hard for the teacher to read but hard for him to correct and even harder for you to revise.

Unless your teacher asks you to put your name at the top of each page, it is a good idea to put the identification on the back of the last page:

Abraham Antwhistle
English 81-B
October 1, 1967

One advantage to this system is that your instructor can read what you have written before he knows that it is yours. What you have written is judged on its own worth, entirely separate from any impression your earlier work may have made on the teacher.

Following the form required and being neat will help to put your instructor in a friendly frame of mind when he reads your paper, but be careful not to overdo it. Frills intended to make the professor warm and cozy in his mind actually may have just the opposite effect. One such execrable extra is the attempt to distract him from what you have written by the way you have decorated your paper. Art work belongs in art class and not in the margins or on the cover of your English paper. Pictures clipped from magazines may impress a seventh-grade teacher, but they will only annoy a college teacher unless he has asked for them. The only design you need to concern yourself with is the orderly design that underlies your writing.

Another way to put your instructor in an unhappy mood is to hand your paper in late. When you miss a class, as everyone must now and then, you are responsible for getting the assignment and doing it just as promptly as if you had been there. If you get the seven-year measles or if all four of your great-grandfathers die the same weekend, your teacher is likely to sympathize with your need to miss some classes and will surely make arrangements to accept your papers after they are due. If your car fails to start on a cold morning, your teacher may sympathize with that problem, too. Sometimes his own car needs to be pushed. But if you say cheerfully, "Oh, I didn't do that because I was absent Tuesday," your teacher may be more angry than sympathetic, and if he accepts the paper at all, your grade will probably suffer.

Even if you follow all of these suggestions, you will not immediately become "good in English." You will only have made the job of learning to write, learning to express your ideas in good, plain English, a little easier. If you aren't sure what we mean by "plain English," read on.

Key Words

Some words are so important in an English class that you must be doubly sure you understand them thoroughly. Unlike the difficult words given in the vocabulary exercise, these key words deserve more than vague understanding. You must not just guess at them; you must be sure. Think about these questions so that when the class discusses them you will have something to say. Your teacher may even want to give you fifteen minutes to write out your answers. If he does, you'll be glad you thought about them ahead of time.

1. *Punctuation* might be defined as the written signs that stand for pauses and stresses we use when we speak. Do you think this is a good definition? Does it include all the punctuation marks you use? Can you think of any that are left out? If we decide to use this definition, what are we saying about the purpose of punctuation?

2. *Spelling* might be defined as using the letters of the alphabet to represent the sounds we hear when we speak a word. How well does this definition fit your own experience with spelling? Where does it not fit? If we use this definition, what do we mean when we say that someone "misspells" a word? What is your reaction when someone else "misspells" a word that you are sure about?

3. *Conventional usage* might be defined as punctuating with the same signs, spelling in the same way, and making the same word choices as do the educated people in your area. One question that this definition suggests is whether everything educated people say or write is clearer than the things poorly educated people say or write. Do you think, for instance, that "he doesn't" is any clearer than "he don't"? The first one is "good usage"; the second is often marked "illiterate"—that is, uneducated. Do you ever judge people by the word choices they make? Some people do. Do you care whether such judgments are made about you?

4. Three books that writers often use to help them in the *revision* of what they have written are a *dictionary*, a *handbook*, and a *dictionary of current usage*. What kind of information do you look up in your dictionary? Can you always find what you are looking for? Give an example of information included in your handbook that is not easy to find in your dictionary. Do you own a dictionary of current usage? If you don't, find one in your library or your bookstore and examine it carefully. Can you find any information in it that is not included in your handbook?

Vocabulary

To get the full meaning of what you are reading, you don't have to know every word well enough to give a clear definition of it, but you should be able to guess at the right meaning as you read. To double-check yourself, see whether you can pick the right meaning of the following words when you have three or four choices. If you pick the right definitions, you probably know the words well enough to get by, but if you get some words wrong, you should look them up in the dictionary. If the dictionary gives more than one meaning, you will have to decide which of the meanings most nearly fits the way the word is used in this chapter. To help you find how the words are used in context, the words are listed in the same order in the vocabulary quiz as in the chapter. Check to see whether your new knowledge changes your understanding of what you have read.

1. A *sadistic* person is one who   ————
   (a) takes pleasure in mistreating others
   (b) takes pleasure in hurting himself
   (c) takes pleasure in helping others
   (d) collects figures and facts

2. A *monomaniac* is a person who   ————
   (a) has lots of money and gloats over it
   (b) has an extreme fondness for monorail transportation
   (c) is overly enthusiastic about just one subject
   (d) is so crazy he should be put in an institution

3. *Osmosis* is   ————
   (a) a method of cell division
   (b) a process of absorption
   (c) nearsightedness
   (d) deliberate hard work

4. To write *forcefully* means   ————
   (a) to use lots of large words
   (b) to avoid hard words
   (c) to threaten your reader
   (d) to write vigorously and convincingly

5. Two things that are *intertwined* are   ————
   (a) so wound together that it is hard to separate one from the other
   (b) built with a piece of string running down their centers
   (c) completely different from each other
   (d) exactly alike

6. Something is *hampered* if it is   ————
   (a) encouraged and made easier
   (b) slowed down and made harder

(c) hidden in a clothes basket
(d) accelerated at a breathtaking rate

7. An attitude is *unjustified* if it is
   (a) not approved by a qualified judge
   (b) approved by a qualified judge
   (c) difficult to defend reasonably
   (d) easy to defend reasonably

8. *Trivial* points are those which are
   (a) not very important
   (b) out of date
   (c) third on the list
   (d) very important

9. *Agony* means
   (a) tremendous pain and great suffering
   (b) excitement and joy
   (c) a person who is hired to work for somebody else
   (d) a bird which is now extinct

10. Things that are *obvious* are
    (a) unimportant
    (b) too painful to mention
    (c) too difficult to attempt
    (d) clear or easy to see

11. An *unfounded* rumor is one that has
    (a) gotten lost
    (b) no basis in fact
    (c) the ring of truth about it
    (d) come to light accidentally

12. *Execrable* means
    (a) easily excitable
    (b) excellent
    (c) more than is needed
    (d) very bad indeed

13. To *distract* someone is to
    (a) cut him into pieces
    (b) call his attention away from what he is doing
    (c) praise him
    (d) accuse him unjustly

Exercises

Exercise 1. To be done *in class* in ink. Three-minute time limit.

1. Read everything before doing anything.
2. Make an X in the upper right-hand corner of this paper.
3. Draw a circle around the X.
4. Make three dots under the circle.
5. Poke a hole through the paper under the dots.
6. Write your initials, in small letters, on the back of the page.
7. Tear out this page.
8. Circle numbers 1, 7, and 13.
9. Cross out the other numbers.
10. Poke a small hole through the center of the paper.
11. Write the numbers from 10 to 1 down the right margin of this side.
12. Write the numbers from 1 to 10 up the left margin of the back.
13. Write your name in the upper left-hand corner of this side.
14. Draw a square on the back of this paper.
15. In the square write the day, month, and year you were born.
16. Print "OK SO FAR" under the square.
17. Draw a line from the upper right-hand corner to the lower left-hand corner of the front.
18. Draw a line from the upper right-hand corner to the lower left-hand corner of the back.
19. Fasten this page back in the book.
20. After reading the whole page, do only 1, 7, and 13.

II

Why Are You Writing This, Anyway? Finding the Purpose

Before you begin to write anything, no matter what it is—a check for $2.98, an application for membership in the SLPEG (Suburban League for the Prevention of the Extermination of Groundhogs), a letter to the editor explaining the virtues of drag-racing, or even an English paper—you need to ask yourself the question "Why am I writing this, anyway?" Sometimes the answer is obvious: you are writing the check to keep the collection agency from foreclosing on your new shoes. You are applying for membership in the SLPEG because you believe in groundhogs and are willing to stand up and be counted. You are defending drag-racing because you like it and because you hope to see your name in print.

It may even seem to you that the reason for writing an English paper is somewhat different, though equally obvious: the teacher assigned it, and you have no choice if you want to pass the course. You are writing it because you *have* to. But if you stop to think a minute, you will see that the reason for writing an English paper is not much different from the basic reason behind all writing; it *has* to be done so that the writer will get something he wants. Almost no sane person writes for the pleasure of setting words on paper one after the other. Did you ever hear anybody say, "Goody, goody, I *get* to write a letter tonight"? The natural phrase is "I *have* to write a letter," and the "have" implies, as usual, that the writing is being done, not for its own sake, but because the writer expects some reward or satisfaction, however small, from the thing he has written.

The statement that nobody writes for the fun of it applies just as much to skilled writers as it does to the unskilled. The professional writer may take pleasure in thinking about what he has written, if he thinks it turned out well; but the actual writing is work, not fun. Homer has left no record of the agony he went through in composing the *Odyssey*, but we do know that the manager of the Globe Theatre was always nagging Shakespeare to finish that fifth act by Friday night. In the last hundred years or so, nearly every writer who has analyzed the process of writing has talked about the sweat and strain that go into every paragraph. From Charles Dickens, who spent sleepless nights grinding out another chapter to meet a magazine deadline, to Dorothy Parker, who was so desperately anxious to avoid facing the blank sheet of paper in her typewriter that—to encourage visitors—she hung a sign saying "Gentlemen" on her office door, professional writers agree in saying that they did not write for fun.

Just as Charles Dickens (and even Dorothy Parker, when the gentlemen had gone on back to their own offices) wrote to get the money for the grocery bill, so less skillful writers force themselves to write because they must. Most registered nurses would rather bathe the accident victim in Ward Seven than write out careful directions on how to give the bath. But the student nurse who comes on at ten o'clock will need the directions. Most engineers would rather build another bridge than write an explanation of what went wrong with Pier Seven. But the company demands to know why the pier fell down. Hardly anybody who is shaken and bruised from a collision enjoys writing a report of the accident for the highway patrol and the insurance adjuster. Most professors would rather make their own speeches than summarize what their colleagues said at the conference. Even a worried freshman may not get much fun out of writing home for that extra ten dollars he just must have.

All these people write because they believe something desirable will result from their writing. The nurse believes that her careful directions may spare the patient some unnecessary pain. The engineer wants to make it clear that the bridge collapse was not his fault. The owner of the smashed Volkswagen and the stiff neck hopes to get his car repaired and avoid having his driver's license revoked. The professor hopes his department head will send him to another conference. And the freshman, of course, expects to get his hands on that ten by return mail.

All these writers know, first, that they have to write. But more important, they know *why* they have to write. They have a clear understanding of their purpose, and they are not likely to be sidetracked into forgetting it. The nurse is not likely to break off her directions for turning the patient on his side to complain about the coffee served in the hospital dining room. The engineer is not likely to interrupt his discussion of the strength of concrete mixes to argue against American policy in the Far East. The accident report will contain no comments on how hot it was at the beach or how plentiful the fish were last Saturday. If the professor at the conference breaks off his summary of Dr. Arbuthnot Doolittle's analysis of Aristotle's *Poetics* to tell about the funny thing that happened on the way to his hotel room, the chances are he will not be sent to the conference next year—unless of course he can make his story at once very funny and relevant to Aristotle. Nor is the boy whose aim is ten dollars likely to fill his letter home with a glowing description of the daffodils outside his door—unless, of course, his mother is mad about daffodils and he thinks he can establish some connection between the flowers that bloom in the spring, tra-la, and his urgent need to loosen the family purse strings.

The moral to be drawn from all these examples is just this:

1. the act of writing is rarely pleasant but it sometimes has to be done; and
2. the chances for success in writing are always greater if the writer understands his purpose clearly and keeps that purpose firmly in mind all the time he is writing.

It is probably easier to see the purpose behind a piece of writing if we first look at a few common purposes that make people abandon their natural sluggishness and set pen to paper. One common purpose in writing is to tell other people how to do something, to give directions. That was what the registered nurse was doing. That was what the doctor did when he left the original set of instructions for the nurse. This is what the makers of TV dinners do on their containers—and the makers of dress patterns, and house paints, and do-it-yourself kits of all kinds. Giving you directions for writing well is what we are doing in this book.

Another common purpose is to explain something. The engineer is explaining the technical reasons behind the collapse of Pier Seven into the Po-Po River, taking with it thirty-seven workmen who didn't want a bath. The letter you received from the college registrar last summer was designed to explain college registration. Any piece of writing that defines or compares or classifies or analyzes is explanation. For instance:

Anthropology is the study of man's physical and cultural characteristics.
The cottontail differs from the jackrabbit in several important ways.

Rats, mice, and rabbits belong to the rodent family.
In order to understand the working of a threshing machine, we
must consider each of its separate parts.

Many elementary texts, in science or in English, for instance, are made
up of explanation. Part of what we are doing here is explaining the
difference between one writing purpose and another.

Some occasions call not for explanation but for telling what occurred.
The accident report, if it is to serve its purpose, must contain no analysis
of the unrestrained, illegal, inconsiderate, nincompoopish nature of the
other driver's driving habits. It must contain no directions as to just
where that other driver ought to go. Instead, it must be confined to a
clear and complete account of just what happened.

Newspaper articles are another example of writing that tells what
happened. A front-page news story says, "Thirteen people were killed
in weekend highway accidents," or "A severe earthquake left thousands
homeless," or "The City Council passed a zoning ordinance last night."
But newswriters do not, in their front-page accounts, warn you to drive
carefully, or urge you to send sandwiches and blankets to the homeless,
or tell you the council members are a pack of reactionary idiots. You
may find these lectures and pleas and opinions on the editorial page
or in syndicated columns, but the news story itself, like an accident
report, will tell only what happened.

A fourth common purpose is to summarize what someone else has
written. The professor who shortened Dr. Doolittle's twenty-four pages
of remarks to a single page was summarizing. And so was the assistant
professor who shortened the professor's page to three brief sentences
in his notes with an aside to himself about the windiness of old age.
Some digest magazines have made millions of dollars and gained millions
of readers by boiling down long articles into shorter ones. When you
take your finals at the end of a course, you are compressing into four
or five pages of writing what you think the content of the course has
been. In short, a summary is (like this sentence) any piece of writing
that shortens another piece of writing without changing its meaning
or commenting on it.

Perhaps the commonest purpose of all in writing is to try to get
others to agree with you or to make them do what you want. The boy
who wrote home for money was trying to convince his mother that
he really needed that ten dollars more than she needed to keep it.
Congressman Gruntansqueal's every written word is designed to convince the voters in his home district that he is the greatest statesman
to hit the country since George Washington was laid to rest. Ad writers
try to convince you that Twinkle Toothpaste will make your teeth a

whiter white, that Fatiac automobiles will cut your gasoline bill in half and double your community standing, and that Vital Vitamins will make you captain of the football team. When you sit in church on Sunday, the sermon is designed to convince you that you should mend your wicked ways, or, if your ways are not wicked, that you should love your fellow man. When you were little, your parents tried to convince you that a good child picks up his toys and does not hit his brother with a baseball bat. From the minute you started school your teachers tried to convince you that education is a fine and useful thing.

These five purposes—giving directions, explaining things, telling what happened, summarizing, and convincing others—occur over and over again.

Sometimes these purposes occur separately. But experienced writers know that to accomplish their main purpose, they may need to use more than one of these methods. Before a writer can *convince* you that eating seaweed is nutritious and economical, he may have to *explain* the dietary needs of the human body and the comparative cost of a yard of seaweed and a pound of steak. In order to *convince* you that you too can enjoy a seaweed soufflé, he may need to *tell* you *what happened* the first time he had seaweed for supper. His main purpose was to convince, but he used two other writing methods—explaining, and telling what happened.

Before any writer can blend methods effectively, he must become skillful in using each method separately. A good blend is not a hodge-podge but a carefully prepared mixture. A cook cannot make a good sauce until he can tell an onion from an egg and knows just how much cayenne will improve the flavor without setting a fire in the mouths of the people who eat his sauce. A landscape architect cannot plan a formal garden until he has learned whether rhododendrons grow higher than nasturtiums, whether petunias clash with pinks, and whether lilies bloom in the spring or in the fall. If he throws seeds at random, he reaps chaos. Writing, like cooking and gardening, is a skill that can be learned. Like any other skill, it must be learned one step at a time. By working on each purpose separately, you can learn to give directions, to explain, to tell what happened, to summarize, and to convince. *Then* you will be ready to try blending.

The English teacher may make your first efforts easy for you by assigning a writing purpose and leaving the topic up to you. He may say, "Write a theme about something you believe in, trying to get other people to agree with you." If he does, you know your general purpose must be to convince, and your problem is to say clearly what you believe in, and go on from there. You may say, "Everybody should eat seaweed," or "Pollution of the Columbia River must be stopped."

On the other hand, your teacher may not say what the purpose of the paper must be; he may just assign a topic and let you decide on your own purpose. Perhaps he simply says, "Write a paper on sports." Before you can decide what your purpose will be, your first job is to cut the topic down to size. Obviously, you can't give directions for sports in general. You can't explain all the sports in the world. You can't tell what happened in a game of "sports." And you can't very well be in favor of all the sports there are, or against them all, though you very well may prefer some sports to others.

As you narrow this extremely broad topic down to manageable size, you will do well to choose a sport you know something about—baseball, for instance. Once you have decided on baseball, you may think you have stated your purpose when you say, "My paper is about baseball." You really have not. At last count there were 5,387,422 ways to talk about baseball. The point is not that you are going to say *something* about baseball but *what* you are going to say. What *are* you going to say about baseball?

You might, for instance, say one of the following:

1. College baseball builds character.
2. Parents should fight only in the bleachers during Little League games.
3. Podunk needs a new baseball park.
4. There are several reasons for the size and shape of a catcher's mitt.
5. Softball differs from baseball in several ways.
6. Raglan College defeated the Quadruped Nine last night.
7. When I was dropped from the Quadruped Nine, I discovered it pays to follow directions.
8. To care for a baseball uniform properly, the player must follow seven distinct steps.
9. In his article in *The Baseball World* for August, 1884, Clive Strongney discusses the reasons for calling baseball a typically American sport.

These nine sentences have two things in common: first, they are all concerned with the general topic of baseball, and second, they all suggest what the purpose of the paper will be. Numbers 1, 2, and 3 express the writer's opinion; the writer's purpose will be to make his reader share his belief. Numbers 4 and 5 will lead to papers of explanation. Numbers 6 and 7 will tell what happened: number 6 should lead to an objective report, telling what happened in the game; number 7 should lead to telling what happened in a personal experience. Number 8 will be a paper giving directions; number 9 will be a summary.

Further, and perhaps more important, all nine of these sentences make a clear, definite statement. They are not topics, but *main idea sentences*.

Before you begin to write any kind of paper, you should work out a main idea sentence for it. Your main idea sentence must make clear what the purpose of your paper will be, and it must state the idea or event on which your paper will be based. It must make this statement in the form of a *complete sentence*.

Certainly the statement "I am going to write about baseball" is, in the grammatical sense, a complete sentence. But the sentence that states your main idea must not contain such obvious evasions as "I am going to write about . . ." or "My paper will be about . . ." In testing for the completeness of your idea, you must strike out all such repetitions of the original question ("What are you writing about?") and examine what remains. After you have crossed out "I am going to write about" or "This paper will be about," do you still have a complete sentence? "Baseball" or "Playing baseball" or even "When I played baseball" or "Why I like baseball" are not complete sentences. "When I played baseball" leads to the question "What happened?" and "Why I like baseball" leads to "Why do you?" You have not stated your main idea clearly until you can say, "When I played baseball, I learned that too much practice can sometimes lead to defeat," or "I like baseball because I am good at it." You may not have stumbled on anything very startling or original, but at least you have found a main idea and stated it in sentence form.

Check your main idea to make sure that it is not *too* narrow. "A baseball is round" is certainly a complete sentence, and so is "Our coach's name was Baby Ruth," but neither of them is a satisfactory main idea sentence because, once you have announced the fact, you are left with nothing else to say. As you look at your main idea sentence, the things you could use to support it or complete it should suggest themselves easily. If your main idea sentence is "College baseball builds character," you might say that the players learn sportsmanship, teamwork, and good health habits. It will take you at least a paragraph for each of these subdivisions, and you will discover, as you begin to write, that you have plenty to say. In the same way, "Softball differs from baseball in several ways" calls for a paragraph on each of the major differences, and "To care for a baseball uniform properly, the player must follow seven distinct steps" calls for a paragraph on each of the seven steps. If, when you look at your main idea sentence, you cannot think of three or four paragraphs that would logically develop from it, discard that sentence and find another one.

Once you have your main idea clearly stated, the hard part, deciding what to write, is behind you. But if you begin to write without a clear main idea sentence, you will find yourself floundering. Like the disorganized gardener, you will reap chaos.

Even the most confused student understands the importance of stating his main idea clearly in things that really matter to him. He is unlikely to write

> Dear Mamma:
> This letter is about money.
> With love, your son,
> Rupert Creech

and then think he has taken care of the situation.

Key Words

Without referring back to the chapter, explain in your own words what these terms mean. Be sure to say enough that one term cannot possibly be confused with another.

1. A *topic* is . . .

2. *Narrowing a topic* means . . .

3. A *main idea sentence* is . . .

4. Finding your *writing purpose* means . . .

5. A piece of writing that *gives directions* is . . .

6. A piece of writing that *explains* tells . . .

7. A *report* tells only . . .

8. A *summary* should . . .

9. A paper that tries to *convince* is . . .

Vocabulary

Pick the answer that most closely fits the meaning of the word as it has been used in the chapter. Look up in your dictionary the meaning of all the words you miss.

1. Something that is *revoked* is _____
   (a) spoken aloud
   (b) made official
   (c) recorded in a public place
   (d) cancelled

2. If a situation is *urgent*, _____
   (a) immediate action is needed
   (b) you have plenty of time
   (c) it is essentially funny
   (d) the problem has something to do with cities

3. *Sluggishness* means _____
   (a) eagerness to fight
   (b) quickness of mind
   (c) slowness in getting started
   (d) clumsy shape

4. An *elementary* explanation is one which is _____
   (a) simple and easy to understand
   (b) confused and twisting
   (c) connected with storms and bad weather
   (d) highly sophisticated and technical

5. Behavior that is *unrestrained* is _____
   (a) cautious
   (b) insane
   (c) uncontrolled
   (d) sane

6. If someone calls you a *reactionary*, he probably means that _____
   (a) he agrees with your politics
   (b) he thinks your political attitudes are out of date
   (c) he thinks your political attitudes are too liberal
   (d) he thinks you advocate violent overthrow of the government

7. If you read an *editorial* in last night's paper, you read _____
   (a) a straight report of the news
   (b) an advertisement
   (c) a recipe
   (d) an acknowledged expression of opinion

8. A *syndicated* newspaper column is one which _____
   (a) is always written locally
   (b) is published the same day in several different news-
       papers across the country
   (c) is published first in one newspaper and then reprinted
       by another one without permission
   (d) the newspaper refused to print because it is too
       obscene

9. If you are offered a *soufflé*, nobody would laugh if you said, _____
   (a) "No, thank you, I'm allergic to eggs"
   (b) "Yes, please, I love chocolate and pecans"
   (c) "I'd rather not; I don't understand foreign plays"
   (d) "No, I have to wear a back brace"

10. A *hodgepodge* is _____
    (a) a mammal that burrows underground
    (b) an electric hedge cutter
    (c) a jumbled, confusing mixture
    (d) a native of northern England

11. Anything that is in a state of *chaos* is _____
    (a) very close to heaven
    (b) badly in need of washing
    (c) earsplittingly noisy
    (d) completely confused and disorganized

12. *Pollution* means _____
    (a) making something dirty and impure
    (b) taking a survey of public opinion
    (c) acting as a police officer
    (d) filtering water

13. To hide behind an *evasion* means _____
    (a) to avoid the real issue
    (b) to enter a country in the rear of an army
    (c) to stand behind a heavy curtain with a design woven
        into it
    (d) to use forged papers

14. ***Floundering*** means _____
    (a) trying to catch a large, flat fish
    (b) going out with other men's wives
    (c) fishing without a license
    (d) acting without purpose or direction

Exercises

Exercise 1. Which purpose (giving directions, explaining, telling what happened, summarizing, or convincing) is expressed in each of these sentences? Notice that you are not being asked whether you think the sentence would be a good main idea for a paper, but only to decide what its purpose is.

1. In 1492 Columbus landed at San Salvador. _____

2. Take a cup of flour, three table-spoons of sugar, a pound of nut-meg, and sift them together. _____

3. The human body is composed of skin, flesh, bone, and blood. _____

4. All college students should be required to take five years of mathematics. _____

5. *Macbeth* is the story of an am-bitious man who, egged on by his wife, killed his king in the hope of gaining a kingdom. _____

6. Yesterday seven cars, a gasoline tanker, and two trolleys collided at the corner of Fourth and Main. _____

7. The United States ought to recog-nize Red China. _____

8. The United Nations should not admit Red China. _____

9. The gist of the pamphlet was that Senator Hoaxshell is in favor of lower taxes and more services. _____

10. My little brother fell off the barn roof yesterday. _____

11. Children shouldn't be allowed to climb on barns. _____

12. Barns are used to store hay and grain and as shelter for various farm animals. _____

13. Mrs. Creech's article on the Gera-nium Society first gave the history of the group, then listed its aims

and accomplishments, and concluded with an appeal for members and money.

_____

14. Striking a match in a room filled
with escaping gas usually causes
an explosion.

_____

15. The newspaper reports that Justice Clark, in writing the decision
on the Civil Rights case, said that
Congress has a clear right to regu-
late interstate commerce.

_____

16. Food prices are too high.

_____

Exercise 2. Which of the following are clear statements of a main idea? Which are merely topics, expressed in such a way that you cannot tell what the main idea would be? Mark *M* for main idea, *T* for topic.

1. Our trip to the beach last summer.   _____

2. This paper will be about digging clams.   _____

3. Razor clams are different from all other kinds of shellfish.   _____

4. Clamming is a major factor in the prosperity of many
   coastal towns.   _____

5. Clams.   _____

6. Telling how to dig clams.   _____

7. Using a clam gun is an unsporting way to catch clams.   _____

8. State game laws should be more strictly enforced.   _____

9. State game laws should be less strictly enforced.   _____

10. Selling night crawlers.   _____

11. Arsenic for everybody.   _____

12. My part in the senior play.   _____

13. Freshman football. _____

14. Sports are for jerks. _____

15. Before you begin to paint the chair, collect all the things you will need. _____

16. When I painted the chair. _____

17. Raglan College entrance requirements. _____

18. Raglan College should lower its entrance requirements. _____

19. My book report. _____

20. My book report on *The Ugly American.* _____

21. The book *The Ugly American* shows some of the weaknesses of American foreign policy. _____

22. What I think of registration. _____

23. Why I hate to have snakes in my bed. _____

24. My paper is about snakes in bed. _____

25. The TV show last night. _____

26. The late movie on TV. _____

27. The late movie last night, *The Loneliness of the Long Distance Runner*, was the story of a juvenile delinquent and his conflicts with society. _____

28. Tigers, jaguars, and house cats all belong to the feline family. _____

29. There were three major causes of the Whitman Massacre. _____

30. This paper is about the Whitman Massacre. _____

31. Yesterday I parked my car on a small boy on a bicycle. _____

Exercise 3. Decide which of the following main idea sentences are too broad, which are too narrow, and which are suitable for a theme of 500 words. Mark *B* for broad, *N* for narrow, and *S* for satisfactory. Be prepared to explain your decisions to the class.

1. Programming an IBM 087 is easy if you follow these seventy-three distinct steps. _____

2. There are many different kinds of computers, and each of them has a distinctly different usefulness. _____

3. Computers are useful for three very good reasons. _____

4. I have five sisters and one brother. _____

5. My brother is a fink. _____

6. I have known many different kinds of teachers. _____

7. Sir James Frazer's classical study of ritual and myth, *The Golden Bough*, is in twelve volumes, with a thirteenth volume containing an index. _____

8. In *The Golden Bough*, Sir James Frazer traces similar themes in myth, religion, folklore, and ritual. _____

9. *The Golden Bough* is a good book. _____

10. All books are interesting. _____

11. Last year I took a long trip with my family. _____

12. I got really to know my family during a long trip we took last year. _____

13. A football is oval. _____

14. During the NAACP convention we heard three speakers, each of whom stressed the need for tolerance. _____

15. There were three different speakers at the NAACP convention. _____

Exercise 4. All of the following topics are too broad for a 500-word paper—or a 5000-word paper, for that matter. For each very broad topic, suggest three narrower topics. For instance, if you begin with the broad topic *War*, you might narrow it to:

WAR: Causes of the American Revolution
The GI in World War II
The possibilities of disarmament
Foot soldiers in Caesar's army
The War of Jenkins' Ear
What the White Paper says about Vietnam
The gains made at the Battle of the Bulge
What is a tactical victory?
Fifteenth-century weapons
Duties of a first sergeant in the U.S. Army

Although we have given ten narrowed topics, notice that you are being asked to find only three for each broad topic.

1. children _____

_____

_____

2. sports _____

_____

_____

3. responsibility _____

_____

_____

4. reference books _____

_____

_____

5. civil liberties _____

_____

_____

6. higher education _____

_____

_____

7. study habits _____

_____

_____

8. music _____

_____

_____

9. vocations _____

_____

_____

10. history _____

_____

_____

Exercise 5. Write a possible statement of a main idea for each of the following topics. If the topic is too broad, narrow it before you write your main idea statement. For instance, the topic *sewing* might be narrowed to "method of hemming a dress," and then the main idea statement might be:

There are three acceptable ways to hem a dress: straight machine sewing, blind stitching done by machine, and hand stitching. (explanation)

Or the broad topic *public officials* could be narrowed to "the Pleasantville Dogcatcher," and the main idea statement might be:

The Pleasantville Dogcatcher has the easiest job in town. (convincing)

Name the purpose of each sentence. Try for some variety. Use each writing purpose at least once but not more than four times.

1. college admission requirements _____

_____

_____

_____

2. going steady _____

_____

_____

_____

3. the United Nations _____

_____

_____

_____

4. college basketball _____

_____

_____

_____

5. books _____

_____

_____

6. pets _____

_____

_____

7. high school principals _____

_____

_____

8. foreign language _____

_____

_____

9. farming _____

_____

_____

10. television _____

_____

_____

_____

11. music_____

_____

_____

_____

Exercise 6. Now try your hand again at identifying the purpose of each of these statements. Some of them would be suitable for main idea sentences, some would not, but each sentence has a *purpose*.

1. John Wilkes Booth shot Lincoln during a performance at the Ford Theater.

2. Be sure to indicate the source of all the quotations you use.

3. My father wrote a two-page letter, but all he actually said was that I had been spending too much money and that he was going to cut my allowance.

4. Victoria, British Columbia, is located on an island in Puget Sound.

5. Before you insert the thingama-bobble, give the whatchamadink three quick twists to the right.

6. Dr. Whoosis, in his article "Kiss Your Troubles Good-by," says he has scientifically proved kissing is the chief cause of rainy weather.

7. Place the patient on his right side, make sure he has not swallowed his tongue, and pull both his arms sharply upward away from his head.

8. There are three hundred shopping days until Christmas.

_____

9. Close cover before striking.

_____

10. When George's grandmamma was told
    That George had been as good as gold,
    She promised in the afternoon
    To bring him an immense balloon.

_____

11. And so she did, but when it came
    It got into the candle flame,
    And being of a dangerous sort
    Exploded with a loud retort.

_____

12. The moral is that little boys
    Should not be given dangerous toys.

_____

13. Go West, young man, go West.

_____

14. In his Gettysburg Address, Lincoln said that it was more important for the living to try to preserve democratic government than to honor the men who had died fighting for it.

_____

15. All Gaul is divided into three parts.

_____

16. In *Animal Farm*, George Orwell tells the story of some pigs who take over the management of a farm.

_____

Exercise 7. For each of the following topics, write

1. a main idea statement for a paper giving directions;
2. a main idea statement for a paper of explanation;
3. a main idea statement for a paper telling what happened;
4. a main idea statement for a paper to convince.

For instance, the topic *house fires* might lead to these main idea statements:

GIVING DIRECTIONS: Even if you wake up some night to find smoke pouring out of the kitchen, you may be able to save the house if you do three things coolly and quickly.

EXPLAINING: The Home Fire Underwriters' Association lists the four most frequent causes of home fires.

TELLING WHAT HAPPENED: A four-story house in East Ignitia burned to the ground last night.

CONVINCING: Every home-owner should carry fire insurance.

1. my English class

GIVING DIRECTIONS _____

_____

_____

EXPLAINING _____

_____

_____

TELLING WHAT HAPPENED _____

_____

_____

CONVINCING _____

_____

_____

2. rabbits

GIVING DIRECTIONS _____

_____

_____

EXPLAINING _____

_____

TELLING WHAT HAPPENED _____

CONVINCING _____

3. the state legislature

GIVING DIRECTIONS _____

EXPLAINING _____

TELLING WHAT HAPPENED _____

CONVINCING _____

4. the Fifth Amendment

GIVING DIRECTIONS _____

_____

_____

EXPLAINING _____

_____

_____

TELLING WHAT HAPPENED _____

_____

_____

CONVINCING _____

_____

_____

5. cheating

GIVING DIRECTIONS _____

_____

_____

EXPLAINING _____

_____

_____

TELLING WHAT HAPPENED _____

_____

_____

CONVINCING _____

_____

_____

6. school spirit

GIVING DIRECTIONS _____

_____

_____

EXPLAINING _____

_____

_____

TELLING WHAT HAPPENED _____

_____

_____

CONVINCING _____

_____

_____

7. gardening

GIVING DIRECTIONS _____

_____

_____

EXPLAINING _____

_____

_____

TELLING WHAT HAPPENED _____

_____

_____

CONVINCING _____

_____

_____

Exercise 8. From your daily newspaper bring five paragraphs, each illustrating a different kind of purpose. Be prepared to present your paragraphs in class to see whether the other students agree with you.

III

You Be the Boss for Awhile: Giving Directions

So far this book has been telling you what to do. Now you get a chance to be the boss for awhile and give some directions of your own. If you've never written any directions, you may think it's easier and more fun to tell someone else how to dig a ditch or scrub a floor than it is to do the digging or scrubbing yourself. But giving directions is not easy unless you know what you are doing. You have to understand two things: how to do whatever it is that you are telling someone else to do, and how to get that knowledge down on paper clearly enough so that your reader can follow your directions.

Your choice of subject is limited to something you know something about, just as it is in any paper you write. If you have never seen the insides of a stereo amplifier, you would be foolish to try to tell someone how to build one. Or, if you have just enrolled in bowling for beginners, you are probably not expert enough to write a paper on how to avoid throwing a gutter ball. If you try to write such a paper, you can do nothing but repeat your bowling instructor's directions. He's the expert; let him write the paper. As for you, choose a subject you do understand, preferably something you have done so often or so well that what you have to say will be worth reading.

Before you begin your paper, work out a main idea sentence. The main idea sentence for a paper giving directions must include two things:

1. what the directions will cover;
2. any important things the reader needs to have or do in order to follow the directions successfully.

For instance, you might say, "The important thing to remember when you deliver a baby is to see that everything to be used is sterile." (Such a sentence would make a useful main idea if you are a neighborhood midwife.) If you are giving directions on something that requires less specialized knowledge, you still need to include the same two things.

You can't change a tire without the proper tools.

(Notice that this main idea sentence tells what the job is—changing a tire—and what is needed—the proper tools.)

Almost anybody can make rich, creamy fudge if he's careful to measure the ingredients exactly.

(This main idea sentence tells what the job is—making fudge—and the main thing to watch out for—using exact measurements.)

Although it is true that there are many ways to skin a cat, the best way is to kill it first.

(Here the reader is told what the job is and what he should do before he begins the actual job.)

Beneath your main idea sentence, list all the steps needed to do the job, whatever it is. Check to see that you have not omitted any of the steps. Because you are dealing with a subject you are very familiar with, you may leave out some steps that seem obvious to you. Just remember that they may not be so obvious to the reader. If you are giving directions for making fudge, don't jump from mixing the chocolate and sugar with half a cup of milk to stirring the mixture when it reaches the soft-ball stage. Your reader may not realize that fudge has to be cooked, or, even if he does know enough to put the kettle on the stove, he may not know whether to use high, low, or medium heat, or whether to expect the soft-ball stage to arrive in five minutes or two hours. It's your job to see that he has all the information he needs, and that he has it in the right order. For instance, a main idea sentence for a paper giving directions on how to start a car might be:

If your car won't start because the motor is cold, there are a few easy things you can do that should help.

Here is a list of the steps that might be included in such a paper:

1. pull out choke
2. step on clutch

3. take car out of gear
4. turn on ignition
5. if no start, turn off again
6. step on accelerator and hold down
7. with accelerator down, turn ignition on again
8. car starts

Are these steps in logical order? They look OK, though the first step could just as well come after the second and third as before them. With the main idea sentence written and the steps listed in logical order, the groundwork is done, and nothing remains but to write the paper.

Like any other paper, a paper giving instructions must have an introductory paragraph. For short papers, three hundred to five hundred words, a paragraph of introduction is sufficient. A ten-page essay may have as much as a page of introduction, and a book may have a whole chapter. The length of the introduction is relative to the length of the writing. The purpose of an introductory paragraph is to tell the reader what the paper is going to be about, and to give him a chance to decide whether to continue reading. The introductory paragraph becomes a contract between the writer and the reader. Once you undertake to develop some idea, you must not go beyond what the first paragraph promises to do, nor may you do less than it promises. If your first paragraph promises to tell your reader how to deliver a baby, then your paper must be strictly limited to the problem of delivering babies. You must not drop the baby and begin telling your reader why you are against birth control.

Besides a clear statement of the main idea, the introductory paragraph to a paper giving directions may contain some reasons for doing the job at all. Further, it may contain a complete list of the things needed to do it, if they have not been mentioned in the main idea sentence. The first paragraph certainly should contain any information the reader needs before he can start the job.

Writing the rest of the paper, then, is fairly easy. All you have to do is take up each thing on your list, item by item. Since you have already arranged all the steps in the right order, you are spared the agony of wondering what you should say first and what you should say next, a problem that is sometimes bothersome in other kinds of papers. Remember that if you leave out a step, you must not write, "Oh, by the way, I forgot to tell you that before you take the tire off, you have to jack the car up." Even the laziest student, finding himself in this fix, will realize that he must throw out that page and start over, this time keeping his directions in the proper order.

Just as papers of directions need an introduction, so they must have a conclusion. Your final paragraph need not be very long, but it ought to give the reader the feeling that he has come to the end of the directions, not that you got tired in the middle and just stopped. The conclusion to a short paper may contain only one sentence:

> Fudge made according to these directions has never been known to fail.

> Now you are ready to put the tools back into the trunk of the car and go on to work.

If your paper is longer or the subject more complicated, you may want to summarize by briefly reviewing the main steps and warning the reader of some hazard he must take care to avoid. The chief thing to remember is that the purpose of the conclusion is to make the paper sound finished.

Just because you have written the conclusion, however, don't think your work is over. The worst is over, to be sure, but you still need to do the careful detective work involved in improving your writing. Read through what you have written. Do you find anything that goes beyond what you promised to cover? If so, strike it out. Did you leave out anything you promised to include? If so, put it in where it belongs.

Is everything you have said absolutely clear? Clarity is important in any kind of writing, but it is essential in giving directions. Short sentences are more likely to make for clarity than long, involved ones. The statement "Go two blocks south and one block west" is much simpler and clearer than

> Although I'm not absolutely sure just how you get there, I think if you go south past Hawmeyer's drugstore—that's the one with the green front across from the bank—and then on past that to the first stop light you see, and then turn up the hill—no, the hill comes a block later but you can see it from the corner—and then turn left—no, right—and turn back to the grocery store, the one with the hole in the window where the woman got shot last summer—and go about a block farther, you ought to see it right across from the city park.

"Go two blocks south and one block west" is not only clearer, but it is more likely to inspire confidence. Remember that if you are doubtful about the directions you are giving, you have no business giving them in the first place. Nothing weakens writing like a continuous stream of apologies. Avoid such phrases as "although I'm not sure," "I think that," "it seems to me," "in my opinion," and "it is my belief that. . . ." Strike these namby-pamby phrases wherever they occur.

Another way to write clearly is to take your reader with you as you move from one step to the next. Sometimes this transition from step to step occurs almost automatically. It is natural to number the steps by saying, "First, remove the spare tire from the trunk," and "Second, jack up the car." Other words and phrases also help to suggest the order of events:

> You begin by . . .
> Next . . .
> Then . . .
> After you have . . .
> The last step is to . . .
> Finally . . .

These transitional phrases make for smoother, easier reading, but overusing any one of them (*then* you do this *and then* you add this *and then* you do that *and then* . . .) becomes tiresome.

Another common, but perhaps less obvious, way of taking the reader with you is to pick up an important word or phrase from the end of the preceding paragraph and refer to it in the first sentence of the next paragraph. For example, in this chapter we ended one paragraph by saying, "The chief thing to remember is that the purpose of *the conclusion* is to make the paper sound finished," and we began the next paragraph with "Just because you have written the *conclusion*, however. . . ."

Beginning writers often realize that they need some way of getting the reader from one point to the next but they don't know what the best way is. They don't understand transitions well enough to use them smoothly, but they feel uneasy without them. Sometimes such writers say, "Now I have told you how to jack the car up and the next thing I am going to tell you is. . . ." This sort of comment on what has already been said does serve as a transition, but it is so flat-footed and awkward that it hinders as much as it helps. If the reader isn't already aware that he has been told how to jack the car up, there is something wrong with the way the directions have been written; they need to be made clearer. If he does know already, then he doesn't need to be told again.

Rather than announcing what you have said, and then announcing what you are going to say, you should rely on transitions that show how your ideas relate to each other in time and space or on transitions that echo an important word or phrase. Make your transitions sound easy and natural. Lead your reader by the hand; don't pull him by the nose.

You must not only lead the reader by the hand from paragraph to paragraph, you must take care of him within the paragraph, too. One way of taking care of the reader is to maintain the same attitude toward him all the time. If you begin by speaking directly to him, you must keep on speaking directly to him throughout the rest of your paper. "Before one can change their tire, you must stop our car" is almost frightening. Is *our* car trying to run over *their* tire, and are *you* chasing behind trying to grab the bumper before *one* is smashed to a bloody pulp? If you mean to say, "Stop the car before you change the tire," then say so.

Check your paper to see that you always speak to your reader in the same way. If you are speaking directly to him, the most natural way is to say "you," "your," or simply, "do this," "don't do that." This method—addressing your reader as though you were speaking to him face to face—is probably the best for giving directions.

When you write about your personal experiences, you say, "I went," "I saw," "I drove." Such papers are about *you*, and in them it is natural to say *I* and *me*. Feeling natural will make your writing sound natural. Some handbooks will tell you, however, that less personal writing purposes—explanations, factual writing, papers intended to convince—should avoid both *I* and *you* and instead use more impersonal expressions such as *people, others, students, anybody*. It is true that avoiding *I*, *me*, and *you* will make your paper sound more formal. But if you are more comfortable writing directly to your reader, by all means do so. Being comfortable may very well help you to write more clearly. Trying to write impersonally, especially at first when you are struggling with what you want to say, is sometimes too much of a strain.

In trying to write impersonally, some writers say "one should," "one tends," but *one tends* to become annoyed by this habit, *doesn't one*? Saying *one* when you mean *people* sounds affected and can easily be avoided. If you must choose between affectation and a naturalness that may sound almost too informal, by all means be natural. Such a sentence as "One should not stay in the bathtub for more than four hours at a time" inspires the flippant reader to say, "O.K., but should two do it?"

Address the reader any way you like—use *I*, *you*, *he*, or *people*—but be consistent. Don't confuse your reader by skipping haphazardly from one pronoun to another within a single paper.

Readers will also be confused if they cannot tell which of two things a pronoun stands for. If you say, "Rupert told Claude *he* had made a mistake," your reader cannot tell who made the mistake. Sometimes the situation gets even more confusing: "When the people left their cars, the parking lot attendants cleaned *them*." What got cleaned, the people or the cars?

Sometimes the reader is confused because the writer uses pronouns without making clear what they stand for: "Tansy missed the premiere, *which* caused many raised eyebrows." Why were the eyebrows raised? Were Tansy's friends astonished that she didn't turn up after she had paid for her ticket? Or had the actors in the first scene taken off too many clothes? "I'm majoring in education, but I don't know whether I'll ever be *one*." If the writer keeps on at that rate, the chances are good that he will not become a teacher—or was becoming a teacher what he meant? It doesn't make much difference what the cause of the confusion is. Your job is to make whatever you are saying perfectly clear.

Examine the following student theme:

Moving the Motor

If you drive a car at all frequently, you have probably experienced times when you just couldn't get it to start. If, as is often the case, your motor is just cold, there are a few steps you can take which should help in starting the car.

The first thing to do is to pull out the choke. (Some cars have no manual choke, and in this case, all you can do is hope that the automatic choke works.) If you have a hand choke, pull it out all the way.

Next, if you have a car with manual shifting, step on the clutch and take the car out of gear. If you drive a car with an automatic transmission, make sure it is in neutral.

After you have pulled out the choke and disengaged the gears, you are ready to turn on the ignition. Do so, and see if your car starts. If it doesn't start within a few seconds, turn off the ignition. If the engine keeps turning over without starting, it may become flooded, which only makes it worse.

Instead, after turning the key off, step on the accelerator and hold it all the way down for about ten seconds. *Don't pump it.* Pumping can also flood the engine. Still holding the throttle down, turn the ignition on again. If your car is going to start, this try should do it.

If your car starts, you are off for school; if it doesn't, call a mechanic.

Does the introductory paragraph contain a main idea sentence? Yes, but it is not the first sentence. The first sentence gives reasons for the directions; the second sentence has the main idea. The main idea sentence tells what the theme will be about (starting a car) and suggests that these directions will work only under certain conditions (if the failure to start is because the car is cold).

Now check the theme for completeness. Are any necessary steps left out? The student tells you to pull out the choke, disengage the gears, and turn on the ignition, but what about the starter? Perhaps all the cars he has driven have the starter connected with the ignition, but do all cars?

The order is all right. It follows the plan that has already been checked.

Notice that the student has avoided all namby-pamby phrases. He does not pretend to be an absolute authority, but he is writing about something he is familiar with, and his writing is straightforward and unapologetic.

Is the theme clear? The writer does address the reader as "you" all through the paper and thus avoids jumping from pronoun to pronoun within the same theme. Are there any pronouns which can stand for more than one thing? In paragraph 3, the writer tells you to "make sure it is in neutral," but does *it* refer to the car or the transmission? Do we need to know whether *it* means the car or the transmission? Unless the difference is confusing, worrying about what the *it* refers to is just quibbling. The fourth paragraph, however, says that to keep the engine turning when it is not starting may cause *it* to "become flooded, which only makes *it* worse." The first *it* is the engine, but what is the second one? Can we make an engine *worse*? Or does the student mean that a flooded engine will make the *situation* worse? Is this pronoun confusion more serious than the one in paragraph three? Probably so, since putting a car in neutral is about the same as putting its transmission in neutral, but making a motor worse (perhaps damaging it) is quite a bit different from making the situation worse (not necessarily damaging the motor, but adding to your general frustration).

Does the student use transitions to take the reader easily from point to point? Most of the transitions in this theme are the ones which are natural to themes giving directions. Paragraph 2 begins with "The first thing to do . . ."; paragraph 3 begins with "Next . . ."; and paragraph 4 begins "After you have . . ." These transitions show the order of the steps. The transition between paragraphs 4 and 5 echoes an important idea. In paragraph 4 the writer has said ". . . turn off the ignition." He begins paragraph 5 by saying . . . "after turning the key off. . . ."

Although this student theme is slightly confusing in one place, most of it is perfectly clear, and no doubt it seemed entirely clear to the student as he wrote it. Your sentences may seem clear to you at the time you write them, but if you put your paper away for a day or two before rereading it, you may find confusions that you did not notice before. Reading your paper aloud to yourself also helps, and it is even better to read it to somebody else, if you can find someone who will put politeness aside long enough to tell you when you are confusing him.

After you have changed everything that needs changing, go back through your paper for one final check:

1. Have you done everything your first paragraph promised and no more?
2. Have you included all the necessary steps in logical order?
3. Have you cut out all the apologies?
4. Have you used enough transitions to take your reader comfortably from point to point?
5. Have you talked to your reader as the same person all the way through?
6. Is the meaning of each pronoun unmistakable?
7. Does your last paragraph fit with your first paragraph and make your paper sound finished?

If your answer to all these questions is "yes," you are almost through. Copy the paper carefully, hand it in, and hope for the best.

Key Words

Here are some of the important terms used in this chapter. Without referring back to the chapter, see whether you can answer these questions about them.

1. The *main idea sentence* of a paper giving directions ought to contain two things. What are they? Why are they useful?

2. In a paper giving directions, what does the *introduction* do that the main idea sentence does not do? In what sense does the introduction serve as a *contract* with the reader? Can introductions do more than serve as a contract?

3. How does the *conclusion* of a paper differ from simple stopping?

4. Describe in your own words what the word "clear" means when applied to themes. Is it true that *clarity* is particularly important in papers giving directions? Why? Why not?

5. What is a *transition*? Describe the kinds of transitions. How do they contribute to clarity?

6. How can the careful use of pronouns contribute to *clarity*? Explain two things you can do to avoid pronoun confusion.

Vocabulary

Pick the answer that most closely fits the meaning of the word as it has been used in the chapter. Look up in your dictionary the meaning of all the words you miss.

1. If a knife is *sterile*, it is   _____
   (a) free of germs
   (b) stolen
   (c) dull
   (d) a promotional gift

2. A *midwife* is most likely to assist in   _____
   (a) cleaning house
   (b) recovering from a divorce
   (c) cooking
   (d) having a baby

3. When you *inspire* someone you   _____
   (a) make him free of germs
   (b) breathe or blow on him
   (c) stimulate him
   (d) make him sweat

4. A *continuous* performance is one that   _____
   (a) is condemned
   (b) occurs seldom
   (c) keeps on happening
   (d) is favored only by politicians

5. A person making *apologies* would be making   _____
   (a) a dessert made of apples
   (b) forthright statements
   (c) regretful excuses
   (d) atomic experiments

6. *Namby-pamby* phrases are phrases   _____
   (a) quoted from a regional dialect
   (b) correctly limiting meaning of papers
   (c) adding great vigor and directness
   (d) weak and pointless, adding nothing but words

7. If you address your reader *consistently* throughout your
   paper, you will be   _____
   (a) using the same system throughout

(b) considering his texture and density
(c) putting a mailing tag on him
(d) changing needlessly from one pronoun to another

8. An *impersonal* paper   ————
   (a) strongly impresses the reader with the writer's personal opinions
   (b) keeps the writer out of it as much as possible
   (c) often addresses the reader directly
   (d) is unsigned

9. An action that is *affected* is   ————
   (a) spontaneous
   (b) natural
   (c) artificial and put-on
   (d) unrehearsed and honest

10. A *flippant* person is probably   ————
    (a) an acrobat
    (b) a pancake cook
    (c) polite
    (d) given to wisecracks

11. To act *haphazardly* means to   ————
    (a) act consistently
    (b) proceed cautiously
    (c) proceed without any plan
    (d) proceed with fear

12. A *premiere* is a production that is   ————
    (a) being put on for the first time
    (b) attended by the prime minister
    (c) simple and easy to understand
    (d) being put on for the last time

13. There is nothing "wrong" with *formal language*, but it is best suited to   ————
    (a) conversation between friends
    (b) serious and important occasions
    (c) papers giving directions
    (d) letters written home to mother

14. *Sequence* means   ————
    (a) the second thing in line
    (b) a shiny decoration used on ladies' dresses
    (c) the result of a previous act
    (d) the order in which things happen

15. If you are *quibbling*, you are _____
    (a) playing an outdoor game
    (b) planting a garden
    (c) fussing over trivial matters
    (d) betraying your country

Exercises

Exercise 1. Write a main idea sentence for a paper giving directions for each of the following:

1. How to sharpen a pencil _____

_____

_____

_____

2. How to change a diaper _____

_____

_____

_____

3. How to shorten a skirt _____

_____

_____

_____

4. How to find an article in the *Reader's Guide to Periodical Literature*

_____

_____

_____

5. How to bathe a canary _____

_____

_____

6. How to wrap a package for mailing _____

_____

_____

_____

7. How to make a _____ (*discuss an object you are familiar with*)

_____

_____

_____

8. How to _____ (*fill in the blank with something you know how to do.*)

_____

_____

_____

9. How to _____ (*use your imagination.*) _____

_____

_____

_____

Exercise 2. Here are the plans for three different papers giving directions. The steps the writer plans to cover are there, but they are listed haphazardly. On a separate page, list them in the order that seems to you most sensible.

1. *How to start a campfire without matches*

    dry leaves may be substituted for paper
    pair of glasses can be used as a magnifying glass

twigs should be shaved very fine
when small twigs are burning well, larger branches can be added
collect plenty of paper, twigs, branches, and logs
put on small twigs after the paper or leaves catch on fire
paper must be dry
sun must be out to shine through the glasses
put on the logs
hold glasses so that sun shines on paper or leaves

2. *How to plant sweetpeas*

seeds should be planted in the trench about an inch deep
fertilizer should be worked into soil
soil must be raked very smooth
small trench should be made with trowel
big weeds must be pulled out and small roots raked away
ground should be thoroughly spaded
seeds should be planted in February when soil is not soggy

3. *How to change film in a box camera*

turn the knob until none of the old film can be seen in the window
    opening
make sure the back is tightly in place before taking pictures
work in a fairly dark place
remove the exposed film and wrap it in the foil that you have taken
    off the new roll
insert the new film, being careful not to expose any of it
turn the new film until the first picture can be seen in the window
    opening
switch the spindle to the other side

Exercise 3. Choose three of the topics in Exercise 1 that you
know the most about. For each of them list all the steps needed to do
the job. Make sure the steps are in the right order. Add more numbers
if your plan requires more steps.

1. MAIN IDEA SENTENCE _____

Step 1 _____

_____

_____

Step 2 _____

_____

_____

Step 3 _____

_____

_____

Step 4 _____

_____

_____

Step 5 _____

_____

_____

2. MAIN IDEA SENTENCE _____

_____

_____

Step 1 _____

_____

_____

Step 2 _____

_____

_____

Step 3 _____

_____

_____

Step 4 _____

_____

_____

Step 5 _____

_____

_____

3. MAIN IDEA SENTENCE _____

_____

_____

Step 1 _____

_____

_____

Step 2 _____

_____

_____

Step 3 _____

_____

_____

Step 4 _____

_____

_____

Step 5 _____

_____

_____

Exercise 4. Rewrite these sentences to avoid any confusion caused by pronouns.

a. Compare a Ford with a Chevy. It's a much better car.

_____

b. George Orwell wrote a lot about Charles Dickens. He was a good writer, he thought, and was always very pleased when he had finished a book.

_____

_____

_____

c. Put two cups of milk in a bowl. Then we add one egg. The cook should then beat to a froth. This will give a richer taste to our French toast. One should dip the bread in his batter, but they shouldn't drop into the frying pan. Put them in gently. One should watch it all the time if we want good French toast. Then serve them.

_____

_____

_____

_____

_____

_____

d. A person shouldn't buy things they can't pay for if you don't want to be put in jail.

_____

_____

e. John told Jim he made a mistake.

_____

_____

f. I've been on hundreds of airplane rides, but I've never learned to fly one.

_____

_____

_____

g. Have the children take off their clothes and then wash them.

_____

_____

h. If a dog bites one, he should run home.

_____

_____

i. My major at college is nursing, but I don't know for sure if I really want to be one.

_____

_____

_____

j. People should show more affection to their children. If you give your children more love, juvenile delinquency will decrease in the United States, but most parents don't think about that when they are annoyed with them.

_____

_____

_____

_____

k. To clean the tables, wait until the students get up, then wipe them off with a damp cloth.

_____

_____

_____

l. One should be well prepared before they go to his or her test.

_____

_____

m. Everyone should comb their wig carefully, especially if you wear it in the shower.

---

n. All members of the student body should know the candidates before you vote.

---

o. Running for office is fine if you like being one, but I don't.

Exercise 5. Be prepared to explain in class what is wrong with each of these introductory paragraphs for papers giving directions.

1. This paper is about cakes. I don't approve of cake mixes, although many people are using them these days. Buy some flour.

2. Get hammer and nails ready. Clear a space in the garage. Don't forget a saw. And don't forget some glue. Make sure you have enough room.

3. I spent the summer working as a flagman on a construction job. They were building a bridge. If you want to build a bridge, get some heavy equipment and some men.

4. After you bathe your dog, dry him. But don't get soap in his eyes.

5. This undertaking is not very hard and it doesn't take much equipment, so that's a good thing. It doesn't cost much either. Get the things you will need together in one pile and make sure you haven't forgotten the most important thing. Now you are ready to begin.

6. The first thing to do is put a good layer of undercoating and let it dry. Before that the wood should be sanded. Sanding is the biggest part of the job, but painting an old chair is a very good way to make it look like new.

7. A kid I know is a real shark at playing basketball, even though he hasn't even seen one for maybe a year. They make it seem real easy. There are four steps in throwing the ball.

Exercise 6. Rewrite the introductory paragraphs in Exercise 5, making sure that your introductions include a clear statement of the main idea and a list of the things needed to do the job if they have not been mentioned in the main idea sentence.

Exercise 7. Write introductory paragraphs for themes using the main ideas and steps you worked out for Exercise 3.

Exercise 8. List and explain all the transitions used on pages 15 and 16 of this text.

Exercise 9. Copy five transitional devices used in one of your other textbooks. Explain the way in which each of these transitions takes the reader from point to point.

Exercise 10. Find a magazine or newspaper article of at least eight consecutive paragraphs. Clip the article and bring it to class with the transitions underlined. In choosing your article, you should
1. find one that uses good transitions;
2. avoid straight news stories and fiction, since neither of these makes much use of the kind of transition we have been talking about.

Exercise 11. Write a paper on one of the subjects you used for Exercise 7. Before you turn it in, ask yourself all the questions listed on page 49.

Exercise 12. Giving directions for getting from one place to another involves a special kind of skill. Write a paper in which you do one of these things:

Explain to someone how to get from the center of town to wherever you live, either by walking or by using public transportation.

Explain to a friend how to drive a car from one place to another two or three miles away. Choose a route that involves at least three turns or choices.

In either of these papers, be sure to identify landmarks clearly enough that your reader will be able to follow your directions.

IV

What Do You Mean?
Explaining

Whenever someone says, "What do you mean?" he is asking for an explanation. He doesn't want to be told how to do something, he doesn't want to know what happened, and he doesn't want an argument. He just wants something explained.

Perhaps the simplest form of explanation is the one you get when you look up a word in a dictionary. Dictionary definitions tell what a word means. But many words or concepts are too complicated to be completely explained by a three- or four-word definition. It takes three or four sentences to explain even a simple word like *chair* clearly enough to distinguish it from a *davenport* or *bench*. You will find that it takes at least three or four paragraphs to explain concepts like *loyalty* or *justice*. And there are terms that require even more detailed explanation. People have written entire books explaining the meaning of such terms as *democracy* and *totalitarianism* and still not covered everything that could have been said.

When you are asked to write a paper defining such a concept, you will need to begin with a generalization, a statement broad enough to cover most situations in which the term might be used. "Loyalty means refusing to abandon the people or ideas you love" is a generalization. In explaining what you mean by such a word as *loyalty*, the generalization will be your main idea sentence, but you will need to back up this general statement by giving some examples.

The easiest way to see the connection between generalizations and the examples that explain them is to begin with the idea of *general* and *specific* words. We can explain *general* by saying that the more things a word refers to, the more *general* it is. The fewer things a word refers to, the more *specific* it is. Thus *general* and *specific* are relative terms. The word *dog* is more specific than *animal*, less specific than *bulldog*. *Bulldog*, in turn, is less specific than *Tige*, Buster Brown's bulldog. In the same way, *human being* is more general than *college student*. *College student* is more general than *Raglan College freshman*. *Raglan College freshman* is more general than *Rupert Creech*. If you begin with *human being*, *Rupert Creech* is about as specific as you can get.

Sometimes you have to use general words to include all the people or things you are talking about, but people understand you more clearly the more specific you are. If you say to your father, "Lots of people I know get one hundred dollars a week for pocket money," he is likely to respond, "Who, for instance?" Your father is not questioning your veracity; he just wants *specific* words. Some occasions, of course, demand general words. In the comment, "Students who turn their papers in late will be penalized," *students* is more general than *Rupert Creech* or *Tansy Ragwort*. The teacher who made the statement, however, meant not only Rupert and Tansy but all fifteen other students in the class. Notice that the teacher did not say *human beings* or *mammals*, since he was not expecting papers from other members of these more general classes. A safe rule to follow is: *choose the most specific word that will fit the subject you are discussing.*

Just as words can be more general or less general, so statements can be more general or less general. A generalization includes many things, a specific statement indicates one particular thing. If the general statement and the specific statement are related, we say that *the specific statement is an example of the generalization*. If you begin your paper with the generalization, "Loyalty means refusing to abandon the people or ideas you love," your reader, like your father, may say, "Who, for instance, refused to abandon what?" Then you give examples. You might say, "The faithful old dog who refuses to move more than four inches from his dead master's bathrobe is showing canine loyalty," or "Barbara Frietchie, leaning out the window and crying, 'Shoot, if you must, this old gray head, but spare your country's flag,' is displaying loyalty to her country."

Examples can be very useful, but they can also be misleading. You probably don't mean that the only two ways of showing loyalty are clinging doggedly to an old bathrobe or offering your head in defense of the flag. Usually when you give examples, you must include a big enough variety to hint at all the kinds of loyalty you can think of.

Even if you don't give examples, you should mention other kinds of loyalty. You might add the generalizations, "Loyalty means sticking up for your friends when other people are running them down," or "Loyalty means working hard for something you believe in and not complaining that you get no credit for the work you do."

Even after you have listed every kind of loyalty you can think of, you may have to add some generalizations explaining what loyalty is not: "Loyalty does not mean giving up your right to say what you think," or "Loyalty does not mean blindly following directions you don't believe in." In explaining what loyalty is not, you need cover only those things that might be confused with it. You don't need to say, "Putting enough salt in the potatoes has nothing to do with loyalty," or "Polishing your shoes is not loyalty."

Whatever it is you are defining—love, sociology, free enterprise—one good way to go about it is to start with a generalization and support it with specific examples. It is probably wise to give your best example first and to use examples of what you do not mean later. And remember that the assignment is to define, not to defend or attack. Don't come out in favor of whatever you are defining, whether it's love, sociology, or free enterprise, and, of course, don't come out against it. Just tell what it is.

Here is a student theme defining *courage*.

Courage

Courage is a quality which has been valued and praised in every society in every century. Courage is the ability and the desire to hold true to principles and stand up and be counted without thought of personal gain or loss.

People often consider the war hero who plunges through a wall of fire to rescue his smoldering buddy brave, but unless he was really thinking just about his good friend, Archie, he was not demonstrating true courage.

On the other hand, America's classic example of cowardice, Benedict Arnold, may have demonstrated the greatest courage if, when he sold out to the British, he did so because of his personal convictions and a belief that in becoming a traitor he was actually promoting the best good for the most people.

Courage is not always shown in big acts, either. The grimy little boy who can go up to his teacher and stammer, "Mr. Legree, I'm sorry, but I cheated on that test," is probably displaying as much courage as the White House aide who says, "Mr. President, I'm sorry, but I lost that last dispatch." Both of these people feel strongly enough about honesty (although apparently the third grader had a bit of a struggle) to admit to their higher authorities that they have made a mistake. Often confessing to somebody else that you have done something wrong requires the highest kind of courage.

The word "courage" comes from the Latin word *cor* which means "heart." Courage, then, is an affair of the heart which requires complete devotion of the mind and the body.

Do you understand what this student means by courage? That is, has he made his meaning exact enough that you can say to yourself, "*This* kind of behavior he would call courageous, but *that* kind he would not"? For instance, would the writer think that pulling a drowning baby out of a pond showed courage? What would he say about joining a peace march from the city hall to the courthouse? What would he say about driving ninety miles an hour in a forty-mile zone? Diving off the high board on a dare even though your knees are shaking? Parachute jumping? Refusing to take a drink even though everybody else calls you a sissy? All these kinds of behavior are sometimes called courageous; the job here, however, is only to decide whether or not they come under this student's definition.

The paper begins with the generalization that "Courage is the ability and the desire to hold true to principles and stand up and be counted without thought of personal gain or loss." This generalization, which is also the main idea sentence, would apparently rule out what is usually called "physical bravery": a willingness to risk getting hurt or killed. Apparently parachute jumping, driving at high speed, and accepting dares would not come under his definition.

That the writer means to omit this kind of behavior is emphasized by his example of what courage is *not*: rescuing a friend during a battle, the writer says, doesn't count. But why it doesn't count is not made very clear. How can we tell what the war hero was thinking about? If he is modest, he is likely to say, "Aw, that was nothing"; if he wants to build himself up as a real hero, he may say, "All I could think about was that they were going to get Archie!" For his example to be very useful, the writer ought to come straight out and say that risking physical danger is not the kind of courage he means.

More helpful are the two examples showing what courage is. In the first, the student suggests that Benedict Arnold might have been motivated by a real belief in the British cause. In the second, he says that confessing a fault is a courageous act. Both examples show people standing up for their beliefs. In other words, they show *moral courage*.

The paper would be better if the student said in his introduction that there are two kinds of courage, physical and moral, but that he is concerned only with moral courage. If he limits his definition to moral courage, we will be fairly safe in saying that the writer would find that joining a peace march and refusing a drink were courageous acts. The marcher believes in demonstrating for peace; the nondrinker believes in abstinence.

The last paragraph is an attempt to make the paper sound finished by restating the definition. Half of the attempt succeeds; the paper doesn't just stop in midair. But the restatement of the definition is much less successful. The final sentence sounds more like a definition of *marriage* than of *courage*. The last paragraph needs to be rewritten.

The second draft of the same theme is not perfect, but it is certainly much better. All of the new material in the second draft has been underlined so that you can see the changes more easily:

Courage

Courage is a quality which has been valued and praised in every society in every century. Everybody admires people who show courage, but not everybody agrees about what courage is. Actually, there are two kinds of courage, physical courage and moral courage. Physical courage means not being afraid to get hurt. Moral courage is the ability and the desire to hold true to principles and stand up and be counted without thought of personal gain or loss. Physical courage is easier to see than moral courage and is more likely to be praised. Because moral courage seldom gets any medals, and because it is really harder to achieve, the person who has moral courage is showing true courage.

People often consider the war hero brave. They admire a man who plunges through a wall of fire to rescue his smoldering buddy. But even though he risked his life for his good friend, Archie, he did not have to use any moral courage. Everybody believes in saving friends.

On the other hand, America's classic example of cowardice, Benedict Arnold, may have demonstrated the greatest courage if, when he sold out to the British, he did so because of his personal convictions and a belief that in becoming a traitor he was actually promoting the best good for the most people.

Courage is not always shown in big acts, either. The grimy little boy who can go up to his teacher and stammer, "Mr.

Legree, I'm sorry, but I cheated on that test," is probably displaying as much courage as the White House Aide who says, "Mr. President, I'm sorry, but I lost that last dispatch." Although apparently the third grader had a bit of a struggle, both of these people feel strongly enough about honesty to admit that they have made a mistake. Often confessing to somebody else that you have done something wrong requires the highest kind of courage.

The word "courage" comes from the Latin word *cor* which means "heart." Courage, then, means that if you believe with your whole heart that something is right, you act according to your belief.

In this version the student has narrowed his definition, taken care of the confusion in the second paragraph, and rewritten his conclusion. In addition, he has changed two sentences to make them read a little more smoothly. One of these changes is in paragraph 2 and one of them is in paragraph 4.

Notice that in both versions the student has used specific words wherever he could. He has given the buddy a name, so that we think of him as a person rather than as a vague "friend." He has let us see the little boy as "grimy" and told us that he "stammered" when he made his confession. He has let us hear both the child and the aide by giving us their own words rather than his indirect version of what they said. The choice of specific words helps to make this paper interesting, and using specific words will make your papers more interesting too.

Perhaps the assignment is to explain two things that might be confused with each other. The kind of explanation which points out the differences between two similar things is called *comparison*. In writing a theme of comparison, you must explain how two similar ideas or things are alike and then deal with their differences.

As usual, you will need a main idea sentence. If you want to distinguish between a mother figure and a great teacher, you may say, "Mothers and teachers are alike in some ways and very different in others." Then go on to work out the likenesses and differences. Did you learn a lot about writing sentences from your year in junior high with Mrs. Ellipsis, or did she mostly just help you plan the Christmas party and pass the cookies with warmth and understanding? Certainly both mothers and great teachers offer you advice and both are concerned with your proper development. Mothers, however, concentrate on keeping you cozy and making you happy. Great teachers are concerned with offering you new ideas, and they don't care much whether the ideas make you comfortable or not. A teacher who becomes a mother figure, therefore, is one who is more concerned with mothering than with teaching. Of course, some teachers have ten kids, and some mothers teach school. But that doesn't mean you can't establish a difference between mothers and teachers.

Just as you can compare people, you can also compare purposes. For instance, you might examine the difference between vocational subjects and liberal arts subjects. You can take both for college credit and both prepare you for life. But vocational courses train you to earn your living and liberal arts courses help you to examine and enjoy life.

All sorts of things can be compared: insects and bugs, toads and frogs, Republicans and Democrats. Whatever you are comparing, the requirements are the same: *you must say how the two are alike and how they are different.*

You may begin with likenesses and go on to differences, or begin with differences and go on to likenesses. Your order will depend on what you want to emphasize. If your main idea is that, in spite of some differences, the two things are really much alike, discuss the differences first. If your point is that the two things seem much alike but are actually very different, discuss the likenesses first. The way you have phrased your main idea sentence will help you to decide what order you will follow.

Here is a student theme comparing two games:

Ping Pong and Tennis

In many ways ping pong and tennis are very much alike. The major and most outstanding difference, of course, is the difference in size of equipment.

In ping pong, as in tennis, each player is equipped with a paddle or racket. The object of both games is to get the ball over the net and still keep the ball inside a certain area. Also, in both games, there are numerous restrictions about where the ball must be served, where the server must stand, and how the score is counted.

But also, the two games have very obvious and important differences. Of course there is a difference in size of equipment, but there is also the difference in exertion needed for each game. Table tennis, as ping pong is sometimes called, can be a very exciting and enjoyable game for almost anyone. But tennis, although exciting and enjoyable, takes much more exertion— running, jumping, etc. For this reason tennis would be limited to those persons in at least average, if not slightly better than average, health.

It would probably seem to an observer of these sports that a person who was good at tennis would also be good at ping pong. In some cases this is so, but actually it can be just the opposite. The person who stands out in tennis, for that very reason, might be horribly poor at ping pong, and vice versa. So, as a general rule it would be wise to stick to one sport or the other.

The introductory paragraph of this paper states that there are some similarities and at least one difference between ping pong and tennis. It implies that the paper is going to compare and contrast, and suggests that the writer is going to concentrate mostly on the similarities. But does the paper concentrate on the similarities and treat the differences lightly? No, it covers the similarities in paragraph 2, and spends the rest of the paper, including the conclusion, on the differences. Thus the introductory paragraph, though it does suggest the purpose, does not state the main idea clearly enough to serve as a contract between the writer and the reader.

Further, paragraph 3 seems to contradict paragraph 1. Paragraph 1 calls the size of the equipment the "major and most outstanding difference." But does he need to say both "major" and "most outstanding"? If the terms mean about the same thing, using both adds nothing but words, and one term or the other can be omitted. Paragraph 3 talks about the difference in exertion required for each game, and suggests that health would limit the number of people who could play tennis. To avoid having more than one "most important" difference, the writer might have called the first difference, size, the "most obvious," and the second difference, exertion, the "most important," since anyone can see the difference in size, and the consequences of overexertion, although they are often quite serious, are less easy to see.

Besides the misleading introduction and the inexact wording, there is also a problem of order. It confuses the reader to have to jump from the specific difference mentioned in paragraph 1, to the specific similarities in paragraph 2, and then back to differences in paragraphs 3 and 4. It would be easy to get rid of this confusing order by rewriting the introduction something like this:

> Even though at first glance ping pong and tennis look very much alike, they are really very different. As anybody who has played both games knows, the differences are more important than the similarities.

The last paragraph of the paper has two major faults in it. First, the writer says that a "person who stands out in tennis" might be poor in ping pong "for that very reason." But being outstanding in tennis is not necessarily a "reason" for anything. We don't know why being good in tennis means being bad in ping pong until the writer explains it to us. The other fault in paragraph 4 is the last sentence, where the writer suggests that the reader "stick to one sport or the other." This advice would perhaps be a good enough conclusion for a theme of directions, but a theme of explanation ought to explain, not advise. The student might say:

> The person who stands out in tennis might be *very* poor at ping pong and vice versa. The thing that makes him win a tennis game—slamming a serve as hard as he can—may make him lose the ping pong game because he will hit the ball clear into the next room. On the other hand, the ping pong expert who stands at the center of the table returning every serve may not be able to run fast enough to reach the tennis ball. Both games require skill, but the skills they require are not the same.

Perhaps the theme would be improved by even more rewriting. Yet as it stands, it does make a fairly successful attempt to explain by comparing.

Sometimes you need to explain one term: *definition*. Sometimes you need to explain two somewhat similar terms or things: *comparison*. And sometimes you need to explain the connection between a number of things that are somehow related to each other: *classification*. You are writing a theme of classification whenever you explain things by sorting them into piles and then resorting each pile into smaller groups. Your sorting process must not be haphazard but must be based on some kind of system.

If you are classifying animal lovers, your main idea sentence might read, "People who keep animals as a hobby can be separated into two main groups, wild animal keepers and tame animal keepers." In explaining the first group, you might go on to say that some exceptional people do keep wild animals. They de-smell skunks, they tame cougars, and they cuddle lion cubs in the corners of their davenports. But as Hilaire Belloc pointed out in a poem about people who keep frogs, "they are extremely rare." In explaining the second group, you might say that the people who lavish their loving care on domesticated animals are a much larger group. But making intimate companions out of many kinds of tame animals is also rare. Not many people pamper pigs, moon over cows, or dote on draft horses. Instead, people tend to make pets of cats, dogs, horses, shetland ponies, guinea pigs, or white Easter rabbits. Domestic animals, of course, can be divided into those which can be trained to respect wall-to-wall carpeting, and those best adapted to life in the great outdoors. You can keep on subdividing until you are tired, or, better, until your point has been made. Any paper that makes its point by beginning with a general group, subdividing, and then subdividing again is following a plan of *classification.*

For instance, the plan of this book depends on classification. We began by dividing writing purposes into five general groups: giving directions, explaining, telling what happened, summarizing, and convincing. In this chapter we are subdividing explanation into four more groups: defining, comparing, classifying, and analyzing. Classifying will be further subdivided if we go on to say that not only ideas, such as the writing purposes we have been talking about here, but also people or things can sometimes be explained more easily if they are classified.

The thing to remember about classification is that you can take only one step at a time. Making a chart of your classification will often help you to decide what steps to take. A chart showing the classification of writing purposes would look like this:

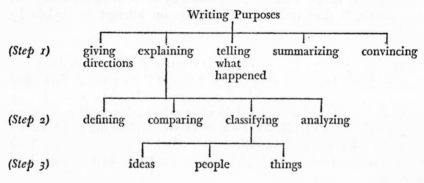

Because our special interest was in discussing classification, we did not subdivide all the divisions in the first step, or in the second step. Notice, however, that we did not jump from the first step to the third, and that we did not combine the first and second steps in order to get to the third step faster. Instead, we followed the route that led through explaining and classifying and then stopped with the third step, the subdivisions of classification.

If you make your chart carefully and follow it step by step, the order of your classification paper will take care of itself.

Here is a student theme of classification:

The Bookstore

"Hey, Sam! There's the college bookstore. Let's go buy a book or two. Maybe we can impress some teachers." So the two boys wandered into the bookstore and stopped about two feet inside the door, astonished and confused by the collection of reading material spread out in front of them. "How are we going to find anything in all this mess?" Sam asked.

But soon one of the boys saw a sign marked TEXTBOOKS. He glanced in that direction, saw a copy of his history book, *Through the Ages with the Sages*, shuddered, and turned toward the other sign: LEISURE READING. "Hey, let's go look at these paperbacks. 'Leisure' means 'fun,' doesn't it? If we're going to buy books, we may as well enjoy it."

In the leisure reading section there were still more signs: FICTION and NONFICTION. Sam thought nonfiction would be more likely to impress the professors, but he took one glance at Hobbes' *Leviathan* and decided he wasn't up to it. Moving over to the fiction racks, he found still more signs: CLASSICS and CONTEMPORARY. Still hoping to find something they might get credit for, they examined a few classics. But Sam had read some Cooper in the eighth grade, and he decided fairly quickly that *The Last of the Mohicans* was not his idea of leisure reading. They went on to the contemporary section.

There the signs offered a choice among SCIENCE FICTION, MYSTERIES, HISTORICAL NOVELS, WESTERNS, and HUMOR. The two boys saw and discarded *Marooned on the New Moon*, *Who Killed Rock Cobbin?* *The Last Days of Bombay*, and *Custer's Next-to-Last Stand*. That left HUMOR. But even here there were signs. Sam decided, after one look at *Why Bigamy Is Preferable to Bachelorhood*, that he didn't want SATIRE, so they went on to SLAPSTICK. Here, at last, Sam found a book that he thought he might enjoy. He hauled out his nickels and dimes and pennies and bought a copy of *I Lost My Mother-in-Law in a Bookstore*.

"Gee, I'm not surprised the old girl got lost," Sam said as they left. "If they didn't have some kind of system, nobody could ever find anything in there!"

If you look for a main idea sentence in the first paragraph of this theme, you will not find it. Nevertheless, the student who wrote this paper did have a clear main idea sentence in his head, and if you look back at the first paragraph, you can make a fairly good guess at what it was. By the time you have read the whole theme, you should be able to work it out yourself: *Books can be classified into two main divisions, textbooks and books for leisure reading.*

Although the writer has not stated his main idea, he has used his introduction to gain interest. Watching two boys discover a classification system makes for livelier reading than simply being told what the system is. In spite of beginning with conversation, however, this introduction does serve as a contract. The introduction makes it clear enough that the paper will try to make order from the confusing array of books. If the rest of the paper did not classify the books into some kind of system, the reader would feel cheated.

Beginning with conversation implies another promise, too. The reader expects to be told a story, and he is told one. In other words, the writer has blended telling what happened with explaining, but he never lets his eagerness to tell a story interfere with his main purpose, classifying books.

Pretty obviously, the student who wrote this paper had a good time doing it. He has amused himself by making up book titles; he mentions only two that are real books, *Leviathan* and *The Last of the Mohicans.* But again, he did not let the fun he was having distract him from his main purpose. The books he mentions in paragraph 4 are clearly examples of five possible subdivisions of contemporary fiction, and the writer has been careful to see that the examples follow exactly the same order as the subdivisions.

In spite of the lively and informal writing, this theme succeeds in following the assignment clearly and well. It is very easy to make a classification chart showing the system that has been followed. Notice that the student has taken only one step at a time:

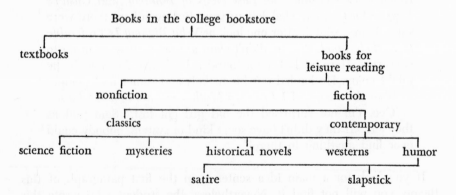

The fourth method of explaining is *analysis*. Things that cannot be defined or compared or classified can often be explained by analysis—

explaining a whole thing by examining it piece by piece. For instance, you can best write a theme explaining how a carburetor works by explaining the mixing chamber, the air intake, the gas intake, and the jet that regulates the proper proportion of gas and air. (Main idea sentence: A carburetor cannot operate unless it has a mixing chamber, an air intake, a gas intake, and a jet.) Or you can write a paper explaining the alarming cost of a wedding by analyzing the cost of providing the bridesmaids' dresses, paying the minister's fee, renting the tuxedos, paying a singer and an accompanist, buying the cake and punch, and hiring somebody to serve the food and a janitor to clean up the mess. (Main idea sentence: Everything about a wedding costs money, from buying the bridesmaids' dresses to hiring someone to clean up when it is all over.) Whenever your paper explains the whole by explaining the relationship of the parts, you are analyzing.

In analysis, the order will depend on what it is you are analyzing. If you're analyzing a carburetor, deal with the parts in the order in which they contribute to the total action. If you are analyzing the cost of a wedding, you can choose between beginning with the most expensive item and working down or with the least expensive and working up.

Here is a student theme of analysis:

How a Camera Works

Most people think that cameras are hard to understand because they often see a lot of lenses, flash attachments, tripods, and other fancy gadgets which are sold with cameras. However, all cameras work on the same principle, and the gadgets are merely extras. If you analyze the four parts of a simple box camera you will discover exactly how a $500 imported job works—the principle is the same, only the extras are different.

First there is a light-proof box which holds the film. It can be a fancy camera or an old shoe box, just as long as it keeps the light out. The inside of the box has to be completely dark or else the film may be spoiled and come out streaked or completely blank.

Next is the film. In most cameras the film is rolled across one end of the camera, but it doesn't have to be. It can be just a single piece of film taped to one side of a light-proof shoe box. The film must not be exposed to light before the picture is taken.

Third is the lens, or opening. This is on the side of the box opposite the film, and it is through the hole that the light comes to hit the film and expose it.

Fourth and last is the shutter, which opens and closes the lens or opening. Obviously you can't leave the opening uncovered all the time or else you would expose your film before you were ready to, and would probably ruin the picture.

Thus we see how the four parts work. The shutter opens and lets light through the lens and onto the film in the dark box. The lens is covered and the picture has been taken. As for the difference between my shoe box camera and the fancy model? You'll have to ask the man who sells them. I don't understand it myself.

Notice that this theme is not telling the reader how to build a camera or even how to operate one. If the student had done either of those things, he would have written a paper of directions. The difference should be clear if you compare the second paragraph of "How a Camera Works" with this paragraph from a theme called "How to Build a Simple Camera."

To build a simple box camera you will need a sturdy shoe box, some heavy wrapping paper, a roll of masking tape, an ordinary pin, and a small piece of cardboard. To operate the camera, you will also need a roll of film of any size.

The first step is to . . .

Next you . . .

After you have read the analysis paper, you know how a camera works, but you probably cannot tell from reading this paper how to build one. If you had read only a paper on how to build a simple camera, and if the directions were complete, you might be able to build a camera without understanding how it worked. The writer who knows what his purpose is will be better able to stick to giving directions, if that is what he means to do, or to analyzing, if he means to explain.

The first paragraph of "How a Camera Works" clearly states the purpose and the main idea: an analysis of cameras to explain how they work. Further, it catches the reader's attention by telling why the paper is being written: to remove some of the confusion about cameras.

Does the order of the parts analyzed seem clear? It seems so to us, since the parts are presented in much the same way that we load, then use a camera: starting with the box, then the film, then the operation of the shutter. This order is made even more clear through the use of transitions. Notice how the paragraphs are introduced, from paragraph 2 on through the theme: *First . . . Next . . . Third . . . Fourth . . . Thus. . . .*

Does the conclusion make the paper sound finished? It does, both by summing up the analysis that has already been given, and by referring back to the introduction and picking up the idea that was introduced earlier—that the principle applies to all cameras. Further, the writer ties the last paragraph to the first two paragraphs by repeating the comparison of the shoe box and the $500 camera. This repeating not only finishes the theme, but it also ties the whole thing together very nicely.

Some readers might be annoyed by the constant reminder not to expose the film, at the end of paragraphs 2, 3, 4, and 5. Maybe the paper would be better if some of this repetition were left out. Otherwise, there is not much wrong with this paper. In fact, it is pretty good.

Defining, comparing, classifying, and analyzing are certainly not the only ways of explaining things, but they are four of the most common ways of answering the question, "What do you mean?"

Whichever of these methods you use, you are forgetting your purpose if you stop explaining the high cost of weddings and begin arguing for elopement; or if you say what a wonderful gadget a carburetor is; or if you bemoan the disappearance of the dodo as a household pet; or if you insist that more people ought to be loyal. The words *should* or *should not, ought* or *ought not, good* or *bad, better* or *worse,* express opinion. They have no place in explanations.

After you have written the main idea sentence of your paper, you are more likely to stick to the job of explaining and not be sidetracked into saying something is *good* or *bad.* The student who starts by saying, "Loyalty is a feeling of devotion toward a country, a belief, a group, or another person," may still be tempted to say, "Everybody ought to be loyal," but he will be less likely to say it after making such a good start. The student who starts by saying, "To understand the workings of a carburetor, it is necessary to examine each of the important parts" may resist the temptation to say, "The carburetor is the greatest invention that has ever been made."

When you have worked out the order your paper will follow, and when you have gone through your plan carefully to make sure that each point is an explanation and not an opinion, start writing. As you write, remember that these separate points are somewhat like women, each with a particular charm, each worthy of undivided attention. But just as two women in the same house may bicker and bite in competing for your attention, so will two of these points clash if you dump them into the same paragraph. Keep each woman in her own house and each point in its own paragraph.

Of course there are some niceties that will help. If you can leave one point gracefully and take up the next one smoothly, you will have a pleasanter theme, just as you will have a happier life if you can move from woman to woman—that is, visit your mother without offending your wife—without jolting either one of them. In an earlier chapter you had some practice in transitions, especially such simple devices as saying *then, next,* and *finally,* or *first, second,* and *last.* By now you may have discovered that smooth relations between paragraphs, like smooth relations with women, is largely a matter of experience.

The problem of saying what you mean is much like the problem in any other kind of writing. Decide what you want to explain, find the method of explanation that will best do the job, list the things that must be said, arrange them in reasonable order, and give each point a paragraph of its own. Check your first paragraph to make sure that it contains your main idea; check the rest of your paper to make sure that it does what your first paragraph promised; check your final paragraph to make sure that it relates clearly to the idea presented in the first paragraph. Put your paper away to cool, and when it is thoroughly cold—in a day or two—go over it to make sure that everything you have written makes sense.

If you follow these directions with care, your reader should have no trouble understanding what you mean.

Key Words

Here are some of the important terms used in this chapter. Without referring back to the chapter, see whether you can answer these questions about them.

1. There is the same kind of relationship between *generalizations* and *examples* as there is between *general* words and *specific* words. In your own words, explain the relationship.

2. What is the difference between writing that *defines* and writing that *compares?* Are the two entirely separate?

3. Both *classification* and *analysis* explain things. How do they differ? How can we tell whether we have a paper of classification or a paper of analysis?

4. Explain what is meant by *order* in themes. What is the best order for a paper of definition? For a paper of comparison? For a paper of classification? For a paper of analysis? How do *paragraphs* and *transitions* contribute to both *order* and *clarity?*

Vocabulary

Pick the answer that most closely fits the meaning of the word as it has been used in the chapter. Look up in your dictionary the meaning of all the words you miss.

1. A *concept* is _____
   (a) a general idea
   (b) an army draftee
   (c) a public performance
   (d) a small organ-like instrument which is squeezed

2. If you *distinguish* two concepts, you _____
   (a) do them great honor
   (b) erase them
   (c) make the difference between them clear
   (d) eliminate the difference between them

3. To *abandon* people or ideas is to _____
   (a) dance about in a loose or immoral way
   (b) desert them
   (c) dessert them
   (d) talk about them critically

4. When we say that "general" and "specific" are *relative* terms, we mean they are _____
   (a) joined by blood or law
   (b) connected by family
   (c) dependent upon each other
   (d) entirely separate

5. A good synonym for *veracity* would be _____
   (a) untrustworthy
   (b) given to mild exaggeration
   (c) truthfulness
   (d) a short distance from a city

6. "Late papers will be *penalized*," means that late papers will be _____
   (a) accepted
   (b) refused
   (c) accepted only if written in ink
   (d) graded down or otherwise handicapped

7. An example that is *particular* (not general) would be _____
   (a) fussy in its habits
   (b) specific
   (c) broad enough to cover a great many things
   (d) made up of many small parts

8. *Canine* loyalty would be _____
   (a) loyalty of a dog for his master
   (b) characterized by a sharp, longish tooth
   (c) easily and rapidly shifting
   (d) loyalty to the ninth power

9. *Abstinence* means _____
   (a) refusing to take even a little of something
   (b) being permanently stained
   (c) not being present
   (d) having a bad temper

10. If you *lavish* your money, you will _____
    (a) wash it
    (b) hoard it
    (c) keep it in your lavatory
    (d) spend it recklessly

11. People who *moon* over cows _____
    (a) like cows only at night
    (b) are absurdly fond of cows
    (c) turn into cows during a full moon
    (d) reverse nursery rhymes

12. *Pamper* means _____
    (a) to pelt with small wads of paper
    (b) to keep on a restricted diet
    (c) to keep carefully penned up
    (d) to spoil through kindness

13. If you *dote* on bagpipes, you _____
    (a) are excessively fond of them
    (b) play them poorly
    (c) play them very skillfully
    (d) are senile and doddering

14. Someone is *adapted* to his neighborhood if he _____
    (a) hates it
    (b) loves it
    (c) becomes easily lost and frustrated there
    (d) is adjusted to it

15. ***Elopement*** is the act of _____
    (a) marrying after a long formal engagement
    (b) running off to be married
    (c) marrying between races
    (d) abandoning the bride at the church steps

16. If you ***bemoan*** the passing of the buffalo herds, you _____
    (a) are extremely pleased
    (b) are extremely relieved
    (c) regret it as a tragic loss
    (d) sing softly to their memory

17. If you ***bicker*** with your parents, you _____
    (a) argue with them over trivial points
    (b) get along with them very well
    (c) disagree with them only about politics
    (d) correspond with them by mail

Exercises

Exercise 1. Put these groups of words in order, from the *most general* to the *most specific*. For instance, the group of words *building, shelter, school, classroom building* should be arranged to read:

2   1   3   4

building   shelter   school   classroom building.

1. book, publication, *A Tale of Two Cities*, novel

2. food, grape, fruit, Concord

3. flats, clothing, shoes, black patent leather with bows

4. tools, equipment, wrenches, crescent wrenches

5. animal, human being, Indian, Sitting Bull

6. mammals, living things, females, Mae West

7. Protestantism, Christianity, religion, Presbyterianism

8. music, art, Beethoven's Fifth, concerto

9. bongos, drums, musical instruments, noisemakers

10. transportation, Volkswagen, automobile, four-wheeled vehicle

11. Annie Rooney, child, girl, biped

12. furniture, wood product, stool, colonial milking stool

13. writing implement, pen, Never-ready Ballpoint, Rupert's new green Never-ready

14. meal, breakfast, cereal, oatmeal

Exercise 2. For each of these words, find one word or phrase that is more general and one word or phrase that is more specific.

GENERAL		SPECIFIC
_____	orphan	_____
_____	house	_____
_____	child	_____
_____	chair	_____
_____	actress	_____
_____	swimming	_____
_____	people	_____
_____	vegetable	_____
_____	book	_____
_____	teacher	_____
_____	dogs	_____
_____	textbook	_____
_____	baby	_____
_____	human being	_____
_____	sewing	_____
_____	janitor	_____
_____	dish	_____
_____	sport	_____
_____	hobby	_____
_____	man	_____

Exercise 3. For each of the following generalizations, find a specific example that illustrates it.

GENERALIZATION: Smoking is bad for the health.
SPECIFIC EXAMPLE: Aunt Agatha smoked a carton of cigarettes a day every day of her life, and died at age fifteen.

This exercise is intended only to help you distinguish between specific situations and generalizations based on them. *Sound generalizations must be based on more than one specific situation* (see Chapter VIII). After you have examined these generalizations, you may want to think about whether you can trust them for all situations, for some, or for only a few.

1. Everybody who likes dogs can be trusted.

_____

_____

2. Driving on ice is dangerous.

_____

_____

_____

3. Competent drivers are as safe driving in icy weather as in any other kind of weather.

_____

_____

_____

4. Music cheers people up.

_____

_____

_____

5. Children without brothers or sisters are usually spoiled.

_____

_____

_____

6. Getting your feet wet is likely to lead to pneumonia.

_____

_____

7. State patrolmen are kind and considerate to motorists.

_____

_____

_____

8. State patrolmen are rude and inconsiderate.

_____

_____

_____

9. Telephones are a great help and convenience.

_____

_____

_____

10. Telephones are a nuisance.

_____

_____

_____

Exercise 4. Write generalizations based on these specific situations.

1. A small Boy Scout helped an old lady across the street.

_____

2. A man in Battle Creek died from the bite of a mad dog.

3. Algernon Creech, a college graduate, died in the poorhouse.

4. My mother got some spoiled meat from a chain grocery.

5. Barbara Frietchie showed loyalty when she offered her own head in protection of the flag.

6. My Uncle Bertram lives in a nice modern house with lots of glass in it. Last Saturday he threw rocks at the kids playing in his front yard, and last night the kids heaved a brick through Uncle Bertram's big front window.

_____

_____

7. I bragged about my car without knocking on wood, and the next day I had trouble with the fuel pump.

_____

_____

_____

8. Old Man Tuttle went to bed every night at 8 P.M. and got up every morning at 6:20. He died at the age of one hundred and three, when a truck ran over him. When he died, he had a million dollars in the bank.

_____

_____

_____

9. When I got home last night, I asked my mother why the house looked so clean. She told me she had just bought a new broom.

_____

_____

_____

10. Socrates was killed for questioning the beliefs held by most of the people of his time.

_____

_____

_____

Exercise 5. What generalizations are illustrated by these examples? When you have answered this question, ask yourself if the generalizations are sound.

1. My cat fell off the roof and broke its neck, trying to find out what was in the chimney.

_____

_____

_____

2. I failed advanced basket-weaving twice, so I'm sure to pass it this time.

_____

_____

_____

3. My lot is a hundred feet long and fifty feet wide, so it must have an area of five thousand square feet.

_____

_____

_____

4. Somebody must have built a fire in that old cabin; there's smoke coming out of the chimney.

_____

_____

_____

5. When we were at the beach last summer, we put a thermometer into the tea kettle and discovered that when the thermometer registered 212°F., the water was boiling.

---

6. Rupert raced his new Thunderbird against Algernon's Model T, and won the race.

---

7. Tansy always sits in the front row, wears plenty of make-up, and laughs at all the professor's jokes. She's sure to get an *A* in his class.

---

8. Mr. Peterson has lots of friends who are members of the John Birch Society. He must be a member himself.

---

9. Rupert is sure to pass history. He hasn't missed a single class.

---

10. Madge Fairlygood has taken a course in Marriage and the Family, so she is bound to make a good wife.

Exercise 6. The following theme of classification has its sentences scrambled. Rearrange the sentences into a complete well-ordered theme, containing an introduction, a body, and a conclusion. If you have kept each point in its own paragraph, you should come out with six paragraphs.

Traveling by car, however, is tiring, and the driver runs the risk of falling asleep at the wheel if he is traveling alone. People who want to get from Portland, Oregon, to San Francisco have a choice of four methods: car, bus, plane, or train. A few years ago there was a boat, too, but now the regular passenger boats no longer run and the only water travel is by private motorboat or by freighter. The bus is the cheapest method, but buses offer very little in the way of sightseeing, and the trip can become very boring. Airplanes are by far the fastest method of travel, but they are also by far the most expensive. Since the freighters run for their convenience rather than for the convenience of the passengers, neither motorboat nor freighter is practical enough to be considered. The train trip is more expensive than the bus ride, and less expensive than the plane trip. Meals at bus stops are hurried and not very good. The man who goes by private car can leave whenever he wishes, travel as fast as the law and his own state of exhaustion will allow, and choose whatever route suits his fancy. Each of these methods of travel has its own advantages and its own drawbacks. If the traveler has money to burn, and is not put off by the death statistics, he will choose the plane trip. Moreover, the traveler whose legs stiffen when he sits in one position for several hours may find the bus ride very uncomfortable. The traveler must decide whether he values speed, economy, sightseeing, or comfort, and make his choice accordingly. Trains travel through the high mountains and offer their passengers dazzling varieties of natural scenery. Then all he has to do is fill his gas tank or buy his ticket, and the slowest of these methods will get him to San Francisco in less than twenty-four hours. Cramped legs can be stretched by a walk down the aisle and the food is usually good, though expensive, on a train.

Exercise 7. Write a main idea sentence for a paper of *definition* for any five of these topics. If you think any of these terms is too broad, define only one of its possible meanings. For instance, in defining *love*, you might limit yourself to the love of a child for his parents or to puppy love or brotherly love.

1. patriotism _____

_____

_____

2. duty _____

_____

_____

3. evolution _____

_____

_____

4. honesty _____

_____

_____

5. good books _____

_____

6. education _____

_____

_____

7. love _____

_____

_____

8. a conservative _____

_____

_____

9. a liberal _____

_____

_____

10. a beatnik _____

_____

_____

Exercise 8. Choose two topics from Exercise 7 and make plans for a paper of definition. This is not a reference project; choose topics you already know something about. Be sure you can defend the order of each step in your plans.

Definition of _____

Introduction (*use your main idea sentence here*) _____

_____

_____

Examples of what _____ is:

  1. _____

     _____

     _____

  2. _____

     _____

     _____

  3. _____

     _____

     _____

Example (or examples) of what _____ is _not_:

  1. _____

     _____

     _____

  2. _____

     _____

     _____

  3. _____

     _____

     _____

Conclusion (*use a variation of your main idea here*) _____

_____

_____

_____

Definition of _____

Introduction (*use your main idea sentence here*) _____

_____

_____

_____

Examples of what _____ is:

1. _____

_____

_____

2. _____

_____

_____

3. _____

_____

_____

Example (or examples) of what _____ is *not*:

1. _____

_____

_____

2. _____

_____

_____

3. _____

_____

_____

Conclusion (*use a variation of your main idea here*) _____

_____

_____

_____

Exercise 9. On a separate sheet, write an introductory *paragraph* and a concluding *paragraph* for a paper of definition, using one of the topics you have already outlined. Base these paragraphs on the introductory and concluding sentences, as they appear in your plan. Be sure the introductory paragraph makes clear what you are going to do and that the conclusion relates to the introduction and makes the paper sound finished.

Exercise 10. Write a theme from the plan you made for Exercises 8 and 9. Remember that you will make your examples clearer if you refer to a definite situation and use specific words. Before you hand in your theme, underline all the transitions between paragraphs.

Exercise 11. Write a main idea sentence for a paper of comparison for any five of these topics.

1. insects and bugs _____

_____

_____

_____

2. *B* students and brownies _____

_____

_____

_____

3. toads and frogs _____

_____

_____

_____

4. softball and baseball _____

_____

_____

_____

5. Republicans and Democrats _____

_____

_____

_____

6. community colleges and four-year colleges _____

_____

_____

_____

7. fascism and communism _____

_____

_____

_____

8. two teachers you have had _____

_____

_____

_____

9. comic strips and television cartoons _____

_____

_____

_____

10. two makes of cars _____

_____

_____

_____

11. ready-made and home-made clothes _____

_____

_____

_____

12. rock-and-roll and cool jazz _____

_____

_____

_____

13. two books you have read _____

_____

_____

_____

   Exercise 12. Choose two topics from Exercise 11 and make plans for papers of comparison. This is not a reference project; choose topics you already know something about. Be sure you can defend the order of each step in your plan. The emphasis in this plan will be on differences rather than likenesses (see page 71).

Comparison of _____ and _____

Introduction (*Use your main idea sentence here.*) _____

_____

_____

_____

Ways _____ is like _____:

   1. _____

   _____

   _____

   2. _____

   _____

   _____

3. _____

_____

_____

Ways _____ is different from _____ :

1. _____

_____

_____

2. _____

_____

_____

3. _____

_____

_____

Conclusion (*Use a variation of your main idea sentence here.*) _____

_____

_____

_____

This comparison should emphasize likenesses.

Comparison of _____ and _____

Introduction (*Main idea sentence here.*) _____

_____

_____

Ways _____ is different from _____:

1. _____

   _____

   _____

2. _____

   _____

   _____

3. _____

   _____

   _____

Ways _____ is like _____:

1. _____

   _____

   _____

2. _____

   _____

   _____

3. _____

   _____

   _____

Conclusion (*Variation of main idea sentence here.*) _____

_____

_____

_____

     Exercise 13. On a separate sheet, write an introductory paragraph and a concluding paragraph for a paper of comparison, using one of the topics you have already outlined. Base these paragraphs on the introductory and concluding sentences as they appear in your plan. Be sure the introductory paragraph makes clear what you are going to do, and that the conclusion relates to the introduction and makes the paper sound finished.

     Exercise 14. Write a theme from the plan you made for Exercises 12 and 13. Before you hand in your theme, underline all the transitions between paragraphs.

     Exercise 15. Write a main idea sentence for a paper of classification for all of these topics.

1. furniture _____

_____

_____

2. food _____

_____

_____

3. hobbies _____

_____

_____

4. sports _____

_____

_____

5. college subjects _____

_____

_____

6. dogs _____

_____

_____

7. art _____

_____

_____

8. cars _____

_____

_____

9. clothing _____

_____

_____

10. buildings _____

_____

_____

Exercise 16. Choose two of the main idea sentences from Exercise 15 and make classification charts which take at least three steps. See the chart on page 74 for a sample. Be sure the charts you make are related to the main idea sentences they are supposed to illustrate.

1. MAIN IDEA SENTENCE _____

_____

_____

_____

Step 1

Step 2

Step 3

2. MAIN IDEA SENTENCE _____

_____

_____

_____

Step 1

Step 2

Step 3

Exercise 17. Write an introductory paragraph and a concluding paragraph for a paper of classification, using one of the topics you have already outlined. Be sure the introduction tells the reader what you are going to classify, and that the conclusion relates to the introduction and makes the paper sound finished.

Exercise 18. Write a theme from the plan you made for Exercises 16 and 17. Remember to take only one step at a time in the subdivisions. Before you hand in your theme, underline all the transitions between paragraphs.

Exercise 19. Write main idea sentences for papers of analysis for any five of these topics.

1. a stapler _____

_____

_____

2. a coffee pot (any type) _____

_____

_____

3. a cigarette lighter _____

_____

_____

4. difficulties of English spelling _____

_____

_____

5. a carburetor _____

_____

_____

6. the cost of going to college _____

_____

_____

7. system of checks and balances in American government _____

_____

_____

8. the causes of your failing _____
                (Write in the name of some course.)

_____

_____

9._____
       (Write in something with which you are familiar.)

_____

_____

10._____

(Write in something with which you are familiar.)

_____

_____

Exercise 20. Choose a topic from Exercise 19 and make a plan for a paper of analysis. This is not a reference project; choose a topic you already know something about. Be sure you can defend the order of each step in your plan. Use this chart in making your plan.

Analysis of _____

Introduction *(Use your main idea sentence here.)* _____

_____

_____

_____

1. _____

_____

_____

2. _____

_____

_____

3. _____

_____

_____

Conclusion (*Use a variation of your main idea sentence here.*) _____.

_____

_____

_____

Exercise 21. Write an introductory paragraph and a concluding paragraph for a paper of analysis, using the topic you have already outlined. Base these paragraphs on the introductory and concluding sentences as they appear in your plan. Be sure the introduction tells the reader what you are going to classify, and that the conclusion is related to the introduction and makes the paper sound finished.

Exercise 22. Write a theme from the plan you made for Exercises 20 and 21. Remember, after breaking the whole down into pieces, to show how each piece relates to the whole. Before you hand in your theme, underline all the transitions between paragraphs.

V

Telling What Happened: Objective Reports

Reports are not concerned with telling people how to do things or explaining how things operate. Instead, reports tell what *was* done, how something *did* operate. From your income tax report, which tells how much money you made last year, to the food commissioner's report on wheat consumption, which tells how many loaves of bread were eaten by how many people, reports are restricted to telling just what *did* happen.

Life is full of occasions that call for reports. Some activities require so many of them that there are special forms to guide you in deciding what to say. An income tax form is an example of such a ready-made guide. An accident form is another. After you have rammed the back of the patrolman's car with your English racing bike, which has four speeds forward and no brake, the state patrol will be so curious to know what happened that they will not want to depend on your unaided account. They will provide you with a printed form. And your insurance company will be so eager to read what you have to say about this little $800 mishap that they will provide a second form, complete with questions. Your answers to these questions will be your report. On such reports, if you read carefully and answer honestly, you can hardly go wrong.

But other occasions require reports, too, and there are not always forms to act as guides. The secretary of the Southeast Boston Geranium

Culture Society writes the minutes of the last meeting—a report. A biochemist runs a series of tests on lung cancer in white mice treated with nicotine and writes up his experiment—a report. A welfare worker visits a widow living in two rooms with thirteen children and no visible means of support and writes up the visit for his supervisor. A family doctor discovers an epidemic of a rare kind of post-nasal drip and writes up his discovery for a medical journal. James Bond smashes a sinister secret spy ring which was about to steal all the gold in Fort Knox, sink the island of Great Britain, and poison everyone in Greenland, and writes a blow-by-blow account to his chief, M. You sign up for Chemistry 101 and write your experiments in your notebook. All these things are reports.

If these reports are any good, they will have several things in common, even though they deal with very different kinds of events. All good reports are *clear* and *precise*. They never leave the reader guessing. Good reports are *orderly*. The reader is never in any doubt about what happened first, what came next. Good reports *stick to the subject*. The reader is never left saying to himself, "What does that have to do with it?" Good reports are *complete*. They never cheat the reader by leaving out any part of what happened, even though the writer may not like it. Good reports are *accurate*. They get the facts straight and present them to the reader honestly and fairly. Most important, good reports are *objective*. They tell the reader what happened, not what the writer thinks about it.

We can see that good reports are much like good directions or good explanations. As you checked your pronouns so that none of them would confuse your readers, you were working for clarity and precision. Reports need that kind of check, too. As you wrote your directions, you tried to use short sentences, choosing the simplest words you could think of that would still express precisely what you meant. You didn't tell your reader to turn left at the "first institution of learning" when what you meant was the first schoolhouse. Instead, you told him that the school was red, and perhaps you added that it was made of brick, two stories high, and on the northeast corner. The same rule applies to reports. Your job is to tell the reader what happened, not to impress him with all the big words you know. If there is a common, ordinary word for what you are trying to say, it is usually the best choice. The word that everybody knows is the word that everybody is likely to understand.

Before you choose a big word instead of a little one, you should always ask yourself, "Does this big word say any more than that little one? Is it any clearer?" If you are trying to decide between *teacher* and *educator*, you should certainly give *educator* a very close look before you use it. The two words mean almost the same thing, but you won't want to say, "My Aunt Hepzibah has just rented her basement apartment to three *educators*," or "An *educator* I had in the third grade *inculcated* me with a tremendous respect for *philately*." Nor will you want to say, "Put half a teaspoon of *sodium chloride* in the soup." In such sentences, these big words are just a way of showing off. If your third-grade teacher taught you to like stamp-collecting, or if you want the soup salted, you'll do better to choose *teacher, taught, stamp-collecting*, and *salt*.

But in some reports the ordinary word will not do as well. Ordinary words are a poor choice if they are so vague and general that part of your meaning is lost. If you are writing a chemistry report, instead of helping with dinner, you will surely need to say *sodium chloride*, not salt. In chemistry, there are many kinds of salts; a good chemistry report will make clear which salt you mean. Use big words rather than little ones whenever the big words are needed for precision.

What do we mean by precision? Precision means exactness. It means hitting the nail on the head, not half an inch to one side. It means using a quarter-inch socket on a quarter-inch nut, not a sixteenth or a three-eighths. In writing, precision means taking care to find, not the big word or the little word, but exactly the right word for what you mean, instead of some other word fairly close to it. Your words will not get across what you say at all, much less do it precisely, if you use them carelessly, without worrying about what other people understand the words to mean. You must not say *idiom* when you mean *idiot*, *precede* when you mean *proceed*, *drudge* when you mean *grudge*, *sadistic* when you mean *statistic*, *shackles* when you mean *shambles*, or even *read* when you mean *red*.

Such irresponsible disregard for words results in mindless gibberish:

> I have a drudge against that idiom who preceded through the read light into my car. Then the idiom would not even report the sadistics to the police, and here my car is in shackles!

As a report, this paragraph fails in more than one way. It isn't exact and it isn't objective, but its main failure is that it isn't clear. The moral should be obvious: don't use a word unless you are absolutely sure of its meaning.

Although you should pick little words instead of big ones when the meaning is the same, and never use any word unless you are sure what it means, you don't need to be content with a fifth-grade vocabulary. You are constantly running across new words that may help you to express yourself more precisely. But don't use these new words only for their fine sound. Use them when they really do make your meaning clearer.

Just as each word used in a report must be clear and exact, the order must be clear and exact, too. The right order for a report is much like the right order for giving directions. When you were telling someone how to do something, you began with the first step and went on to the next. When you are telling someone what *has been* done, you should tell him what happened first, what happened next, and how it all ended. Another way of saying it is that reports should be arranged in chronological order. Don't let your report read like this:

> The meeting was closed. Just before it closed Mrs. Creech asked if there was any new business. Before that the secretary read the minutes of the previous meeting. About the middle of the meeting Mrs. Dreadnaught read her paper on the inbreeding of the new Blush Pink Tinkerbell. All the members agreed it was the most satisfactory meeting they had had this year.

Such minutes make clear only that the Southeast Boston Geranium Culture Society needs a new secretary with a better sense of order.

Another thing a report has in common with giving directions is that both of them must stick to the subject. The minute the writer becomes sidetracked, the minute he gives his reader a chance to say, "What does *that* have to do with it?" he is getting off the subject. The second secretary of the Geranium Society will not last any longer than the first if she writes:

> After the meeting was called to order, the minutes of the previous meeting were read. It rained the day of the last meeting, but as I was writing this today I could not help notice what a nice day it is today, and how much nicer it would have been last time if we had had some sun for our meeting. Geraniums never look so beautiful as they do in the sun. There was no old business. My son Gerald is secretary of his Boy Scout troop and I always have to help him write up their minutes and every time it seems that most of their meeting is devoted to old business. The president called for new business. . . .

We will never get to find out what the new business was, because as the secretary reads the minutes all the members of the Geranium Society will rise to their feet shouting, "What do your son and the sunshine have to do with it?" and elect a third secretary. The third secretary will have less difficulty if she keeps firmly in mind that her job is not only to tell what happened in chronological order, but also to restrict herself to telling what happened at the meeting at the home of Mrs. Algernon Creech on May 10, 1888.

It is easy enough to see that the secretary included too much in her report; it is not nearly as easy to tell what she may have left out. Perhaps the Geranium Society voted to increase the dues twenty-five cents a year. Even if the secretary voted against the motion, and even though she hopes everybody will forget it, she must not leave it out of the minutes. And the biochemist reporting on his mice experiment must make his report equally complete if it is to have any value for anyone. He cannot say:

> Last week I inoculated some mice with a nicotine solution in some sugar water. The mice squealed like everything when the needle went in. Now about half of them are still looking all right in the cage, but my sister is sorry because she's scared to death of mice.

Such a statement is incomplete in two ways. It is incomplete because it is inexact. We need to know when the writer began the experiment, how many mice were inoculated, how much nicotine and how much sugar the solution contained, and what he means by "about half" and "looking all right." But his statement is incomplete for another reason, too; he has forgotten to tell us what happened to the half that do not seem all right. Did they die? Did they sneak out through a hole in the cage? Have they been moved to another cage because they did not look all right? Since the purpose of the report is to tell the reader what happened to the mice that were shot full of nicotine, a complete report *must* include two pieces of information not given here: how many mice were there? And what, *exactly*, happened to each one of them?

The writer needs to begin again, taking out the two comments that have nothing to do with the way the experiment turned out, and putting in exact information that will give the reader a complete account of the things that matter. This time he will not tell us that his sister is afraid of mice, or that the poor mice squeaked and squealed. Instead, he will say:

> On September 16, 1966, I inoculated twenty white mice with 10 milligrams of nicotine in a 2 per cent sugar solution. On September 17, five of the mice refused to eat. On September 18, ten refused food and four would not move, although they were still breathing. On September 19, five mice were dead, six refused food, and nine appeared to be eating and moving normally.

Even this report could be made more complete. The writer could tell us at what hour the injections were given, whether the mice that died on the nineteenth were the same mice that wouldn't eat on the seventeenth.

In deciding whether you ought to add more details to your report, ask yourself two questions:

1. Do these details have something to do with how the event turned out?
2. Can the reader understand exactly what happened without them?

In reporting that unfortunate encounter between the English racing bike and the patrolman's automobile, it really doesn't matter what color the bike was, but it matters a good deal what color the traffic light was. If you leave out the information that the light was red, your report will certainly be incomplete.

A complete report will always include *who* and *what* and *when* and *where* and *how much*. It will be exact in the details it gives, and precise in the words it uses. But none of this completeness and exactness will do much good unless the details are accurate. The writer who says, "The experiment took place last month" or "sometime in September" is not being exact. "March 1" and "September 14" and "September 16" are all *exact* dates, but only one of them is *accurate*. In the same way, "some nicotine" is inexact. "One per cent" and "2 per cent" and "3.5 per cent" are all exact, but only one of them is accurate. For the reader who wants to do the experiment himself, lack of accuracy can be disastrous.

Whenever a report includes dates and numbers and quantities—and most of them will, for reports deal in exactness—the dates and numbers and quantities must be right. You can't just guess at them, you have to know. And you must be careful to see that what you know is what you actually put down in your report. Reports are no place for careless mistakes. It won't improve the report much to have the writer say afterward, "Oh, I didn't mean *three*. I knew Mrs. Brown had thirteen children. I must have left the *one* out by accident." By that time, the Welfare Department will have cut Mrs. Brown's food allowance down so much that those ten children you carelessly eliminated will be getting pretty thin. Accuracy means getting it exact *and* getting it right.

If you have been careful to see that your report is clear, precise, and orderly; that it sticks to the subject and is complete enough to include everything that matters; and that it is exact and accurate, you have only one more thing to worry about: *objectivity*. Probably objectivity is the most important characteristic of a report. *Objectivity* is the opposite of *subjectivity*. When you write *objectively*, you keep yourself out; when you write *subjectively*, you put yourself in.

A person who writes subjectively sees everything so much in relation to himself that what he says is of very little use to anybody else. Of course everybody sees things from his own point of view, simply because it is physically impossible to *be* anybody else. However, it is possible to be aware of this tendency and to make a great effort to see things from a neutral viewpoint. When you write from a neutral viewpoint, you are writing objectively.

To be objective means to keep opinions out of your report. But before you can keep opinion out, you must be able to distinguish between factual statements and opinion statements. Factual material is anything that can be checked. If somebody tells you it's raining outside, he has made a factual statement. What he says may not be accurate. *It does not have to be true to be a factual statement.* Factual statements are simply statements that can be checked, and unless you are sick in bed, you can go out and see whether it is raining. If, on the other hand, he tells you that the weather is perfectly horrible, he has given you his opinion. You cannot possibly check his statement. While you both mean the same thing by *rain*, you may have quite different ideas about *horrible* weather. Maybe he likes storms and thinks calm, sunny days are horrible.

Perhaps you have been told that Mudville is a large and prosperous town. Is the speaker offering a factual statement or giving his opinion? Though what he says may seem like fact, it is really opinion, because the words *large* and *prosperous* are subjective and depend on the experience of the speaker. If you live at a crossroads with thirty other people, Mudville may seem huge. But if you grew up in New York or San Francisco, Mudville may seem like the nether end of nowheresville. If you are used to a place where nobody can afford shoes for school, and bacon with the beans is a notable feast, supermarkets and store-bought shoes may look like prosperity. But if you have been spending your winters at Palm Beach and your summers in Switzerland, the sight of Mudville's ordinary citizens may move you to ask whether Mudville is on the federal list of depressed areas.

All words like *large, small, horrible, wonderful, prosperous, poor*, are subjective. They depend on the user's point of view, and each one of us has his own idea of what they mean. None of them can be checked. If you are told that Mudville has a population of five hundred people and that its business district contains two filling stations, two grocery stores, one bank, and a tavern, all of which have been painted in the last two years, you can, if you want to, go to Mudville and count the people, count the businesses, and look at the paint. On the basis of these facts you can form your own opinion about Mudville's relative size and prosperity. But if you write a report of your trip, you must give your readers factual information and let them form their own opinions.

Most of the knock-down, drag-out fights you get into in the student center can be avoided if you remember that some terms always rest on opinion. Was Ty Cobb a *greater* player than Babe Ruth? Is baseball a *better* game than basketball? Are the teenagers of this generation *worse* than their parents were? You can argue until your tongue turns black in your mouth, but you probably won't get anywhere until you define your terms. Defining your terms means that you and your opponent must decide what you mean by *greater, better, worse*. Once you agree that greatness in baseball can be measured by home runs hit, bases stolen, dollars earned, or fan mail received, you have pushed the discussion out of the realm of opinion into the realm of facts. Now you have something you can check. In the same way, you must agree on what makes a *better* game, what sort of behavior is *worse* than another, before you can get beyond the "It is too"—"It is not" stage of an argument. *Greater, better, worse*, are opinion words. Before your opinion can be worth anything, you must show the objective facts that the opinion rests upon.

Since the purpose of reports is to tell what happened, the writer's job is to limit himself to what happened, not to interpret it. The student is reporting what happened in his English class if he says, "The teacher marked my paper *A*, Scotch-taped a red rose on the front, and kissed me on the forehead as I went out the door." He is interpreting if he says, "The teacher was impressed by my paper." The first includes only events that can be checked; the second tells what the student thinks the events mean.

Once you see the difference between factual statements and opinions, it is much easier to keep obvious interpretations out of your reports. All you have to do is go back through what you have written and cut out the opinion. Then instead of the opinion, put in the facts.

It is much harder to get rid of the opinions that creep in with the words you use in reporting the facts because your own attitude toward what happened always tends to influence your choice of words. Perhaps one day you came out to your car to find the right wing window smashed, the door of the glove compartment open, your sunglasses gone, and four boys walking away. You think you know what happened, but can you fairly say, "Four greasy-looking punks broke into my car, stole my sunglasses, and were scared away when they saw me coming"? Of course you can't. This statement is full of booby traps. Take the term *greasy-looking*. You may have thought you were giving a description, but if the boys are to be caught, then you must say what was greasy-looking about them. Were they all wearing dark leather jackets, oil-stained Levis, and sideburns? Or did the term *greasy-looking* come into your mind only because you resented the loss of your sunglasses?

What about the word *punks*? What is a *punk*, anyway? Do you mean that the boys were between sixteen and eighteen? Do you mean that they were small and undernourished? Or do you simply mean that you didn't like them much?

You said they broke into your car, but did you, or anyone else, see them doing it? You said that your sunglasses were stolen, but are you sure that your mother didn't borrow them? You said the boys were scared away by your approach, but do you really know any more than that they left just as you came up? Your report would be more objective if you said, "Four boys dressed in black leather jackets and black Levis were standing by my car and walked away as I came near it. I found the right wing window smashed, the glove-compartment door open, and my sunglasses gone."

Using words that force the reader to accept your opinion of what happened is called *slanting*. When you called the boys "greasy-looking punks," you were slanting *against* your subject. A friend of the boys, hearing that they were suspected of taking your sunglasses, might say, "Four considerate young men, seeing the lights left on in a battered old jalopy, were thoughtful enough to go out of their way to turn the lights off." The friend is slanting, too, but *for* the boys instead of against them. Both *considerate* and *battered old jalopy* are opinion terms. If the lights actually were left on, and the friend was trying to be objective, he should have said, "Four young men went over to turn off the lights of a 1926 Essex." It is possible to slant either for or against, but in reports you will not want to slant at all.

To avoid slanting, select words that neither purr nor snarl. S. I. Hayakawa invented these terms to describe words that express approval (*purr words*) or disapproval (*snarl words*). Talk about a *woman of about seventy* instead of an *old hag* or a *sweet old lady*. Say, "The car went through the intersection at twenty-five miles an hour," not "The car tore recklessly down the street" or "crept along at a snail's pace." Say *came noiselessly* rather than *sneaked*; *said* rather than *snarled* or *whimpered*; *walked unevenly* rather than *staggered*. Try as hard as you can to make your report objective. Give the reader the facts, and let him make his own interpretation.

Writing a good main idea sentence will not insure that your report is objective any more than it will insure that the report is complete and accurate. But as usual a good main idea sentence will help. The main idea sentence for a report should make clear what event is being reported, when the event took place, and, unless it would be obvious to the reader, where. The main idea sentence should tell who—or, in the case of the mice, what—took part in the event. Above all, the main idea sentence needs to be definite and objective, since it will set the tone for the rest of the report. Here are some main idea sentences that would do for several different kinds of reports.

> The regular meeting of the Southeast Boston Geranium Culture Society was held at the home of Mrs. Algernon Creech on May 10, 1888.

> On September 16, 1966, twenty white mice were inoculated with 20 milligrams of nicotine in a 2 per cent sugar solution.

> Mrs. Prunella Brown, 406 Dead End Street, receives $19.22 a month from her father-in-law, a sum she says is inadequate to feed and clothe her thirteen children.

> Since December of last year, fifteen severe cases of black nasal discharge have occurred in residents of Drain, all cases occurring in people living within 200 feet of the town incinerator.

> I apprehended and was forced to kill in self-defense seventy-five secret spy agents and one innocent bystander this morning, August 17, 1958, at 2:00 A.M., in the lobby of the Liberty Theater in Bury-Your-Dead, Wyoming.

Notice that all these main idea sentences give exact details. They include names, addresses, dates, and numbers. With two exceptions, they avoid using opinion words. Although the fourth main idea sentence uses the word *severe*, the writer is careful not to say that the discharge is caused by the incinerator; he says only that the victims live within a certain distance, 200 feet. The fifth main idea sentence uses the phrase *innocent bystander*. Here it is apparent that *innocent* is not really an opinion word. Used in connection with *bystander*, it means that the seventy-sixth man killed just happened to be hanging around and was not really connected with the spy ring. (The opinion word *inadequate* in the third sentence is part of what Mrs. Brown said; that she said it is factual, even if she used an opinion word.)

Most of these main idea sentences might serve as the first sentence of the report itself. Reports need much less general introduction than other kinds of writing need, because reports are always written for a special audience. Your chemistry report is intended for your chemistry professor, and you can hardly expect the police department or even your history professor to care much about it. Your accident report is written for the police, and perhaps your insurance company, and you cannot expect to sell it to the confession magazines no matter how hard you work on it, unless you change it from a report into another kind of writing.

Since you have a ready-made audience, there is less need to try to interest people in what you are reporting. The purpose of a report is to give information, and people who do not want to be informed about what happened will not read your report anyway. Entertaining comments are not likely to increase the number of readers, but they will certainly annoy the readers you have. The police seldom read an accident report for laughs. If they want to laugh, they read the *Police Gazette.* Nor is your chemistry professor likely to look for rich glowing prose in your lab report. For rich glowing prose he reads Faulkner. The police will be satisfied with a clear account of what car ran over which pedestrian at which intersection. They will also be interested in knowing whether the pavement was wet or dry, and whether it was night or day. Your chemistry professor will be perfectly satisfied if you can make clear exactly what you put into that beaker, how much heat you applied, and what came out of it. Stick to the facts and the interest will take care of itself.

Just as reports don't need much introduction, they don't need very elaborate conclusions either. A good main idea sentence will have made clear the limits of the event you are covering. When you have come to the end of the event, you have come to the end of the report:

The meeting was adjourned at 4:15 P.M.

By Saturday, September 21, all twenty mice were dead.

Mrs. Brown had one pound of dry beans, half a package of oatmeal, and two cans of apricots in the house. She has no money at all, and will receive none until Algernon can make collections on his paper route the first of the month.

None of the discharges has been completely cured, and the patients are remaining under weekly observation.

By 5:20 A.M. all of the bodies had been removed to the Little Chapel of the Desert Mortuary, and arrangements are being made to notify relatives.

You must resist the urge to use your conclusion to interpret events. Just as you would not end your report by saying, "That was the dullest meeting I ever attended," you must also avoid saying, "This experiment proves that nicotine is a bad thing," or "These people will have to move away from the garbage dump if they want to get well."

Writing a good report is much like filling out a printed report form. The forms ask enough questions that when you have answered all of them, your report is complete. They provide such a small amount of space that you have to be precise. The questions are listed in sensible order so it is impossible to wander here and there. And the forms provide no space for opinion; there are no questions asking whether you resent paying your income tax and no space left on the accident report for you to say how bad you felt about the whole thing. If you imagine, as you write your report, that you are working from a printed form, you won't go far astray.

Remember that the people who read your report trust you to make it both accurate and complete. Honest reports are based on everything that happened. And what good is a dishonest report?

Key Words

Here are some of the important terms used in this chapter. Without referring back to the chapter, see whether you can answer these questions.

1. What is the difference between *reports* and *directions*? In what ways should they be alike? In what ways are they different?

2. Why should you bother to learn new words if ordinary words are usually better? What is meant by *precision* in deciding which words to use? When are unusual words better than ordinary words?

3. Is the *order* of a report more like the order of a paper of directions or the order of an explanation? What should the order be?

4. Explain what is meant by a *complete* report. How can you tell whether you are being complete enough and at the same time make sure you are *sticking to the subject*?

5. What is the difference between *exactness* and *accuracy*? Is it possible to be *accurate* without being *exact*? Is it possible to be *exact* without being *accurate*? If your answer is "yes," give two or three examples.

6. What is the difference between *objectivity* and *subjectivity*? Can people ever be completely *objective*? Can they ever be completely *subjective*?

7. Distinguish between *factual statements* and *opinion statements*. Do statements need to be accurate to be *factual*? Do they need to be accurate to be *opinion*?

8. What are *purr* words and *snarl* words? What do these words have to do with *slanting*?

9. What should the *main idea sentence* of a report contain?

10. What should the *introduction* of a report contain? The *conclusion*?

Vocabulary

Pick the answer that most closely fits the meaning of the word as it has been used in the chapter. Look up in your dictionary the meaning of all the words you miss.

1. "The meatpackers say *consumption* has fallen off this year," means _____
   (a) fewer people are getting married
   (b) fewer calves are being born
   (c) people are eating less meat
   (d) fewer people have tuberculosis

2. When an *epidemic* occurs, _____
   (a) quite a number of people get the same disease
   (b) somebody has a rash on his skin
   (c) many people are taking college courses
   (d) the police are always called out

3. A *sinister* organization _____
   (a) is a sisterhood devoted to charity
   (b) is a sisterhood devoted to giving parties
   (c) functions only at Easter time
   (d) contains a threat of evil

4. *Idiom* means _____
   (a) a person born without much sense
   (b) a person who behaves as though he had no sense
   (c) Latin for idea
   (d) a group of words with a special language meaning

5. A person who *precedes* _____
   (a) goes ahead of others
   (b) goes behind others
   (c) walks with a group of people
   (d) goes on with an action or process

6. A person who *proceeds*   _____
   (a) goes ahead of others
   (b) goes behind others
   (c) walks with a group of people
   (d) goes on with an action or process

7. To be in *shackles* means to be   _____
   (a) battered and damaged beyond repair
   (b) in need of a good cleaning
   (c) handcuffed or chained
   (d) housed in a substandard dwelling

8. To be in *shambles* means to be   _____
   (a) battered and damaged beyond repair
   (b) in need of a good cleaning
   (c) handcuffed or chained
   (d) housed in a substandard dwelling

9. An *irresponsible* person is one who   _____
   (a) refuses to answer questions under oath
   (b) cannot be trusted to do what is required of him
   (c) can always be depended on
   (d) gives deliberately false answers

10. *Gibberish* means   _____
    (a) a kind of stew made from rabbits
    (b) the adjustment of a sail on a boat
    (c) meaningless nonsense
    (d) a man born in East Gibbon

11. To *restrict* means   _____
    (a) to punish severely
    (b) not to permit a person or thing to go beyond certain
        limits
    (c) not to allow a person or thing to do anything at all
    (d) to pull something backwards and sideways

12. A person who has been *inoculated* has been   _____
    (a) given a shot with a hypodermic needle
    (b) graduated from an accredited high school
    (c) trained to fit eye glasses
    (d) the inventor of something totally new

13. An *encounter* is   _____
    (a) an adding machine
    (b) a lining for a pair of shoes

(c) always accidental

(d) a meeting or coming together

14. A *disastrous* event is   _____
    (a) one in which an astronaut takes part
    (b) one in which there are bad consequences
    (c) always the result of an earthquake or flood
    (d) one in which the culprit is arrested

15. Something that is *eliminated* is   _____
    (a) lighted up like a Christmas tree
    (b) shot dead with a machine gun
    (c) cut out
    (d) underlined

16. To take a *neutral* stand means to be   _____
    (a) un-American
    (b) not committed to either side
    (c) opposed to the use of neutrons in warfare
    (d) in favor of exaggerated ideas or behavior

17. A *notable* event is one   _____
    (a) unusual enough to be remembered
    (b) that everybody takes written notes about
    (c) in which all the participants are famous
    (d) for which written invitations are sent

18. A person who *interprets* something   _____
    (a) translates it from English to Sanskrit
    (b) decides what he thinks it means
    (c) breaks into the middle of the event
    (d) signs up to take a course without credit

19. People who are *undernourished*   _____
    (a) do not get enough to eat
    (b) are foreigners
    (c) have not finished the eighth grade
    (d) do not drink enough milk to keep the dairies in business

20. Something that is *inadequate*   _____
    (a) has not been added up properly
    (b) does not behave according to the rules of good manners
    (c) has very little education
    (d) is not enough to meet needs or requirements

21. A person who has been *apprehended* has been _____
    (a) caught
    (b) scared into a state of shock
    (c) unable to understand
    (d) tattooed

22. If you make something *elaborate*, you _____
    (a) embroider it with yarn
    (b) complete it in the chemistry lab
    (c) add a number of details
    (d) clear it with the union

Exercises

Exercise 1. Circle the word or words that seem the best choice. Be prepared to explain your choice in class discussion.

1. Jeremy K. Jerome $\binom{\text{matriculated at}}{\text{went to}}\binom{\text{an institution of higher learning}}{\text{college}}$ for two years.

2. Mr. Penny took half a teaspoonful of $\binom{\text{sodium bicarbonate}}{\text{baking soda}}$ in a glass of $\binom{\text{water}}{\text{H}_2\text{O}}$ before he $\binom{\text{went to bed}}{\text{retired}}$.

3. Just before the shot was fired the victim shouted, "Mr. Sullivan, you are a dirty $\binom{\text{prevaricator}}{\text{liar}}$."

4. To $\binom{\text{quite a bit}}{\text{two ounces}}$ of water in the test tube we added $\binom{\text{a little bit}}{1.5\text{ grams}}$ of $\binom{\text{sodium carbonate}}{\text{washing soda}}$.

5. Mrs. Charity White $\binom{\text{ingests}}{\text{drinks}}$ so many $\binom{\text{inebrious spirits}}{\text{beers}}$ that she is often unable to $\binom{\text{remain gainfully employed}}{\text{hold a job}}$.

6. Consequently, her family finds itself $\binom{\text{in impecunious circumstances}}{\text{without money}}$.

7. When I investigated the property of Barney Snell for evidence of wind damage, I found his front yard littered with $\binom{\text{things}}{\text{rain gutters}}$ and $\binom{\text{stuff}}{\text{shingles}}$.

8. Eastside Hardware $\binom{\text{say they have for sale}}{\text{advertise}}\begin{pmatrix}\text{lots of different odds}\\ \text{and ends}\\ \text{brushes, paints, and}\\ \text{rollers}\end{pmatrix}$.

9. Eddie Oldfield reports that the $\binom{\text{motorized vehicle}}{\text{car}}$ he was $\binom{\text{driving}}{\text{piloting}}$

$$\begin{pmatrix}\text{had a disastrous encounter with}\\\text{crashed into}\end{pmatrix} \text{ a pickup on the } \begin{pmatrix}\text{juncture}\\\text{intersection}\\\text{corner}\end{pmatrix}$$

of Eighteenth and Blandon Drive.

10. The $\begin{pmatrix}\text{encounter}\\\text{accident}\end{pmatrix}$ was $\begin{pmatrix}\text{precipitated}\\\text{caused}\end{pmatrix}$ by a loose $\begin{pmatrix}\text{hydraulic line}\\\text{gadget}\end{pmatrix}$ in Oldfield's $\begin{pmatrix}\text{vehicle}\\\text{car}\end{pmatrix}$.

Exercise 2. In the following lists of details, cross out those details which do not stick to the subject. Be prepared to defend the details you keep.

1. A real estate salesman's report to his boss about some property that has been offered for sale by Cyrus Teasel.

_____ Mr. Teasel not home on date visit was made.
_____ House was locked.
_____ A big dog chased the salesman from the property.
_____ Salesman's car broke down on the way home.
_____ Some shingles missing from Teasel's roof.
_____ House is painted green.
_____ Fence is partly blown over.
_____ Salesman doesn't like Teasel's lampshades.
_____ Salesman doesn't like Teasel's dog.

_____

_____

_____

2. A report to the newspaper of a house fire.

_____ Property owned by Vance Packwood.
_____ Mr. and Mrs. Packwood argue a lot, often in public places.
_____ Address is 17302 Chestnut Avenue.
_____ Fire first noticed at 1:45 A.M.
_____ Blaze extinguished at 6:00 A.M.
_____ Damage to house estimated at $15,000.
_____ Charles Vigor, fireman, overcome by smoke.
_____ Charles Vigor hadn't had much to eat the night before.

_____ Vigor is a cousin of Packwood's uncle on his mother's side.
_____ Packwoods away when fire started.
_____ Packwoods had steak and applesauce for dinner.
_____ Mrs. Packwood may have left the oven going.

_____

_____

_____

3. A report to a car owner about the cost of repairs to his new car.

_____ Left front fender replaced.
_____ New shocks and springs in left front.
_____ New headlight installed.
_____ New grill installed.
_____ New fender repainted.
_____ Expensive metallic paint rather than regular paint.
_____ Four men worked on car for a total of 60 hours.
_____ Bill includes pickup and delivery charge.

_____

_____

_____

4. A report to the Society for the Prevention of Barbershop Garrulity, about barber Snip N. Gabble's fourteen-hour filibuster.

_____ There have been many other complaints.
_____ The barbershop is not very clean.
_____ The linoleum is worn through in several places and the walls have not been painted or cleaned for twenty-seven years.
_____ John Meek entered the Elegant Gentleman's Hair Emporium at 8:00 A.M. and left at 10:00 P.M.
_____ John Meek tried to get out of the chair thirty-three different times, and each time he tried it barber Gabble would open up a new topic of conversation.
_____ John Meek wears glasses, a hearing aid, false teeth, a wooden leg, a wig, and a brace for his back.

_____

_____

_____

5. A report to the Boston Geranium Culture Society by the member who has just returned from a convention of the New York Geranium Growers.

_____ An amusing anecdote about the train accommodations.

_____ A summary of the main convention speaker's address about geraniums and fertilizer.

_____ The kinds of hair styles that most of the New York representatives were wearing.

_____ A description of the three new breeds of geraniums which were introduced at the convention.

_____ The best joke told at the convention.

_____

_____

_____

6. A report to your insurance company about damage to your property, caused by a recent wind storm.

_____ About half the shingles were blown off the roof.

_____ The garage was blown down.

_____ Fourteen chickens blew away.

_____ The TV antenna was knocked down.

_____ Your wife was so nervous that she threw up.

_____ The lights went out.

_____ You couldn't find the flashlight.

_____ You hope the wind doesn't blow like that ever again.

_____

_____

_____

7. James Bond's encounter with the secret spy agents.

_____ The encounter took place on August 17, 1961.

_____ It was 2:00 in the morning.
_____ It was in the lobby of the Liberty Theater.
_____ He was there with a beautiful blonde.
_____ His gun got stuck in his pocket, so he had to use his flamethrower.
_____ Seventy-five spies were burned to death in the theater.
_____ The theater was old and well insured.
_____ The film that was playing was an old Laurel and Hardy comedy.

_____

_____

_____

8. A report to an employer, explaining an expense account.

_____ The client's wife is a good-looking blonde.
_____ The date on which the client was taken to dinner.
_____ A complaint about the meat being overdone.
_____ The number of martinis the client drank.
_____ The amount of the tip.
_____ A detailed account of the floor show.
_____ Dinner for three cost $12.80, tax 51¢.
_____ The client is a dreadful bore.

_____

_____

_____

9. A report of the safety committee.

_____ Four workmen received minor cuts and were treated in the first-aid room.
_____ One man was taken to the hospital for a head injury received when another workman dropped a two-by-four on him.
_____ These statistics cover the period from March 1 to March 31.
_____ All cases have been reported to the state workmen's compensation board.
_____ The railings on the second floor need to be repaired.
_____ Nobody reported any injuries in February.

_____ The sandwiches in the Automat are not being put in every day and don't taste as good as they used to.

_____ Two men were ten minutes late to work last week.

_____

_____

_____

10. A biology report on the dissection of a frog.

_____ The frog smelled bad.

_____ Two students worked together on the experiment.

_____ The scalpels are dull.

_____ The work was done on May 2 and 3.

_____ John kept yawning all the time he was working.

_____ John didn't do his share of the work.

_____

_____

_____

Exercise 3. Remember that a complete report will include all the details that help the reader understand exactly what happened and omit all details that have no real connection with what did happen. Go back to Exercise 2 and use your imagination to supply three more details that should be included in each report.

Exercise 4. Rearrange all the details in each report covered in Exercises 2 and 3, putting them in the right order. Place the proper numbers in the space provided.

Exercise 5. Some of these statements are accurate, and some of them are inaccurate. Using your own information or consulting reference books in your school library, rewrite the inaccurate statements.

1. The Japanese bombed Pearl Harbor on December 2, 1943.

_____

_____

2. There are four cups to a quart, and four pints to a gallon.

_____

_____

3. Thomas Edison invented television.

_____

_____

4. Alaska has an area of less than 420,000 square miles.

_____

_____

5. Seven months of the year have thirty-one days.

_____

_____

6. November 21 has more hours of darkness than any other day in the year.

_____

_____

7. The American Civil War, which began in 1850, lasted until October, 1866.

_____

_____

8. Ulysses S. Grant was a great Civil War general who won three important battles for the Confederacy.

---

9. Lyndon C. Johnson is the thirty-first president of the United States.

Exercise 6. Mark all factual statements with **X**. Mark all judgments or opinions with **O**. In evaluating these statements, consider as fact anything that could have been or can be checked, whether or not you think it is accurate.

1. "The Music Man" is a good musical comedy.   _____

2. "The Music Man" is a bad musical comedy.   _____

3. Today is _____ (*fill in the date and then mark*).   _____

4. Billboards are a nuisance.   _____

5. The library contains 32,000 books.   _____

6. Socialism is a step toward communism.   _____

7. Raglan College has 1,700 students.   _____

8. Modern art is a confused splash of paint.   _____

9. I have been in elective office for twenty-five years.   _____

10. Experience is the best teacher.   _____

11. Thou shalt not kill.   _____

12. He sat on the flagpole fifty-nine days.   _____

13. Senator Hoaxshell will get 59 per cent of the vote. _____

14. Peace marchers are unpatriotic. _____

15. Any typewritten theme always gets a higher grade than a handwritten theme. _____

16. My history professor is a good teacher and a charming man. _____

17. Junior colleges have easier courses than do four-year colleges. _____

18. The Browns had ham and eggs for breakfast this morning. _____

19. Mrs. Brown fixes delicious breakfasts. _____

20. A college degree is a guarantee of a good job. _____

21. Mayor Apple has two telephones on his desk. _____

22. Mayor Ball has six telephones on his desk. _____

23. Mayor Ball is more successful than Mayor Apple. _____

24. Mrs. Brown works from eight to five every day. _____

25. Mrs. Brown neglects her children. _____

26. An atomic war would mean complete devastation. _____

27. The Americans dropped an atomic bomb on a Japanese city. _____

Exercise 7. On a separate sheet, rewrite all the opinion statements in Exercise 2 as factual statements. For example, " 'The Music Man' is a good musical comedy" might be rewritten " 'The Music Man' has run continuously for six years in the same theater." You need not worry about whether the factual statements are accurate as long as you express them in such a way that their accuracy can be checked.

Exercise 8. Mark all factual statements with **X**. Mark all judgments or opinions with **O**. In evaluating these statements, consider as fact anything that could have been or can be checked, whether or not you think it is accurate.

1. The area of New York is six square miles. _____

2. There is one New Yorker per square yard. _____

3. Mrs. Creech says that there is one baby born to every ten New Yorkers every ten seconds. _____

4. There is a relationship between smoking and lung cancer. _____

5. There is no relationship between smoking and lung cancer. _____

6. Algernon crunches when he eats crackers. _____

7. Cheese tastes horrible. _____

8. This book is excellent. _____

9. The name of the book is *Gone with the Wind.* _____

10. All men are pigs at heart. _____

11. My father ate four pounds of sausage for dinner last night. _____

12. Sunday is the pleasantest day of the week. _____

13. In 1803 the first Sunday in April fell on April 1. _____

14. Pencils are made from graphite and cedar. _____

15. Tansy slops when she eats pickled herring garnished with peppercorns. _____

16. All directions should be in capital letters. _____

17. One o'clock is the witching hour. _____

18. The town clock struck three times at one o'clock last night. _____

19. There are five *c*'s in "people." _____

20. Algebra is not only deadly, it is illogical! _____

21. Thomas Edison was the greatest genius in history. _____

22. A knife is a dangerous instrument. _____

23. Rupert is a charming boy. _____

24. Rupert is a stinker. _____

25. Rupert must be some kind of a nut or something. _____

26. Green linoleum is beautiful. _____

27. Rupert was born in Hitter, Miss., in 1903. _____

Exercise 9. On a separate sheet, rewrite all the opinion statements in Exercise 8 as factual statements. Again, don't worry about whether the factual statements are accurate as long as you express them in such a way that their accuracy can be checked.

Exercise 10. In each of the following groups of words, check the most neutral word.

1. _____dog

_____fleabag

_____hound

_____mutt

2. _____policeman

_____dick

7. _____walk

_____stagger

_____strut

_____slink

8. _____howl

_____croon

_____flatfoot   _____sing

_____law-enforcement   _____yodel
officer

3. _____long hair   9. _____hit

_____concert goer   _____clobbered

_____opera buff   _____pelted

_____music nut   _____socked

4. _____entrepreneur   10. _____interrupted

_____Babbitt   _____nagged

_____businessman   _____asked

_____speculator   _____showed admirable
curiosity

5. _____tramp   11. _____eat

_____bum   _____pick

_____unemployed   _____gobble

_____deserving poor   _____dive

6. _____thinker   12. _____orate

_____egghead   _____talk

_____intellectual   _____mumble

_____braintruster   _____harangue

Exercise 11. For each of these unfavorably slanted words, substitute a neutral word or group of words that refer to the same person or thing. For instance, you might replace *egghead* with the words *college professor*, since both terms refer to the same person.

1. old maid _____

2. bonehead _____

3. brat _____

4. ski bum _____

5. tramp _____

6. punk _____

7. sneaked _____

8. waddled _____

9. ranted _____

10. wheedled _____

11. white trash _____

12. skinflint _____

13. dictator _____

14. crook _____

15. guts _____

Exercise 12. Fill in the blank with a word that slants favorably, unfavorably, or one that is neutral—whichever applies.

FAVORABLE	NEUTRAL	UNFAVORABLE
Example: limousine	*car*	*clunker*
1. statesman	_____	babykisser
2. public relations expert	press agent	_____

FAVORABLE	NEUTRAL	UNFAVORABLE
3. electronic wonder	television	_____
4. _____	doctor	sawbones
5. attorney	lawyer	_____
6. _____	janitor	broom pusher
7. lady	_____	dame
8. all-new Philip Morris Multi-filter II	cigarette	_____
9. _____	occupation	_____
10. footwear salon	_____	clodhopper shop
11. uninhibited little dear	_____	nasty little brat
12. epicurean delight	_____	chow
13. virtuoso	_____	fiddler
14. automotive technician	mechanic	_____
15. _____	soup	slop
16. liberator	_____	dictator
17. law-enforce-ment officer	policeman	_____
18. cottage	_____	shack
19. trail blazer	motorcycle	_____

20. _____	teacher	pedant
21. _____	war	atrocity
22. her beloved	_____	her same old steady
23. senior citizen	_____	old guy
24. bourbon supreme	_____	rot gut
25. willowy maiden	_____	scrawny female

Exercise 13. All of these paragraphs were written as reports. Criticize them for *clearness* and *precision*, *orderliness*, *sticking to the subject*, *completeness*, *accuracy* (if you are able to judge), and *objectivity*. Your teacher may assign this exercise either as a writing topic or as a class discussion.

1. The internationalists at Raglan College are supporting the United Nations Organization. Everyone knows that the United Nations has Russians in it, and that the United States is not exactly peacefully inclined toward Russia. The internationalists at Raglan College are betraying the trust placed in them by the taxpayers.

2. The windstorm that struck here October 12, 1962, sure did cause a lot of damage out my way. You would hardly recognize my house, it has changed so much from the way it was last time. Nearly everything was wrecked by the wind.

3. The husky fellow hit the shrimp first. I thought the little guy would be pulverized. Instead, he gave the big guy a karate chop in the guts and one across the ear, laid him out, and stood over him like a banty rooster. Man, what a fight!

4. The meeting of the Raglan College Service Club was called to order at 3:15 in Room 304, Helping Hall, by the president, Louise Smith, on March 8, 1966.
   The secretary, Joan Mills, read the minutes of the December meeting and, after some discussion, they were approved as read.

Louise called for new business, and Elsie Dinsmore mentioned that the party scheduled for June 10 would have to be postponed or cancelled because there would not be any transportation available to the Ghost Town Hotel. Lizzie Borden moved that we charter a bus, and, after some discussion, the motion was carried by a vote of eight to three.

There was no further old business.

Joan Mills had some new business. She suggested that the club sell "No Peddlers Allowed" signs to raise money for the club charity. Candy Christian was appointed head of a committee to look into this possibility. Candy is to appoint two other girls to help her.

The meeting was adjourned at 4:03.

Respectfully submitted,

Elsie Dinsmore
(substituting for Joan Mills, who
sprained her hand)

5. I got to the lab at about eight o'clock this morning, and noticed that the janitor hadn't dusted or swept. I didn't get the place cleaned up till quite a bit later, but I was careful to wash my hands and put away the broom and the rest of the cleaning equipment so that they wouldn't dirty up the lab.

Even though the experiment got started late, I still got the steps done, mostly by cutting down on the time I allowed for each step. There was one step that needed extra equipment, but I found the equipment and that step went OK.

Even though the experiment got started late, I still got through it early enough to be out of the lab before I usually do, and had a nice time with my family the next day. We went to the beach. The experiment was a good one. I think I'll get an A.

6. On March 23, the day after the vernal equinox, I commenced my custodial duties at 6 A.M., Mountain Standard Time, and had just emerged from the antiquated enclosure where the outworn and discarded garments used for increasing the luster of the furnishings are kept when it dawned on my consciousness that all was not well in the oversized edifice devoted to student assemblages.

Making like Sherlock Holmes, I slunk on little cat feet to an orifice and peered in. Some unmitigated scoundrel had come like a thief in the night and molested school property. I was shocked to see the shambles that had been made of those beautiful, expensive folding chairs and all those handsome festooned-with-roses maroon draperies that our gallant Parent-Teachers' Association sold so many stale doughnuts to help pay for.

At 6:30 A.M., Mountain Standard Time, I bounded to the nearest telephone and communicated with Mudville's fearless arm of the law, informing him that I suspected foul play and encouraging him to make an immediate investigation of this unwarranted vandalism.

7. The two years I served with the Peace Corps in Arreta, Bodgiklotsque, from 1963 to 1965, saw several changes in the living habits of the village. When I first arrived with two other Peace Corps volunteers, the one hundred and three natives lived in eight-by-ten huts made of tree bark. Their food was chiefly a root which is native to that region, supplemented occasionally by milk and meat from a flock of about twenty-five small sheeplike animals. There were no public buildings, no school, no teachers, and no government.

In the winter of 1963 we instructed the men of the village in the planting of corn and wheat, and the next spring we helped them to plant and cultivate these two crops. Late that summer and in the early fall, after the harvest, we worked with the village people to erect a twenty-by-forty foot building made of mud bricks, thatched with bark, and glazed with glass brought overland more than a hundred miles by donkeys. This building was used both as a school and a public meeting room. We later encouraged several families to make houses of mud brick, thatched with bark. Five families completed such houses, which were about ten by twenty feet, and when we left in October, 1965, four other families had started to build.

When we left after two years, the people of Arreta, Bodgiklotsque, had two new crops which they used for both food and trade. They had a building usable for a school and a public meeting room. They had a teacher and a mayor. They were holding classes in reading and arithmetic for children and in farming methods for adults. Arreta is not completely changed, but the differences are measurable.

Exercise 14. Write a main idea sentence for a report on each of the following:

1. The actions, during a five-minute period, of a person seated across the room from you

_____

_____

2. A recent visit to an art gallery

_____

_____

_____

3. A concert (a lecture) you recently attended

_____

_____

_____

4. Some peculiar behavior of your car

_____

_____

_____

5. An accident report of an imaginary collision

_____

_____

_____

6. Your trip through the cafeteria lunch line

_____

_____

_____

7. The minutes of a club meeting

_____

_____

_____

8. Your expenditures (imaginary, if you like) for the last week

_____

_____

_____

9. The condition (safe or unsafe, operable or inoperable) of some piece of machinery

_____

_____

_____

10. Any college function you have attended in the last month—a convocation, a dinner, a party, or an athletic event

_____

_____

_____

11. An experiment done, a field trip taken, or a special project assigned for some class

_____

_____

_____

12. Any event of your own choosing

_____

_____

_____

       Exercise 15. Make plans for two of the main idea sentences you wrote in Exercise 14.

MAIN IDEA SENTENCE _____

_____

_____

_____

1. _____

_____

_____

2. _____

_____

_____

3. _____

_____

_____

4. _____

_____

_____

CONCLUSION _____

_____

_____

_____

MAIN IDEA SENTENCE _____

_____

_____

_____

1. _____

_____

_____

2. _____

_____

_____

3. _____

_____

_____

4. _____

_____

_____

CONCLUSION _____

_____

_____

_____

Exercise 16. Write a report using one of the plans you made in Exercise 15. Be sure to check your report for clearness and precision, orderliness, sticking to the subject, completeness, accuracy, and objectivity.

VI

My Hunting Trip
and Other Drivel:
Personal Narrative

Students who are asked to write a paper "telling what happened" often write about their own experiences. They sometimes produce papers that seem to the reader to go on and on:

> I got up early in the morning, I ate my breakfast, I packed the car, I drove there, I set up camp, I ate my dinner. I went to bed. I got up early in the morning. I ate breakfast. I washed the dishes and put the fire out. The country was very pretty. I almost shot the biggest deer I ever saw, but I didn't. We got home very late and very tired, and we all agreed it was the best hunting trip we ever had.

Only the writer's girl can read such drivel, and even she would not put up with it from anyone else. She reads it, not because it is interesting (it is ghastly), but because it was written by somebody she is fond of. She reads with the same lack of critical sense that she shows when she sits for an hour or so contemplating her beloved's cauliflower ear and assuring herself that it is the most distinguished ear in town. Love, as everybody knows, is blind. Other readers, not blinded by love, will put the paper down before they have finished the first paragraph. They realize that such papers are dull, but they also realize a shortcoming which is even *more* serious—the paper *makes no point.*

In writing your own papers, don't lay yourself open to "So what?" or

"Who cares?" Unless you have a definite reason for telling your experiences, and can make that definite reason clear to your readers, there is no difference between a weekend at the beach, your most successful hunting trip, the night the hurricane came, or the time the pigs ate your pet cat. Unless these tales make a clear point, they all have one thing in common: they are valueless. Either throw them away or mail them to your own true love.

You should not, however, throw out all your own experiences. Your experience, what has happened to you, is the only basis you have for writing anything original. In writing factual reports, you avoided interpretation. But in writing about what has happened to you, your job is to interpret your experiences, to find what is meaningful in them. If you can convince your readers that what happened to you means something, not only to you but to them, you are doing more than rambling on about meaningless experiences.

As always, the best way to arrive at the meaning is to put the main idea down in one clear sentence. But the main idea cannot be simply a statement of what happened. "Last fall three friends and I went on a hunting trip" will not do, because the sentence fails to say why the trip was important or what you learned from it. Such a sentence will lead to "I got up early in the morning, I ate my breakfast," and so on and so on till the reader goes to sleep.

One way to get at the significance of what happened is to fit your main idea sentence into one of the following patterns, or something like them. Instead of letting the trip or the event stand alone in the main idea sentence, fit it into the first blank. Then ask yourself what you found out during the experience.

EVENT	SIGNIFICANCE
On a hunting trip last fall, _____.	
During the hurricane last year, _____.	
When we went to the beach for the weekend, _____.	

Even though many kinds of discoveries will fit into the blank, you will not be able to use them all. "On a hunting trip last fall, I discovered that it is 110 miles from my front door to Route 66" is useless for two reasons. First, it is a "So what?" discovery. Nobody except your family, or possibly a prospective buyer of your corner lot, cares how far it is from your house to the highway. But even supposing there were readers who would find this fact a meaningful discovery, what else can you say about it? Once you have said how far it is, you are through. "When we went to the beach for the weekend, I discovered that the tide goes out and comes in every twelve hours" is not very useful either, if you want to tell about your trip to the beach. If, on the other hand, you want to write a paper of *explanation,* telling about the behavior of the tides, "The tide goes out and comes in every twelve hours," might be a good main idea sentence. Notice, however, that your weekend at the beach has faded completely out of the sentence; the tides come in and go out whether or not you are there.

The kind of discovery you are looking for must grow out of the event you are telling about, and it must have a meaning that will carry over into other experiences. When you took that hunting trip did something happen to remind you that safety is important? That inexperienced campers get into trouble? Did you come face to face with a deer and find that the trusting look in those liquid brown eyes made you unable to pull the trigger? Did you discover, in the strain of sharing camp chores, that the football hero you had always admired was a lazy, no-good slob? None of these ideas is very world-shaking, but they all have two things in common: they can be formed into main idea sentences broad enough that you can write a whole paper based on them, and they show why the hunting trip meant something to you. If it meant something to you, it will probably mean something to your reader. If it means something to your reader, what you write will lead to more than boredom and a big *F*.

Like any other main idea, these sentences should serve as a guide to what is included in the paper. If your main idea sentence reads, "On a hunting trip last summer, I discovered that I don't really like killing animals," you must put into the paper only the details and events related to your discovery that you are more humane than you had thought you were.

Don't bother to check the first hunting story for the relation between its details and its discovery. Besides being pointless, the story also is completely without specific detail. What is *early* in the morning? Four o'clock? Seven-thirty? Half-past ten? Did *breakfast* consist of five slabs of bacon, four eggs, half a dozen biscuits, and a pint of orange juice, or was it a bowl of stale tootsy-wootsies and a crust of leftover toast? The writer says the country was *very pretty*, but he fails to tell the reader what it looked like. Perhaps his idea of pretty country is flat, brown fields, neatly divided by painted white fences, and nothing in sight for miles except the horizon. Maybe he likes sagebrush and concrete. Whatever he likes, he must give you a chance to see it with him so you can decide for yourself whether it was *very pretty*. Even though you are supposed to be interpreting, you must not be content with merely giving the reader a bunch of opinion words. Specific details are as important in this kind of writing as in report writing. If the writer does a really skillful job, he may make you aware of beauties in sagebrush and cement that you never dreamed were there.

Of course you must start with details, but you cannot stop there. Even though the following version of the hunting paper has been stuffed with specific details, it is not much better than the earlier version:

> I got up at four-thirty in the morning. I ate a slice of ham, a boiled egg, two and a half biscuits, and a glass of milk for breakfast. I put three cans of beans, a loaf of bread, my old brown suede jacket, Mary's torn sleeping bag, and my new shotgun into the back of my 1956 Dodge sedan. I drove 183.7 miles due north to Ogden's Woods. Natty came with me. We decided to make camp on the edge of a lake that is about half a mile from shore to shore. First we opened the trunk and laid the tent stakes in a pile on the ground. Then we . . .

Have you quit reading yet? Everybody else has. The trouble with this paper is that it reads like a catalogue. It's about as lively as a telephone directory. Too many unselected details can be almost as bad as no details at all. The specific details you include, like the events you select, must have some significance. Does getting up early in the morning have anything to do with your reluctance to shoot the deer? Does what you had for breakfast, or even that you ate at all, really matter? What about stuffing the car with extra clothing, cans of pork and beans, and the sleeping bag with the torn cover? Was your unwillingness to shoot the deer connected with your decision to pitch camp near the lake? Does the reflection of the stars on the slick, thick blackness of the lake connect in some way with how you felt about the deer? In these two pointless accounts of a hunting trip, none of the details and events the writer talked about had much to do with anything. The writer did things or saw things, and he simply wrote them down, without asking himself what significance, if any, they had. If the events have no significance, they must be firmly discarded. But if you start discarding events at this rate, you may ask, what will you have left to write?

The answer, of course, is that you don't discard everything that happened. Rather, you re-examine events in the light of what you discovered. As you stumbled out of bed at four o'clock, did you comfort yourself with visions of the venison steak you would eat next winter? Did you tell your mother, as she loaded your plate with slices of ham, that she could stop worrying about the high cost of meat? As you rode out to camp with your old friend Natty Bumppo, did you keep boasting about the sureness of your aim and the steadiness of your finger on the trigger? As you stared at the cold yellow stars mirrored in the lake water, did you see yourself as the Great American Hunter, a kind of twentieth-century Daniel Boone, complete with everything except the coonskin cap? In other words, did the size of your expectations before you met the deer face to face in the brush contrast with the smallness of the way you felt when you couldn't bring yourself to shoot him? If what went before relates to what went after, put it in; but as you write, make the relationship clear.

You can also use what you saw and did after your meeting with the deer, as long as you use the same test. You can record your apparently pointless conversation with Natty Bumppo, but you must make it clear that your hesitation in answering, "No," to his question, "See any deer?" was because you couldn't decide whether to tell him what you had found out about yourself. You can include what you had for supper if you emphasize that your appetite for pork and beans was greatly increased because you hadn't killed the pig. You can describe the beauty of the pointed fir trees against the drab gray sky or the quiet splash of lake water against the rocks if you pause to remember that your camp is deer country, not man country, and that the great stag you didn't kill is alive to drink from the lake after you have gone home.

This particular treatment of a hunting trip may strike your reader as sentimental or silly—especially if he is the first in his crowd to fill out his deer tag. But even if he calls you a clod, at least he's not saying, "So what?" His reaction proves you have made him see what you saw and understand how you felt about it, even though he may not agree. You have made your point.

In writing papers that tell what happened to you, there are two things you should keep in mind. First, you use your main idea sentence in a slightly different way than in other kinds of writing. In giving directions, in explaining, in reporting, your main idea sentence usually appears in the introduction, often as the first sentence in the first paragraph. In papers of personal experience, it may not appear at all. Even though you must know before you begin to write that your main idea is "During my hunting trip last summer, I discovered that the football hero I had always admired was a lazy, cowardly slob," you will probably not begin your paragraph with that discovery. Instead, you may start something like this:

> Last summer, when Tarzan Peterson invited me to go elk hunting with him and his cousin, I couldn't have been more flattered. I had known Tarzan for nearly ten years, first as the second-grader who could chin himself more times than any other kid in school, then as the junior high school strongman who claimed he could lick anybody in school, the teacher included, and finally as the star halfback of Podunk's winning team, the big shot that all the prettiest girls mooned over and all the fellows envied. I thought he was a real hero.

What this paragraph is doing, of course, is building Tarzan up, so that when you show him for the slob and coward he is, you can knock him down effectively. Your new view of Tarzan as a quite unheroic hero may not be clearly stated until the end of the paper, and maybe even then it will be only implied: "That fall, when the adoring crowd of seniors made themselves hoarse shouting Tarzan's praises, my shouting was pretty restrained. I'm not sure I even whispered."

The second thing to remember is that papers telling what happened to you must be told in easy, natural-sounding language. Hunting excursions, trips to the beach, leads in the senior play will all be more convincing and more interesting if they sound as though they were written in the informal language of conversation. Making your language sound stilted and pedantic is another quick way to bore your reader. If you begin your paper by saying,

> Last summer, an individual I had been acquainted with for several years invited me to accompany him on an elk hunt. He then informed me that one of his relatives would also accompany us.

you will have spoiled the flavor of your paper. Your reader will be quick to recognize that most people do not refer to the boys they know as *individuals*; that *know, go with,* and *told* are more natural words than *acquainted with, accompany,* and *informed*; and that "Then he told me" is a more normal word order than "He then told me." In informal accounts of your own experience, if you would feel silly saying it, don't write it.

The catch here is that what you write must *sound as though* it were the language of conversation, without really being a copy of what you would say. Perhaps a safer practice is to write the way *you wish you talked,* rather than the way you actually do. When we talk, most of us are careless about the way we use our pronouns. We say *he* or *she* and expect our hearers to see the person we are looking at. We let *this* and *that* and *which* stand for whole blocks of earlier discussion and trust our hearers to ask us what we mean if they are confused. We say, "A guy sure has to have a lot of money when you run for office in this county," when we mean, "Anyone who runs for office in this county has to have a lot of money." We depend on gestures, on the tones of our voices, on scowling and smiling, to convey part of our meaning for us. In writing we must be more precise. We must be careful that what our pronouns stand for is clearly understood, but we must do it so naturally and easily that our readers are not conscious of how careful we are being.

Another thing we do when we talk is use incomplete sentences. We say a word or two here, a phrase there, and let the rest of what has been said help us out. A perfectly normal conversation might go something like this:

"Coming?"

"Guess not."

"Oh, gee. Why?"

"Mom won't let me."

"What's the matter? Worried about you or something?"

"A fussbudget, that's what she is."

"Will she ever let you?"

"If my dad says."

"Will he?"

"Nope."

To the speakers, such fragments are probably perfectly clear, but written down just as they were spoken, they sound incomplete.

When we talk, we not only use fragments, we often repeat ourselves without any awareness of sounding like a stuck phonograph record:

"My, this is a good dinner. This is one of the best meals I ever ate. My, this is good. I was just telling Angie that I sure like the way Auntie Mame fixed this meat. It tastes awfully good. Henry, don't you think this is good? I think this is the best meat I ever tasted. It's sure good."

If everybody is enjoying the dinner, probably nobody will find this series of remarks very repetitious, and Aunt Mame will be pleased about the whole conversation. But written down, the comments get boring. Both fragments and repetitions ruin writing.

When you write your experiences down, you may, if it is easier for you, write them down *exactly* the way you would talk; but before the paper is finished, you must go back and complete the fragments and cut out the repetitions. Even if you are quoting what someone said, leave in just enough repetition and just enough fragments to make the conversation sound natural. Don't overdo it.

You will probably also notice, if you have honestly written down just what you would say, that in talking you string your sentences together, using almost no connectors except *and* and *so*:

We went to the concert and we saw Aunt Mame and Uncle Henry in the balcony and we waved and whistled but they didn't see us, so Cassie went around during intermission and she couldn't find them, but we did see Aunt Mame after it was all over and she said they'd been kind of hidden behind a big palm so I guess that was how we missed them, and anyway, Uncle Henry doesn't like us to call attention to ourselves in public and I guess it is just as well he didn't see us.

As you revise your sentences into smooth writing, you will want to get rid of this stringy effect by using words that show more precise relationships: *nevertheless, in spite of, although, before, while,* and a good many others.

> *While* we were at the concert, we saw Aunt Mame and Uncle Henry in the balcony. *Although* we waved and whistled, they didn't see us. *When* Cassie went around during intermission, she couldn't find them. *Nevertheless,* we did see Aunt Mame after it was all over. She said we probably missed them *because* they had been *somewhat* hidden behind a big palm. *Since* Uncle Henry doesn't like us to call attention to ourselves in public, I guess it is just as well he didn't see us.

Adding six connectors, all different, makes this paragraph sound much better. Notice that one other change has been made. The sloppy phrase, *kind of,* has been changed to *somewhat.* This change helps, too. Varying the connectors you use not only gets rid of the tiresome overuse of *and* and *so,* it also helps you to write sentences of a more normal length.

If you are in the habit of punctuating every third sentenec with "dagnab it to perdition" or phrases even more profane, you will have to strike out those expressions too. If your conversation is ninety-three per cent slang, you'd better reverse the proportions. Seven per cent slang, if it is carefully chosen, may give flavor to your writing, in much the way that pepper flavors soup. More than seven per cent, however, will make your writing unacceptable, just as too much pepper makes the soup inedible. Some teachers want all slang phrases eliminated from student writing. They believe, with only too much justification, that using slang is only an excuse for not finding the accurate expression in standard English. These teachers too, however, will want your writing to sound natural, not stilted.

Just as some slang expressions will give spice to your personal experience papers, so some personal experience will give tang to your other writing. When you wrote a paper explaining what you meant by *loyalty* or *courage* or *honesty,* you were using what had happened to you or to someone you knew. The difference between what you did then and what you are doing now is largely a difference of approach. In explaining what you meant by *courage,* for instance, you began with the meaning and looked for an experience that would illustrate it. You decided to tell the story of Adeline jumping into the creek to pull the poodle out because her behavior seemed a good example of bravery. You included the information that the poodle could swim and Adeline couldn't, because Adeline's lifelong fear of water was what made her action really brave.

In other words, because you recognized the significance of the story you were telling, because you knew what point you wanted to make, you found it fairly easy to decide what to put in and what to leave out.

When you write papers to convince, you will find it much easier to get other people to agree with you if you can support your beliefs by your own experience. A reader is much more likely to suppose you know what you're talking about if you can let him see in operation the evil you are deploring and show him why you are concerned with the problem.

Here is a student theme of personal experience:

No Help in Sight

Because I am the middle daughter in a family of seven, I have never had to be very self-reliant. As a matter of fact, whenever I was unsure of anything, all I had to do was ask one of my older brothers. Since I didn't have to depend on myself for anything, until last summer I had always been afraid that I wouldn't be much good in an emergency.

But on the Fourth of July my little brother and I were out in the car alone, cutting sticks for a weenie roast the family was going to have later. Freddy was about twenty-five feet away from where I was hacking away at a hazel bush when all of a sudden he let out a yell. I turned around to ask what the matter was, but when I saw the blood running down his leg, I didn't stop to ask questions. I just took one look and ran over to him. Apparently, when he was trying to cut off a branch, the knife had slipped. Anyway, there was a gash about two inches long in his thigh, and he was bleeding like a stuck pig.

My first thought was, "Oh, my gosh, I wish Chuck or Seymour was here!" Then I realized that I would have to be the one to help Freddy. I happened to be wearing a bandana scarf, and I took it off and pressed it hard against Fred's leg. He was crying, but he helped me hold it in place. Luckily, the car was only a few yards away, and I got Fred over to it without letting the makeshift bandage slip.

I don't think I ever drove so fast before. I made the usual fifteen-minute trip in about seven minutes. I decided in the car to take my brother directly to the hospital. It was lucky I did, because the doctor there said that Freddy couldn't have lost much more blood. What's more, he said that if I hadn't put the pressure bandage on, Freddy might have died.

Of course, I'm not glad Freddy cut his leg, but every time I see his scar I can't help thinking that I did know what to do in an emergency. I can get along by myself.

This student theme is an excellent example of a paper using personal experience. The first paragraph introduces the writer and prepares us for the significance of her experience. The language throughout is natural-sounding and full of specific detail: "hacking away at a hazel bush," "about twenty-five feet away from where I was," "made the usual fifteen-minute trip in seven minutes." She makes use of slang only once, "bleeding like a stuck pig," and though the image is neither pleasant nor original, the phrasing is undeniably effective. The conclusion carefully qualifies the main idea sentence—"Of course, I'm not glad Freddy cut his leg"—and ends with a clear statement about the significance of the event: that the writer can do all right by herself during an emergency.

It's not easy to write personal experience papers which make a point, use significant details and events, and sound natural. Such papers take more thinking out than a series of generalizations or a catalogue listing details. But they are certainly a great deal easier to read, and they may earn a "very good" or two in the margin of your paper. Further, they provide excellent practice in examining and explaining the meaning of your experiences. The ability to find the significance in what has happened to you will make you much more skillful in two other kinds of writing: explaining and convincing. By learning to use your own experiences in your explanations and your arguments, you, like other skillful writers, have arrived at the place where you can blend your purposes, keeping the lesser purpose, telling what happened, subordinated to the more important, explaining or convincing.

And besides, if you can make your experiences significant, you can be sure you are not writing drivel.

Key Words

Here are some of the important terms used in this chapter. Without referring back to the chapter, see whether you can answer these questions.

1. How can you distinguish between telling what happened in an objective report and *telling what happened to you*? How are they alike?

2. What is meant by finding the *significance* in an experience? What is one way of finding it?

3. Explain some differences between the *language of conversation* and the *language of writing*. Be sure you can list at least three characteristics of conversational language.

4. How does using *normal word order* keep your writing from sounding *pedantic*?

5. In what way is using *slang* the opposite of sounding *pedantic*? Can you work out a satisfactory definition for *slang*? Do the other members of the class agree with your definition?

6. What are the two most common *connectors* in conversational language? List at least eight other connectors which can give variety to your writing.

Vocabulary

Pick the answer that most closely fits the meaning of the word as it has been used in the chapter. Look up in your dictionary the meaning of all the words you miss.

1. To call something *drivel* means that you _____
   (a) think the thing is silly and worthless
   (b) think it has been out in the rain
   (c) think it is used in golf or hockey
   (d) admire it

2. To call something *ghastly* means that you think it is _____
   (a) a vision from another world
   (b) shockingly bad
   (c) amazingly good
   (d) wearing an old sheet

3. When you *contemplate* something, you _____
   (a) put it on a heated plate
   (b) draw a design showing a cross-section
   (c) revise it
   (d) look at it and think about it

4. To be *humane* means to be   _____
   (a) a featherless biped
   (b) given easily to anger
   (c) kind and good
   (d) a member of the race of man

5. *Version* means   _____
   (a) writing poetry
   (b) the same account, retold
   (c) honesty
   (d) treason

6. When you *discard* something, you   _____
   (a) put it aside
   (b) file it in a cabinet
   (c) ask for a reshuffle
   (d) use a disk-shaped comb on it

7. *Drab* means   _____
   (a) a woman of the streets
   (b) colorless and dull
   (c) an old horse
   (d) a two-wheeled carriage

8. A *sentimental* story is one which   _____
   (a) has a moral
   (b) is excessively tender
   (c) is always about young lovers
   (d) is harsh and unrealistic

9. Writing that is *stilted*   _____
   (a) goes about on long sticks
   (b) flows gracefully
   (c) reads awkwardly
   (d) is seldom still

10. A *pedantic* person   _____
    (a) fusses over trivial details
    (b) goes about on a bicycle
    (c) has foot trouble
    (d) is a foot specialist

11. When you *imply* something, you   _____
    (a) state it over and over again
    (b) suggest it rather than state it
    (c) make it move more smoothly
    (d) hinder it rather than help it

12. A *gesture* is   _____
    (a) a court clown
    (b) an expressive motion
    (c) a punctuation mark
    (d) a kind of ballad

13. A word that *conveys* meaning to someone else   _____
    (a) confuses him
    (b) costs him money
    (c) enlightens him
    (d) carries him from one place to another

14. A *fragment* is   _____
    (a) an expensive perfume
    (b) a piece of the whole
    (c) an ancient relic
    (d) a bad odor

15. When you *vary* your usage, you   _____
    (a) give it some variety
    (b) intensify it
    (c) fill it with slang
    (d) make it pedantic

16. A *profane* speaker is one who   _____
    (a) takes money for what he says
    (b) takes great pains to speak correctly
    (c) swears a good deal
    (d) avoids coarse and unseemly language

17. *Proportion* means   _____
    (a) having a good figure
    (b) a second helping
    (c) having a purpose in life
    (d) the relation of one part to another

18. Something that has *tang*   _____
    (a) also has ting
    (b) belongs to a Chinese union
    (c) has flavor and zest
    (d) isn't worth a dang

19. A thing that is *inedible* is   _____
    (a) impossible to erase
    (b) very difficult to erase

(c) not fit to eat

(d) only half alive

20. A person who offers *justification* is offering   ____
    (a) reasons that explain his actions
    (b) a bribe
    (c) an introduction to a member of the Supreme Court
    (d) reduced prices

21. *Deplore* means   ____
    (a) to be sent out of the state
    (b) to remove unwanted hair
    (c) to maneuver troops
    (d) to regret something keenly

22. If something is *subordinate* it is   ____
    (a) less important than something else
    (b) more important than something else
    (c) more outstanding than something else
    (d) the first thing you think of

Exercises

Exercise 1. In these sentences, replace the generalizations with specific detail. Be sure the details support the generalization. For instance, "My uncle is very generous" could be rewritten as "Uncle Peter gave a thousand dollars to help crippled children get medical care," or "Uncle Peter gave me fifty dollars to get some new shoes."

1. We ate a good breakfast. _____

_____

_____

_____

2. The country was very pretty. _____

_____

_____

_____

3. The museum was interesting. _____

_____

_____

_____

4. John had a dilapidated car. _____

_____

_____

_____

5. The weekend was lots of fun. _____

_____

_____

_____

6. My aunt is a very nice woman. _____

_____

_____

_____

7. My aunt is a cranky old lady. _____

_____

_____

_____

8. Most animals are shy. _____

_____

_____

_____

9. Mr. Peterson had a pleasant house. _____

_____

_____

_____

10. Uncle Hiram is hard to understand. _____

_____

_____

_____

Exercise 2. Rewrite the following sentences to avoid unnatural word order and stilted language.

1. Having completed our efforts at washing it, we then put the car in the garage.

_____

_____

_____

2. Give a cookie to each individual present.

_____

_____

_____

3. Upon departing from the bathroom, turn off the light.

_____

_____

_____

4. Each particular person I met smiled pleasantly.

_____

_____

_____

5. My mother then encouraged me to attempt once again to open the door.

_____

_____

_____

6. I informed my baby sister that some persons don't cry all the time.

_____

_____

_____

7. I made each person present acquainted with my father.

_____

_____

_____

8. It was then ordered that all enlisted persons assemble at the tonsorial parlor in order that they might be divested of most of their crowning glory.

_____

_____

_____

9. Due to the fact that I had not been informed of the examination, I did not do as well as might have been expected or wished for.

_____

_____

_____

10. The captains having shaken hands, the whistle was blown.

_____

_____

_____

11. I, being in the mood to see my girl friend, forthwith began a trip across town.

_____

_____

_____

12. Books, believed sinful, were promptly, by the city fathers, banned.

_____

_____

_____

13. Rejoicing over his immense good fortune, I congratulated my friend.

_____

_____

_____

14. Sleeping in class is not approved of by most educators.

_____

_____

_____

15. My avocation is the exposure of photographic film to light.

_____

_____

_____

Exercise 3. Put these conversational fragments into complete sentences. For instance, "All right?" could be changed to "Is it all right if we park the car on your geraniums?"

1. Got indigestion from eating too fast. _____

_____

_____

2. When I get back. _____

_____

_____

3. Out to lunch. _____

_____

_____

4. Of course, that sounds sort of—don't you think? _____

_____

_____

5. Going to the dance? _____

_____

_____

6. But you don't have to. _____

_____

_____

7. Seven more? _____

_____

_____

8. Too bad. _____

_____

_____

9. Tired? _____

_____

_____

10. John home? _____

_____

_____

11. Salt, please. _____

_____

_____

12. Apparently. _____

_____

_____

13. Canasta, anyone? _____

_____

_____

14. Coming? _____

_____

_____

15. Sounds good. _____

_____

_____

Exercise 4. Rewrite these sentences using more precise connectors. (You may rearrange their order or break them up into shorter sentences.)

1. I was afraid of the water and so I didn't go swimming and so I missed my chance to meet the new boy in town.

_____

_____

_____

_____

2. I don't like to cook and my mother makes me do it and my father complains about it.

_____

_____

_____

3. The bell rings and the students all leave.

_____

_____

4. The speed limit is twenty-five miles an hour and the people drive forty and the police arrest them.

_____

_____

_____

_____

5. Rupert Creech takes Tansy out to dinner and then he doesn't have enough money and so he doesn't pay the bill and the restaurant manager is annoyed and Tansy doesn't like it much either and it embarrasses her.

_____

_____

_____

_____

_____

6. I sat down to play and they laughed and then I played the piano and they whooped and haw-hawed and I cried and they still laughed and so I shot them.

_____

_____

_____

_____

_____

7. When John sits down to write sentences, he never seems to have any trouble and the words just come spilling out of his ballpoint pen and always arrange themselves in nice, neat sentence-length segments but when Sally writes, it seems more like a string of sausages with only one sausage but a long one because she does not break her writing into sentences.

_____

_____

_____

_____

_____

_____

_____

8. It is a bad thing to write terribly long and loosely connected sentences and when people read them, the people get confused and what is the sense of confusing people more when there is already so much confusion all over the world?

_____

_____

_____

_____

_____

9. My teacher always gives me low grades on my papers and when I ask him why he says I am wordy but I don't see how you can write themes without words but he won't change the grade and I don't like it.

---

10. I went to the game Saturday and it was in the last quarter and we were behind and so our star player shot a basket but he missed and the second-string man grabbed the ball and out jumped the guard and made the basket and won us the game.

---

11. I play the piano but my father is tone deaf so he can't tell if I make mistakes and so I don't always correct my mistakes and my piano teacher yells at me.

12. We've been practicing a week and almost everyone knows his lines and I have my costume ready but the man who plays Father doesn't know his lines and so I don't know if the play will be a success but I hope so.

_____

_____

_____

_____

_____

13. Last night I watched the movie on television and so I didn't get up on time and so I had to gulp my breakfast and run to school and so I was late and so now I didn't get the assignment and I will get in trouble if I don't do it.

_____

_____

_____

_____

_____

14. Jane applied for a job but she kept getting turned away but she kept trying and finally she got one and now she has one hundred dollars in the bank.

_____

_____

_____

_____

_____

15. Pete doesn't like to eat spinach and his mother always makes him eat it and he always gets sick when he eats spinach.

_____

_____

_____

_____

Exercise 5. Rewrite these sentences, changing the slang expressions to natural, standard English.

1. Gee, your coat looks keen.

_____

2. He's got bats in his belfry.

_____

3. Jane is an apple polisher.

_____

4. Most of the students in the class wish the teacher would get lost on Friday afternoon.

_____

_____

5. As far as drips go, he's one of the crumbiest guys I know.

_____

_____

6. We crabbed at the teacher for giving us such a filthy assignment.

_____

_____

7. Rupert Creech's grandfather kicked the bucket several years before the turn of the century.

_____

_____

8. Pete really lucked out in the history test yesterday, but then the teacher pulled a fast one and really clobbered the whole class.

_____

_____

_____

9. It was a swingin' blast last night, but everybody got bombed out of their wigs, and then the fuzz made the scene.

_____

_____

_____

10. The boss gave Rupert the old heave-ho, and then his old man gave him what-for for spending too much dough.

_____

_____

11. The teacher was ticked off at Rolf.

12. Senator Hoaxshell is a shoo-in.

13. Professor Jack is a pushover if you come on strong about canasta.

14. I'll bet I can butter up old pruneface by reading Hobbes.

15. Let me clue you, the test is a real winner.

16. John's a goof-off.

17. You don't rate if you don't like to chew the fat.

18. I wish he'd take a powder.

19. There are a helluva lot of exercises on this page.

20. I don't give a damn for any of them.

21. Suzy's more hip than square but her flap is from antiquesville!

_____

_____

_____

22. If you don't dig our lingo, ask your old man. He remembers "23 skidoo."

_____

_____

_____

Exercise 6. Fill in the blanks, making the significance clear.

1. During my usual nap in history class, I discovered

_____

_____

2. When I got my leg broken during football practice, I learned

_____

_____

3. While proving how fast my car can accelerate, I learned that

_____

_____

4. During the blizzard, I discovered that

_____

_____

5. When I was nominated for student council, I discovered that

_____

_____

6. During the final exam in metal welding, I learned that

_____

_____

7. After three months on the girls' field hockey team, I learned that

_____

_____

8. While I was spending five thousand dollars each week for a year, I learned that

_____

_____

9. On a trip to the city dump, I learned that

_____

_____

10. When I saw my own mother doing the frug, I learned that

_____

_____

Exercise 7. Fill in the blanks, using your own experiences.

1. During _____

_____, I discovered _____

_____

2. When _____

_____, I learned _____

_____

3. While _____

_____, I learned that _____

_____

4. During _____

_____, I discovered that _____

_____

5. When _____

_____, I discovered that _____

_____

6. During _____

_____, I learned that _____

_____

7. After _____

_____, I learned that _____

_____

8. On a trip to _____

_____, I learned that _____

_____

9. While _____

_____, I learned that _____

_____

10. When _____

_____, I learned that _____

_____

Exercise 8. List the events you would include in writing papers on any two of the main idea sentences in Exercise 7. Then explain how each event relates to the main idea sentence. For instance, if your sentence in Exercise 7 had read, "When I worked in a restaurant last summer, I discovered that most people are kind and helpful," your plan might begin like this

EVENT I spilled my first order all over the table, and the customer helped me clean it up.
RELATIONSHIP I expected him to complain to the boss; instead, he helped.

EVENT When my father was sick, the boss let me go home early without docking my pay.
RELATIONSHIP I asked him if I could go home, but paying me for time I didn't work was really kind.

1. MAIN IDEA SENTENCE _____

_____

_____

_____

Event _____

_____

Relationship _____

_____

_____

Event _____

_____

Relationship _____

_____

_____

Event _____

_____

Relationship _____

_____

_____

Event _____

_____

Relationship _____

_____

_____

Event _____

_____

Relationship _____

_____

_____

CONCLUSION _____

_____

_____

_____

2. MAIN IDEA SENTENCE _____

_____

_____

_____

Event _____

_____

Relationship _____

_____

_____

Event _____

_____

Relationship _____

_____

_____

Event _____

_____

Relationship _____

_____

_____

Event _____

_____

Relationship _____

_____

_____

Event _____

_____

Relationship _____

_____

_____

CONCLUSION _____

_____

_____

_____

Exercise 9. For each of the events listed in one part of Exercise 8, list on a separate sheet ten concrete details. If the event is the try-out for the school play, you might list such things as:
   auditorium so noisy you couldn't hear the bell
   dachshund wandered across the stage

red velvet curtains, old and dusty
torn prompt book
scratches on the mahogany piano
blond boy with a runny nose
light so dim it was hard to read the script
a shoestring that broke just as you stepped on the stage
the roar of trucks going by outside
clammy hands

In each group of details, circle at least three that are significant in relation to your main idea sentence.

Exercise 10. Write the theme you have planned as you did Exercises 8 and 9. You may use more events and details than you listed in the exercises, but do not omit any of those that are significant.

VII

Making Others See It Your Way: Writing Papers to Persuade

Most of this book so far has badgered you to keep your opinions out of your writings, and browbeat you when you failed to do so. Except when you were interpreting your own experiences, you may have gotten the notion that nobody cares what you think about anything. That is not true. The point is that you must be able to tell the difference between opinions and directions, opinions and explanations, and opinions and reports. There is nothing wrong with opinions, but there are some places where opinions do not belong. Opinions do belong in papers intended to persuade others.

The world is full of persuasive writing. Some of it is open and above-board; some of it hides behind explanations and reports. When you think of persuasive writing, you probably think first of ad writers, for none of us can escape them. Ads are all around us. The radio shrieks at us about newer, bigger, better products. Television issues frank warnings about household germs and offensive body odors. Beautiful people in magazine ads beckon to us from beautiful cars parked on beautifully landscaped driveways in front of beautiful houses. Newspapers squeeze in a dribble or two of world events between the furniture close-outs and the grocery specials. Our mailboxes are jammed with circulars offering everything from life insurance to cemetery lots.

But ad writers are not the only salesmen. Politicians have something to sell, too. Millions a year are spent to persuade you that Senator John

S. Hoaxshell is a plain, earnest farmboy who carries your particular interest engraved upon the gold of his hundred per cent American heart. He persuades a group of laborers that he believes unions were made in heaven, and he persuades a group of businessmen that he believes unions were definitely made somewhere else. In the Senate, he persuades his colleagues that the multimillion-dollar project for a grasshopper sanctuary in his state will benefit the national economy, increase our prestige, and preserve a priceless national resource.

Many other people try to persuade us, too. The public relations man proclaims the merits of his organization; the chairman of the United Good Givers' drive pleads for the poor; the president of the local Teetotalers' Union portrays the evil of drink. Indeed, it is much more difficult to think of people who are not trying to persuade than it is to think of people who are.

You, too, are involved in persuasion. Persuasion is one of the first things you learned and the ability to persuade is still one of your most important assets throughout life. As an infant you cried for a bottle, and as a child you whined for a popsicle. Between these two acts is more difference than meets the eye. Crying for a bottle is simply an expression of a physical necessity: you were hungry, so you cried. But when you whined for a popsicle, you were making a calculated effort to use whining for the result it would bring. You learned to pitch the whine so your parents were moved to pity you rather than to hit you, and you soon learned how much whining you could get away with and which parent could be most easily worked. By the time you were sixteen your cunning had improved and included many other persuasive techniques. You knew when to do, unasked, a favor for your father, when to startle your mother with a kiss. You learned the exact moment when you were most likely to get a favorable response to the question "Dad, may I have the car?"

You probably learned what you know about persuasion without giving it much thought. If you cried, you got your bottle. If you whined too much, you got a swat instead of a sweet. And if you asked for the car without first mowing the lawn, chances are you went without the car. Automatically you learned how to behave to get what you wanted. Maybe you have developed a high degree of juvenile charm. But charm, especially juvenile charm, is not enough to get you through college, let alone through life. Most history professors cannot be wheedled, sociology teachers flim-flammed, chemistry professors bribed, or English teachers jollied into raising a grade from *D* to *C*. In college, as in life, you are rewarded according to your ability to persuade; but you must persuade through sound performance, not merely sound.

In other words, you don't improve the quality of your persuasive themes by smiling at your professor every time you pass him in the halls, nor by laughing, frowning, or making faces. You improve your themes by writing a clear introduction, by supporting your point of view with convincing reasons, and by restating your point of view in the conclusion.

Your point of view, the statement of what you believe and what you are trying to get your reader to believe, too, will be the main idea sentence of your paper. The main idea sentence of a paper to convince is easier to write and easier to recognize than the main idea sentence of other kinds of papers. It is easier to write because all you need to do is ask yourself, "What do I believe?" or "What do I think should be done?" and then state the answer clearly and definitely. Such a main idea sentence is easier to recognize because it usually contains such words as *should* or *should not, must* or *must not, ought* or *ought not, good* or *bad, better* or *worse*—in fact, just the same group of opinion words that you tried to eliminate from your explanations and reports.

Even though your teacher does not assign a definite topic but, instead, simply says, "Write a paper defending some conviction you hold," you will find it fairly easy to find a subject. Almost all of us have convictions on a wide variety of subjects ranging all the way from a belief that the neighbors ought to keep their dog tied up to a conviction that the nations of the world should enter into an agreement for total disarmament. Certainly either of these beliefs could be made a main idea sentence for a paper to convince, but you would probably do better not to use either one of them. Even though you might be able to write an impassioned denunciation of the cads who can't keep their poodles out of other people's petunia beds, nobody else is likely to care as much about it as you do; this belief is too narrow to have much general interest. That the nations of the world should agree to disarm is unsuitable for the opposite reason; this belief is too broad. Most people care about this one, or would if they knew enough about it, but the problem is too big and too complex to be covered in a five hundred word paper. Your job is to select a conviction broad enough that it does concern other people and narrow enough that you can cover it in a short theme. For your first paper, some campus controversy is a safe choice. Do you believe the school lunches are too expensive? Do you resent the removal of the cigarette machine from the student center? Do you think the student newspaper should take a more vigorous stand on national issues? As soon as you decide to write on your belief that cigarette machines should be returned, your main idea sentence is ready-made: "The cigarette machine should be returned to the campus."

You found your main idea sentence so easily and feel so sure of your support for it that you decide to change your usual approach. Instead of making a plan for the paper, you plunge straight into the introduction.

The introduction to a paper of persuasion must do double duty. It must make a contract based on the main idea sentence, telling the reader fairly what the paper will be about. The contract is exactly the same kind of thing you wrote before you began your other themes. But papers giving directions, papers of explanation, and reports are presumably written to satisfy a particular audience about a specific question. The interest is already there. If anyone reads beyond the first paragraph of your paper of persuasion, it will be because he has been hooked by your interesting first paragraph. Thus the second duty your introduction must perform is to make your reader keep reading. You must try to interest him so much that he would not look up from your paper if the entire company of the Bolshoi Ballet squatted and kicked its way through his reading room.

You might start by saying, "Men are weeping." Naturally, your reader will want to know what those big men are blubbering about. So you go on:

> Although cruel authorities are prohibited by law from ripping the bowels from living men or stretching them on the rack, men in power today continue to cripple and maim. A loathsome example of modern torture exists on this campus, where men and women alike weep piteously for the return of the cigarette machine.

That example is both melodramatic and exaggerated, and you probably will not want to use it for your theme. Nevertheless, it is a great deal better than this beginning:

> I believe, although I know that some people don't agree with me, that we ought, in all fairness, to have the cigarette machine returned to the campus.

You don't need to exaggerate, but if you think of some beginning that will make your reader say to himself, "I wonder why he thinks that," you will likely have him reading on to find out. If you can't think of an interesting beginning, there is nothing wrong with a direct approach: "The cigarette machine must be returned to the campus." It may not be very dramatic, but it is straightforward. It is better than the wishy-washy introduction which simpers around so much that it seems the writer is apologizing for the whole thing. And it's better than a beginning which tries so hard to be clever that the reader can't tell what the paper is about.

Even though you may use your charm in the introduction to lure your reader in, you must go on to persuade him honestly. You cannot persuade honestly by repeating your opinion over and over, no matter how many exclamation points you use to emphasize it. You may know someone who seems to get away with this kind of persuasion at home or at work or in the coffee shop. If he pounds the table hard enough and shouts loud enough, he may silence all opposition. But he isn't really getting away with anything, for he has not persuaded people—he has merely cowed them. Shouting and exclamation pointing have no place in the college classroom. Honest persuasion involves reasons. Unless you can convince your reader that your reasons are good, he will not be persuaded by what you say. Before you go any further with your paper, therefore, you decide to form a plan. You must make a list of sound reasons supporting your main idea sentence.

Perhaps when you decided that your main idea sentence would be "The cigarette machine must be returned to the campus," you had not thought much about why you wanted it returned. You smoke yourself, and it certainly would be handy for you if whoever took the machine would return it. It seems right that you shouldn't have to run downtown everytime you run out of cigarettes. You ought to be able to run up to the student union and buy them there. Still, no matter how obviously "right" your opinion may seem to you, nonsmokers are still not likely to care much. Why do you hold your opinion? If you can't think of any better reasons than mere personal convenience, change your mind. Nobody should hold opinions he can't support.

As hard as it is to think of reasons, you decide that thinking of reasons is easier than quitting smoking, which you may have to do if you keep running out of cigarettes on campus. After an hour's head-scratching and pencil-gnawing, you produce some reasons. The removal of the cigarette machine from the campus will, you say,

1. increase the rate of alcoholism among the student body;
2. increase the rate of nervous breakdowns among smokers suddenly unable to satisfy their craving;
3. demonstrate the administration's lack of democratic ideals;
4. encourage immaturity in the students;
5. decrease college income.

You figure that's enough work for one day, and turn in, but the next morning when you go back through the list, you see that two or three of the things you have down are pretty silly reasons. Removing the cigarette machine will probably not turn very many students into alcoholics, nor will very many really have nervous breakdowns for want of a cigarette. Both these reasons are obviously exaggerations, and while one exaggeration might add to the humorous effect of the paper, two will surely weaken it. If you use both of them, the reader may decide that your whole paper is silly and not read any further. So you cut the nervous breakdowns and keep the alcoholism. You can also skip the idea that removing the cigarette machine demonstrates that the administrators don't have faith in democracy. College administrators will not take seriously the notion that the removal of a cigarette machine has anything to do with democratic ideals.

At the end of your agonizing reappraisal you have three reasons left. Removal of the cigarette machine will

1. increase the rate of alcoholism among the student body;
2. decrease college income and thereby increase student costs;
3. encourage immaturity in the students.

These seem to be rather strong reasons for demanding the return of the cigarette machine. The reasons can be used to support your main idea. But you want to use them in the most effective way. To avoid presenting them haphazardly you must decide which reason should come first, which second, and which last. Rather than drawing straws, you decide to arrange them in order of importance, from least to most.

The first reason, though silly, can be used to attract attention, to interest the reader in your argument. The second reason is more serious than the first, but the amount of money involved is small and so the reason does not deserve the most important position. The third reason, encouraging immaturity, is a serious matter. To increase maturity is the point of education. Treating college students like children will encourage them to act like children and defeat the purpose of college.

Now that you have found some reasons and decided on the best order for them, go ahead and write your paper. But remember that reasons, like the opinions they support, must be supported. You cannot properly support your reasons without giving each reason at least a paragraph. Some of the common ways of supporting reasons are using examples, giving statistics, citing authorities, and predicting consequences.

If you use examples, you will be supporting the general reason you have given with a particular instance. Your statement that the removal of the cigarette machine will cause alcoholism is a generalization. You can give an example by saying that Rupert Creech was forced to leave the campus to buy cigarettes, that the nearest cigarette machine was located in a tavern, that poor Rupert had two schooners just to be polite and came into his English class stony blind drunk. Now this is a silly example, but remember that the reason was pretty silly to begin with. You think you can be more serious on the next reason.

Your second reason, that the removal of the cigarette machine will decrease college income and thereby increase student costs, seems to invite statistical support. You dig into the college records and find that the average monthly net income from the cigarette machine was $1.71. When this princely income is divided among two thousand students, it decreases student costs by exactly $.0008 a month. In other words, the removal of the cigarette machine will increase student costs by less than a penny a year. You've found some statistics, but they don't support your reason very well. You see now that any strength your argument may have will need to come from brilliant support of your third reason.

Still game, you reach for your support which will show that removal of the cigarette machine will encourage immaturity in the students. Suddenly you realize that you are not quite sure what immaturity means, or what maturity means either, for that matter. You decide you need some help from an authority, so you knock on your psych professor's door. You explain what you are trying to do, and ask him for a definition of maturity. "One aspect of maturity," he tells you, "is the ability to identify situations that cannot be changed, and to accept them. Only the immature have temper tantrums about things they can't change. And anyway, you can't bring the machine back. Having a cigarette machine on campus is against a local ordinance. If you brought it back, you would be liable to fine and imprisonment."

Your attempt to find authority has fallen flat, and that threat about fine and imprisonment has taken care of the consequences. It is now plain that you cannot support your reasons, and if you can't support your reasons, you'd better change your opinion. Although you hate to scrap the time you've already invested, you realize that you must find another topic. And the time hasn't been entirely wasted. You have learned for yourself that you must know a good bit about your topic before you start to write about it. And you have learned firsthand about the value of planning a paper before writing it.

You grope around for a second topic, this time determined to show your maturity in your choice of a subject. You think of arguing that final examinations should be abolished, or that all professors should grade on a curve, or that the library should be kept open two hours later every night, or that the college newspaper should be censored. You look at these topics in the light of what you learned in the last attempt and discover that abolishing final examinations is the only opinion on which you hold genuine convictions.

You know finals are not a true test of what you have learned in a course because you freeze up in every final you take. And it simply infuriates you to see those students in the back row copying from the information they have written on their white tennis shoes. And besides, you are sure that if finals were abolished, you could focus your attention on the content of the course, where it belongs, rather than concentrating on outguessing the professor about the final. You not only have found three good reasons, but they seem to have come to you in the right order. Your plan is made.

Your next problem is finding support for your reasons. Your first reason, that finals are not a true test of what a student has learned, has come to mind with its support attached. You can explain that you freeze up, that your hands grow cold and your brow clammy, that every item of information you acquired so painfully at four A.M. leaves you when the test is put in front of you. Using your personal experience as an example is all right here, because you are using it to make a point. And it is a fair example because you're dead certain that what happens to you happens to a lot of students.

The second reason is not hard to deal with either. You can say you resent the cheating you've seen going on, and that you felt somewhat better when the fifteen students who were caught cheating during one final exam were put on scholastic probation. Fifteen out of fifty students make altogether too high a percentage. But you also felt sorry for the ones who were caught because you know they were driven to cheating by pure despair, and because they were unlucky enough to be the ones that got caught. When you add your estimate of the number of students who cheated without getting caught, the number goes up from fifteen to thirty, and the reason becomes even stronger.

Your last reason, that students study to pass the final rather than to master the content of the course, seems the strongest. Just the other day you read an article about Raglan College, where final exams have been abolished. Raglan's president said that he never had been convinced that final examinations were a true test of knowledge, and that since finals had been done away with, Raglan had fewer students flunking out, and more students enthusiastic about their class work. You can use that comment just as you remember it. You can go on to say that if finals were done away with on your campus, it would be reasonable to expect the same good results.

The plan for this theme is sound enough. You have listed three reasons for your opinion and supported all of them. You have used examples— your personal experience in freezing up and in seeing other students cheat. You have used statistics—the percentage of students who were disciplined for cheating. You have cited authority—the statement by the president of Raglan College. And you have predicted the consequences— if it happened at Raglan, it can happen here.

These reasons seem so good you begin to wonder why anybody would want to keep finals. One of your professors argued that if you have learned anything in the course, you ought to be able to remember it until the end of the term. However, your point is not that you don't remember it, but that the stress of a two-hour exam, with your whole grade depending on it, is so great that you can barely remember your own name. In writing your paper you may want to quote your professor, then explain why you don't agree with him. It is a good idea to figure out the arguments of the other side and dispose of them. Such foresight can only strengthen your position.

You still have not written your introduction or your conclusion, but often in writing papers of persuasion it is a good idea to write the introduction and conclusion last, after you are sure how you can support your reasons and know what the introduction and conclusion should emphasize.

Put some paper in your typewriter and begin: "That horror of every college student's life, the final examination, ought to be done away with." Then you go on from there. After all, your plan is made. And don't forget to emphasize your main idea in your conclusion: "Everybody would worry less, cheat less, and learn more if final exams were abolished."

Key Words

Here are some of the important terms used in this chapter. Without referring back to the chapter, see whether you can answer these questions.

1. How does the aim of *persuasive writing* differ from other writing purposes we have discussed?

2. How can we recognize *main idea sentences* for papers of persuasion?

3. Can you write a good five hundred word paper based on any of your *convictions*? How does the size of your conviction relate to the quality of your paper?

4. What should the *introduction* to a paper of persuasion contain? Why must it contain more than the introductions to other papers?

5. What is the difference between cowing your audience and *persuading* them *honestly*?

6. Name four ways of *supporting* your convictions.

7. What are the two main ways of arranging the *order* of a paper of persuasion?

Vocabulary

Pick the answer that most closely fits the meaning of the word as it has been used in the chapter. Look up in your dictionary the meaning of all the words you miss.

1. To *badger* someone means to _____
   (a) provide him with a fur coat
   (b) treat him gently and kindly
   (c) keep after him to do something
   (d) treat him like a groundhog

2. To *browbeat* someone is to _____
   (a) hit him with your fist just above his eye
   (b) bully him and scold him
   (c) persuade him with rubber hoses
   (d) knock your head against his

3. A *colleague* is _____
   (a) an associate
   (b) a school
   (c) a portfolio
   (d) a dog

4. A grasshopper *sanctuary* is _____
   (a) a place where grasshoppers can live safely
   (b) a very holy place
   (c) a sacred grasshopper
   (d) a place to worship grasshoppers

5. *Prestige* means _____
   (a) neatly pressed
   (b) something sticky
   (c) agility of the fingers
   (d) reputation or sense of importance

6. If you have *assets*, you _____
   (a) are large and slow-moving
   (b) are set in your ways
   (c) have advantageous qualities
   (d) have several complete sets

7. A person who uses *cunning* is probably _____
   (a) behaving like a baby
   (b) acting with slyness and calculation

(c) too timid to say anything
(d) making a joke

8. A person of *convictions*   _____
   (a) is a convict
   (b) has been a convict
   (c) has strong beliefs about things
   (d) is indifferent about things

9. A paper which is *impassioned* is   _____
   (a) full of strong emotion
   (b) all about making love
   (c) against making love
   (d) against strong emotion of any kind

10. A man who gives a *denunciation* is   _____
    (a) giving a lecture on how to pronounce words
    (b) making an announcement
    (c) giving up tobacco for Lent
    (d) condemning something with vigor

11. *Cads* are   _____
    (a) like mods and rockers
    (b) owners of expensive cars
    (c) definitely not gentlemen
    (d) class-A cods

12. If you are involved in a *controversy*, you are   _____
    (a) taking part in an argument
    (b) taking part in a dance group
    (c) changing from one side to another and back again
    (d) writing modern verse about prison life

13. If something is *loathsome*,   _____
    (a) it rises slowly like bread dough
    (b) it is completely disgusting
    (c) it hesitates to get started
    (d) it is very close to the ground

14. If you *maim* someone, you   _____
    (a) make him the most important person
    (b) mangle and cripple him
    (c) imitate him
    (d) call him names

15. If something is *melodramatic*, it is   _____
    (a) silly and exaggerated

(b) prosy and dull
(c) given a surprise ending
(d) mellow and soothing

16. If you *simper*, you probably _____
    (a) drink through a straw
    (b) wear too many underclothes
    (c) operate a sump pump
    (d) act silly and behave self-consciously

17. To *cow* people means to _____
    (a) bully them
    (b) change them into cows
    (c) milk them for all they're worth
    (d) moon over them

18. An *agonizing* situation is one that _____
    (a) causes you considerable grief
    (b) happens again and again
    (c) makes you drowsy
    (d) earns you some money

19. If you make a *reappraisal*, you _____
    (a) pay somebody another compliment
    (b) take another look at the situation
    (c) take out another loan
    (d) release someone from a previous obligation

20. If you have made yourself *liable* to something, you have _____
    (a) told a falsehood about it
    (b) made yourself able to tell lies about it
    (c) exposed yourself to something undesirable
    (d) made it likely that something good will happen

21. An *ordinance* is _____
    (a) something quite usual
    (b) something quite unusual
    (c) a kind of small organ
    (d) a public regulation

Exercises

Exercise 1. Which of the following are main idea sentences suitable for a paper of persuasion?

_____ 1. The United Nations was established at the end of World War II.

_____ 2. The United Nations contains a Security Council and a General Assembly.

_____ 3. The United Nations should be strengthened.

_____ 4. Cigarette smokers have a higher rate of lung cancer than do nonsmokers.

_____ 5. The sale of cigarettes should be outlawed.

_____ 6. I can't help loving that man.

_____ 7. Final examinations must be given at the end of each term.

_____ 8. An apple a day keeps the doctor away.

_____ 9. You should eat an apple a day.

_____ 10. Compulsory class attendance should be abolished.

_____ 11. An income tax is a fairer system of raising money than a sales tax.

_____ 12. My father pays income tax in two states.

_____ 13. The freedom riders have done a great deal for democracy in America.

_____ 14. I know a boy who is opposed to civil rights.

_____ 15. The voting age should be raised to thirty.

_____ 16. John Milton wrote an essay opposing government censorship of books.

_____ 17. Television programs containing violence have a harmful effect on children.

_____ 18. The British Broadcasting Company does not carry advertisements on its programs.

_____ 19. Censorship of movies and books means that someone in authority decides what the public should see or read.

_____ 20. Look in the entertainment section of the newspaper to find a listing of movies approved for children.

Exercise 2. Read the following introductions to persuasive themes and decide whether you think they are satisfactory. If they are good, you should be able to answer two questions:

1. How do they arouse your interest?
2. What is the main idea likely to be?

If you think they are unsatisfactory, be prepared to explain why in class discussion.

1. I probably won't have everyone's agreement and I know that I'm not an expert on this subject, but it seems to me that cats make better pets than elephants.

2. People are gullible. I know it. You know it. Everyone knows it. There is a sucker born every minute. P. T. Barnum said that. He was an authority. He had a circus, too.

3. The American Medical Association says that cigarettes are bad.

4. James Boswell is the greatest biographer in the world. He wrote *The Life of Samuel Johnson.* Sam Johnson was a huge bear of a man who had scars all over his face and very poor eyesight. He had suffered from scrofula or the King's evil as a child. Sam also had nervous tics and wrote *The Lives of the Poets.*

5. Almost any day you can see students trying to study in the snack bar. You can see them leaning against the walls in the hall, holding an open book. They sit on the steps, even in the rain sometimes, and

write themes. They have to study in these awkward places because all the chairs in the library are full. There is no question about it. We need a bigger library.

6. This subject is debatable. Everybody debates about it. I don't know why. My mother agrees with me that there is only one point of view on the subject.

7. The Bible says, "Thou shalt not kill," but lots of people go to church every Sunday and think they are good Christians. Still, they think killing is perfectly all right if it happens a long way away from them, inside a prison somewhere, where they don't have to see it.

8. The purpose of my paper is to show that eighteen-year-olds should be allowed to vote.

9. My brother Bill got drafted last year. Bill is eighteen years old. He's been driving a car for two years, and he made enough money being a bag boy that he had to pay forty-five dollars income tax. Bill is engaged to be married. Bill can do everything that grownups do, except vote.

10. My brother Bill got drafted last year. Bill is eighteen years old. He's been driving a car for two years, and he made enough money being a bag boy that he had to pay forty-five dollars income tax. Bill is engaged to be married. Bill can do everything that grownups do, except drink.

Exercise 3. Give two examples that support each of the following beliefs.

1. Earning a living can be fun.

---

2. Raglan College needs a new swimming pool.

_____

_____

3. The driving age should be lowered to fourteen.

_____

_____

_____

4. The driving age should be raised to eighteen.

_____

_____

_____

5. All college students should own a good dictionary.

_____

_____

_____

6. Every boy should spend two weeks at a good summer camp.

_____

_____

_____

7. Television programs contain too much violence.

_____

_____

_____

8. Mothers of small children should not work.

_____

_____

_____

9. Senator Hoaxshell is a ninny.

_____

_____

_____

10. Divorces should be made easier to get.

_____

_____

_____

11. Divorces should be made harder to get.

_____

_____

_____

12. All boys ought to take a year of cooking in high school.

_____

_____

_____

13. Skunks make excellent pets.

_____

_____

_____

14. Mayor Sleight is a crook.

_____

_____

_____

15. Going to college is expensive.

_____

_____

_____

Exercise 4. What kind of statistics would support each of the following general statements? Where might you expect to find the statistics? For instance, if the general statement were "Speed kills," the *kind* of statistics that would support it would be the number of fatal accidents caused by driving over the speed limit last year or the year before. These figures could be obtained from the office of the State Patrol, from any automobile association, or from the National Safety Council.

1. It's more dangerous to drive a car today than it was five years ago.

_____

_____

_____

2. Raglan College needs a new swimming pool.

_____

_____

3. Juvenile delinquency is increasing in the Shantucky district.

_____

_____

_____

4. Children of working mothers get into less trouble with the law than the children of mothers who stay home.

_____

_____

_____

5. Aspirin must be good for a person.

_____

_____

_____

6. College costs are increasing.

_____

_____

_____

7. Virginia has a climate well adapted to raising tobacco.

_____

_____

_____

8. The two-cycle gasoline engine is relatively trouble free.

_____

_____

_____

9. It looks as though Senator Hoaxshell is going to win the election.

_____

_____

_____

10. In spite of the larger number of nurses' training schools, there is a greater shortage of nurses now than there was ten years ago.

_____

_____

_____

11. Men who read widely and comprehendingly are more successful than those who do not.

_____

_____

_____

12. Television programs contain too much violence.

_____

_____

_____

13. There is very little segregated housing in Mudville.

_____

_____

_____

14. Driving too close is a major cause of accidents.

_____

_____

_____

15. Girls tend to get better grades in high school than boys do, but boys get better grades in college.

_____

_____

_____

Exercise 5. List the qualifications an authority should have in order to support each of the following general statements. You might mention your authority by the position he holds, not by his name; be more specific than "government expert," however. For instance, if your general statement were, "Speed kills," your authority would need to be someone familiar both with cars and traffic problems. He might be the chairman of the National Safety Council, an experienced state patrolman, or even, perhaps, a professional race-car driver. He should *not* be a nice old man who has never driven a car or the president of a railroad company who is trying to get people to "take the train instead."

1. Farm surpluses are on the decrease.

_____

_____

2. Women are better drivers than men.

_____

_____

3. Fluoride added to a water supply in the proper amount has no detrimental effect on health.

_____

_____

4. The United Nations has helped preserve world peace.

_____

_____

5. Students at Raglan College are more concerned with politics than they were a generation ago.

_____

_____

6. Farm manure is still one of the most satisfactory fertilizers.

_____

_____

7. Writing is not fun.

_____

_____

8. A six-cylinder Whiz is a safer car than a fourteen-cylinder Whoosh.

_____

_____

9. Movie stars don't need to know how to act.

_____

_____

10. The United States must increase expenditures for armaments.

_____

_____

11. The United States must decrease expenditures for armaments.

_____

_____

12. Joseph Conrad was a great author.

_____

_____

13. The history of England is full of tyranny and violence.

_____

_____

14. Television is a cultural wasteland.

_____

_____

15. Television can be credited with raising the general cultural level in the United States.

_____

_____

Exercise 6. For each of the following, write several sentences predicting the consequences and making clear why those consequences will follow. For instance,

> *If you drive seventy miles an hour on a corner marked for twenty-five,* your tires can't possibly hold the road. The car will skid out of control and it would take a very skilful driver to have even a bare chance of coming out alive. The car may roll over; it may plunge into a gully; or it may wrap itself around a telephone pole. Whatever it does, it does of its own accord, and the lucky driver kills only himself, not the people in the other car, coming around the corner at a safe twenty-five.

1. If you elect Senator Hoaxshell, _____

_____

_____

_____

_____

_____

2. If you brush your teeth with Shiney-Kleen, _____

_____

_____

_____

_____

_____

3. If you kiss on the first date, _____

_____

_____

_____

_____

_____

_____

4. If you don't kiss on the first date, _____

_____

_____

_____

_____

_____

_____

5. If you don't elect Senator Hoaxshell, _____

_____

_____

_____

_____

_____

_____

6. If you buy plenty of insurance, _____

_____

_____

_____

_____

_____

7. If the dogcatcher visits your neighborhood, _____

_____

_____

_____

_____

_____

8. If it rains too much in February, _____

_____

_____

_____

_____

_____

9. If the school levy fails, _____

_____

_____

_____

_____

_____

_____

10. If you learn to dance when you are ninety-five, _____

_____

_____

_____

_____

_____

11. If the city refuses to buy snow-removal equipment, _____

_____

_____

_____

_____

_____

_____

12. If the college does not provide more places for studying, _____

_____

_____

_____

_____

_____

_____

13. If children watch too many horror shows, _____

_____

_____

_____

_____

_____

14. If you have regular medical checkups, _____

_____

_____

_____

_____

_____

15. If you fail to put antifreeze in your car, _____

_____

_____

_____

_____

_____

_____

Exercise 7. Write two different main idea sentences for persuasive themes of about five hundred words for each of the following topics. Make sure that your belief is neither too broad nor too narrow. Make sure that one belief does not simply contradict the other. For example, if you say

Billboards should be abolished because they clutter up our cities and spoil the natural beauty of our countryside.

you may *not* say

Billboards should not be abolished because they do not clutter up our cities and spoil the natural beauty of our countryside.

You *may* say

Billboards should be encouraged because they help the consumer to have more freedom of choice.

1. guns _____

_____

_____

_____

_____

_____

2. politics _____

_____

_____

_____

_____

_____

3. foreign aid _____

_____

_____

_____

_____

_____

4. college _____

_____

_____

_____

_____

_____

5. television _____

_____

_____

_____

_____

_____

6. space races _____

_____

_____

_____

_____

_____

7. coffee breaks _____

_____

_____

_____

_____

_____

8. taxes _____

_____

_____

_____

_____

_____

9. censorship _____

_____

_____

_____

_____

_____

10. world government _____

_____

_____

_____

_____

_____

Exercise 8. Choose three of the main idea sentences you wrote for Exercise 7 and give reasons to support each of them. Don't use the same kind of support (examples, statistics, authority, consequences) twice for any one idea. For example:

MAIN IDEA SENTENCE The sale of guns should be limited by law.
1. (least important) Charles Remington, feature writer for *Gunshooter's Quarterly*, article in May issue. (authority)
2. (more important) estimate of unlicensed guns sold in United States, FBI figures (statistics)
3. (most important) shooting of President Kennedy (example)
CONCLUSION Gun laws helpful in preventing tragedies.

MAIN IDEA SENTENCE _____

_____

_____

_____

1. (least important) _____

_____

_____

2. (more important) _____

_____

_____

3. (most important) _____

_____

_____

CONCLUSION _____

_____

_____

_____

MAIN IDEA SENTENCE _____

_____

_____

_____

1. (most important) _____

_____

_____

2. (less important) _____

_____

_____

3. (least important) _____

_____

_____

CONCLUSION _____

_____

_____

_____

MAIN IDEA SENTENCE _____

_____

_____

_____

1. (example)_____

_____

_____

2. (authority) _____

_____

_____

3. (consequences)_____

_____

_____

4. (statistics)_____

_____

_____

CONCLUSION _____

_____

_____

_____

Exercise 9. For each of the plans you made in Exercise 8, write an introductory paragraph and a concluding paragraph. Make sure that your introduction interests the reader and gives him some idea of what the main idea is. Make sure that your conclusion emphasizes the main idea.

Exercise 10. Write a persuasive theme following one of the plans you made in Exercise 8, using the introduction and conclusion you wrote for Exercise 9.

Exercise 11. Pick out some phase of college life that infuriates you and write a letter of protest to the editor of your school paper.

Exercise 12. Write a theme supporting your favorite candidate for office, either campus or political.

VIII

How Good Are
the Reasons?
Unfair Persuasion

When you try to get other people to agree with you, you must give reasons for your opinion and support your reasons. And you have a right to expect supported reasons from anybody who is trying to make you agree with him. But how often do you get reasons? And when you do get them, how good are they?

> Buy Lovely Lady Facial Tissue.
> It's used by Hollywood stars.

This advertisement is an attempt to convince you. The main idea sentence is "Buy Lovely Lady Facial Tissue." The reason given to support the main idea is "It's used by Hollywood stars." This ad shows that reasons can be pretty feeble. The name of the tissue and the claim that stars use it suggests that if you use it, you will be lovely too. The notion is stupid when stated plainly, but the advertisers don't expect you to state it plainly. They just want you to associate the glamor of Hollywood stars with the use of Lovely Lady Facial Tissue. However, look at what has been left out.

You are not told *how many* stars use the tissue. The implication is that all stars use it, but it only takes two to make stars. Nor do you know why they use it. Maybe they were paid to endorse it, or maybe Lovely Lady Tissue Company gave them a year's supply of the stuff and hopes they can figure out something to do with it. Certainly you are not told *how* they use it. Maybe it's so rough they sand their furniture with it. Maybe it's so durable they carpet their apartments with it. Or maybe it's so flimsy they tear it to shreds and decorate their Christmas trees with it. All the ad says is they use it. It doesn't even say the stars like it.

And what is a "Hollywood star," anyway? Boris Karloff and Lassie are Hollywood stars of the first magnitude, but who wants to be like them? "Star" is a word that can be defined several ways. Tansy Ragwort, who had a thirty-second walk-on part as the maid in the movie "What's Become of Raphael Bogislav?," is called a star by her press agent.

But even if the stars were Shirley Temple, Sophia Loren, and Kim Novak, would the reason be any stronger? You would ask a banker about a loan, a jockey for a racing tip, Emily Post for a point of etiquette. These are experts in their fields. But what makes stars authorities on facial tissue? Do they blow their noses more than ordinary people? True, they wipe thick layers of makeup off their faces. But they do that with towels. In the matter of choosing a facial tissue, you are as much an expert as a Hollywood star. You have a nose, and a harsh tissue will not scratch it less, no matter how many Hollywood stars use the same tissue.

Actually, this advertisement does not use reason at all. Instead, it relies entirely on your willingness to respond to pleasant words. The advertiser would not say, "With this paper you can wipe the grime off your worn-out face in a few hurried swipes. And when you're done fussing with yourself, you can just dump the paper in the garbage can." He can sell more tissue if he says, "Lovely Lady Facial Tissue restores morning radiance. Its soft caress smoothes away daytime cares. And when you are once again your fresh and lovely self, the tissue is disposable." *Radiance, soft, caress, smooth, fresh,* and *lovely* are all purr words that tend to put the reader in a good mood, to soften him into buying the tissue. Persuasion that relies on slanted words is common, and it can be deceptive.

Much like the use of slanted words is the use of glittering generalities. These are such sweet and general statements that we feel bound to agree —until we realize they really have no specific meaning. Glittering generalities slant by what they don't say and are used by people who want to avoid definite answers.

Both ad writers and politicians may use glittering generalities and slanted words. There is a big difference, however, between deceiving people about facial tissues and deceiving them about the state of our national defenses. If you are told that wearing three drops of Allure will help you marry a millionaire, you may enjoy pretending to believe it, or you may simply be amused by the ad, and thus be more likely to remember the perfume. If you are told that our national defenses are falling apart because of insufficient funds and that we would be completely at the mercy of any enemy who decided to attack, the deceit involved is no laughing matter. We may not want to hold our ad writers to the absolute facts, but if we cannot depend on our elected representatives to tell us the whole truth, we are in bad shape indeed. We are on our way to recognizing truth when we can tell the difference between honest statements and glittering generalities, between neutral language and slanted words.

For example, Senator Hoaxshell leaves more out of his campaign speeches than he puts in. The senator says he is for God, mother, and country; and that he is against atheists and Freudians and communists (those who are anti-God, anti-mother, and anti-country—according to Hoaxshell). In effect he says, "I love good and hate evil. Since all of you love good and hate evil, you should support me for the Senate." It is probably true that you do love good and hate evil, but what is "good" and what is "evil"? Does everyone always mean exactly the same thing by *good*? By *evil*? Sometimes people react emotionally without stopping to ask whether Hoaxshell's notion of what is good agrees with their own.

To avoid being taken in by such sweet generalizations, you must insist on more specific information. In answer to the question "Will you support the Medicare bill?" (a definite question), the senator says:

> This bill deserves the serious consideration of all thoughtful people. If we are to win the life-death struggle between the American ideal and the communist conspiracy, we must gird ourselves with moral courage and physical strength. Money for defense is essential to the preservation of our way of life. Yet taxation must not be excessive. We must think this thing out and arrive at a satisfactory solution.

What does this answer tell you? The senator seems to be in favor of America and against communism. He is in favor of moral courage, and against physical weakness. He believes in defense and he doesn't want to raise taxes. And it all sounds so good. Unless you are careful you may respond to these soothing comments in the same way people respond to the ad writer's words—with emotion, not reason. You may be so busy agreeing emotionally with the senator's viewpoint that you will forget he was supposed to be talking about Medicare. If you see Medicare as part of the American ideal, you are likely to suppose the senator does too. If you think of Medicare as part of the socialist-communist conspiracy, it is easy to think that Senator Hoaxshell, too, believes Medicare is communist-inspired. Senator Hoaxshell hopes that if he avoids a definite statement, all his hearers will go away believing he sees eye to eye with them.

If you stubbornly insist, as you should, that the senator say something definite about medical aid, he is sure to spoon out the sugar-coating of slanted language. Even though he plans to oppose the bill, he will not say, "Let those crotchety old bums fend for themselves." He won't even say, "I intend to vote against the bill." Instead, he will probably say, "The American way is to allow our older citizens the natural dignity that goes with paying their own bills."

The ad writer gave you sugared words; Hoaxshell gives you sugared words and sugared generalizations. You refuse to be persuaded until you have been given some reasons. What *examples* can Hoaxshell offer? What *statistical support* has he for the stand he takes? Can he back up his position by *appealing to authorities* on the medical expenses for old people? What *predictions* is he making about the effects of the bill? All these devices, properly used, are legitimate forms of persuasion, and if you don't want to be deceived, you must learn to tell the difference between their proper and their improper use.

Examples can be used fairly or unfairly. Senator Hoaxshell exhibits his independent old father as an example of a senior citizen who resents government interference. But his father, who lives in a fifty-room mansion and owns huge blocks of blue-chip stock, is hardly a representative example of a seventy-year-old citizen. And Senator Hoaxshell is misleading you when he uses such an unfair example.

Honest examples can be useful in two ways: They can make the meaning of a general statement clear, and they can help the reader see a problem more vividly. When you said that final exams are not good indications of student learning (a generalization), you illustrated it by students who cheated or froze up during final exams (examples). If there were enough cheaters and freezers in most of the finals you have taken, then cheating and freezing are probably representative enough to be honest examples. Certainly these examples will help your reader to see what you mean by the generalization, "Final exams are not good indications of student learning."

Some words are so general and so subjective in their meaning that they almost always require examples. When you say, "John Smith was brave," you need an example to make clear what you mean by bravery. Does it simply mean that John Smith was completely without fear, or was he so eaten up by fear of spiders that he showed great courage in removing a daddy longlegs from the baby's crib? When you talk about a great revival of religion, do you simply mean that more people put on their new hats and go to church or are you suggesting that more people are really worried about their souls? Only carefully chosen examples can make your meaning clear.

Sometimes the meaning of the word being used is perfectly clear, but the full force of what the word represents is not felt by the reader. In such cases, examples help to drive home the point. Even though everybody knows what *starve* means, "Five thousand starve to death in eastern China" will not disturb the reader nearly as much as the example of one emaciated infant, wailing feebly and hopelessly for the bowl of rice that is not there. Even whole statements such as "Four hundred killed in weekend traffic mishaps" take on more reality with just one headless body, one glimpse of bloody pavement, and one set of grief-shocked relatives.

Examples are used honestly when they lead to a clearer understanding or a more vivid realization, but they are dishonestly used when they tempt the reader to move from only one example or one instance to a generalization. You cannot say that because one baby goes hungry, all the children in town are undernourished; or that because one 1940 car has defective brakes, everyone who drives a 1940 model will be involved in a fatal accident.

Before you make a general statement, you must have enough facts to generalize about. One way of getting enough facts is to make a survey. The result of the survey, if it is fairly made, may provide statistical support for a generalization.

Suppose you want to know how many students in your school smoke. It is glaringly obvious that you can't say, "I smoke; therefore everybody smokes." It is equally obvious that you don't have time to ask all the students in school whether they smoke, unless you drop all your classes and quit your job. But you can make a survey.

Your statistics will not be very reliable if you question only the people in the coffee shop and then say, "Sixteen of the thirty-two people in the coffee shop at nine o'clock Thursday morning said they smoked; therefore, fifty per cent of the student body smoke." If your school has a student body of two thousand, a sample of thirty-two students is not enough anyway. Furthermore, the students in the coffee shop may not be representative of the whole student body. Maybe students who drink coffee are more inclined to smoke than students who do not drink coffee. If you ask fifty people in the library at nine o'clock Thursday morning whether they smoke, ninety per cent of them may say they do not.

A hundred might be a large enough sample, but if you ask only humanities students, you still will not have a good cross section. Maybe humanities students are more likely to smoke than science students. Your statistics will not be reliable unless you have examined enough students and unless those students are representative. If you ask a hundred students, if you make sure that they represent every department on campus, and if you ask them on more than one day and at different hours during the day, you may come up with a pretty good estimate of the number of smokers on campus.

Suppose your estimate shows that thirty-three per cent of the student body smoke. When you present your statistics, be careful not to say, "many students smoke" or "a large number of students smoke" or "the average student smokes" or even "some students smoke," for all these statements interpret the facts rather than state them. One person's *many* is another person's *some*. Is thirty-three out of a hundred *many* or *some* or a *few*? And who is the *typical* student? Is Rupert Creech the typical college student? Or are you? Remember that *typical* and *average*, like *good* and *bad*, *better* and *worse*, are opinion words.

Keep in mind that statistics, like reports, should not be interpreted. You are not justified in saying anything except, "The survey shows that approximately thirty-three per cent of the students on this campus smoke."

When you've finished your survey and have stated it in specific language, your percentage will probably be believed—unless you happen to be campus representative for a tobacco company. If you are trying to sell cigarettes, or even give them away, then you have something to gain by the result of your survey. Sensible people will distrust your figures.

Statistics are fairly used when they are based on enough samples; when the samples have been carefully chosen to be truly representative of the whole group; when the results of the survey are expressed in specific, objective language; and when the persons making the survey have nothing to gain from the outcome.

Giving authorities who agree with you is another way of supporting reasons, but authorities should not be misused, either. Using the name of a famous man who is expert in one field to give evidence for something in another field is a misuse of authority. Winston Churchill was a great and respected man and an expert in politics; but he did not pretend to be, and you should not use him as, an expert on American movie stars.

Winston Churchill, by the way, was a good amateur painter, and his judgments about art might be better than yours. But his value as an authority on art history would certainly be less than that of the curator of the Louvre. In using an authority, you must consider his standing among other experts in the same field, and you must be sure that he has nothing to gain by his testimony.

Quoting an authority out of his field is an attempt to grab off some of the glory associated with his name and graft it on to whatever is being discussed. You would be using glory or guilt by association if you used comments by Harry Truman and Nikita Khrushchev to condemn modern art. These men are politicians, not artists, and your opinions on art are probably as good as theirs. The advertisers were using glory by association when they dragged in the Hollywood stars. Hollywood stars may be experts on acting; they are not necessarily experts on facial tissue.

Glory by association is used to sway people emotionally rather than rationally, and so is guilt by association: "John went to hear the secretary of the American Nazi party speak. John must be a Nazi sympathizer." Or "Russians wear fur hats. John wears a fur hat. John must be a Russian." But John may have been following the advice "Know your enemy" when he went to hear the speaker, and he may be wearing the hat simply because his ears are cold. Guilt by association is a smear technique, never a sound method of supporting opinions or reasons.

Neither is the imaginary *everybody* very good authority to back up opinions or reasons. Your case becomes no stronger if you say, "Everybody is doing it, so I should do it too," or "Everybody else has a new car; I need a new car too." This misuse of authority leads to fads in foods (yogurt, Metrecal), in toys (skate boards and guitars), in clothes (white crew socks and bleeding plaids), in hair-do's (beehive yesterday, what tomorrow?). For one thing, a careful survey would show that *everybody* is a great exaggeration. For a second, and more important thing, even if the survey showed that ninety-nine and forty-four one-hundredths per cent of the population were doing it, you still have not proved it is worth doing. Large numbers of people have supported actions we now think wrong: the Salem witch burnings, the Nazi book burnings, the American lynch mobs. Group pressure is group pressure, not rational thinking.

"Everybody does it" is not good support; neither is "It's always been that way; why change now? A horse and buggy was good enough for my old man and it's good enough for me." A man is not giving sound support for his belief if he says, "We don't need medical care for the aged; grandpa couldn't afford an operation and why should I?" He is only saying that he is afraid of change. The point is not that all changes are either good or bad, but that each change should be judged on its own merits.

Predicting the consequences is another much-used method of supporting an argument, but predictions, even more than examples, statistics, and authorities, can be used unfairly. You are always on risky ground when you attempt to foresee the future, but you can be a good deal more certain in some areas than in others. Suppose you say, "If I put a kettle of water on the stove and turn the burner on high, the water will boil." Almost everybody will accept this prediction. Suppose you say, "If I come to class every day and smile sweetly at the teacher, I will pass the course." Almost everybody will want to ask a few questions. Suppose you say, "If we elect Senator Hoaxshell, everybody in the country will get his dearest wish, but if we elect John Q. Upright, the roofs of our houses will fall in on our heads." At this one, everybody should protest loudly.

Predictions that deal with the physical world are usually fairly safe:

Water will boil at 212°F.

On January 28, 1975, the sun will rise at 7.25 A.M., Central Standard Time.

Low tide tomorrow will be at 8:33 P.M.

Predictions that deal with the behavior of people are much less safe:

Senator Hoaxshell's temper will boil at the mention of the medical aid bill.

My father will rise from bed tomorrow at 7:25 A.M., Central Standard Time.

My automotive teacher will sneeze at 8:33 P.M.

Senator Hoaxshell may have changed his mind about the medical aid bill, smile blandly, and talk smoothly about our responsibility to our senior citizens. Your father may oversleep. Your teacher may have recovered from his hay fever.

Even so, if you know Senator Hoaxshell well and are well acquainted with your father's habits, your first two guesses may be fairly good. If you are predicting something simple about someone you have known for a long time, what you say may often be accurate. But when you move to new situations and attempt to predict the results of something you've never experienced before, then your predictions become less reliable. When you try guessing about complex problems, in situations where many different causes might affect the results, your guesses may become wildly unreliable.

Just as you must keep your wits about you in looking into the future (prediction), so must you keep your wits about you in looking back into the past (analyzing cause and effect). If you forget that most events have several causes, perhaps you will settle for a simple and incorrect explanation. One way you can go wrong is to say that because one thing happened after another thing, the first one caused the second. Before you can say surely that abolishing final examinations at Raglan College improved scholarship, you must find out whether some other changes were made at Raglan College at the same time. Were the entrance requirements changed? Was the grading system altered? And before you accept the notion that walking under ladders brings accidents, you must ask whether the accidents could have been caused by anything else. At ten o'clock poor Rupert Creech walked under a ladder and at ten-thirty he sprained his thumb. Did walking under the ladder cause him to sprain his thumb? Tansy Ragwort caught a bad head cold, sneezed miserably for six days, and on the seventh day tried the new Never-Sneeze cold pill she has been pretending to swallow on the television ads. In four days her cold was gone. Did the pill cure her cold, or did she simply get over it?

At other times when you are puzzled by complex situations, you may try to simplify them by comparing the unknown to the known. Such comparisons can be dangerous if the differences are more important than the likenesses. Comparisons can be fairly made only when the things being compared are alike in significant ways and when the differences have nothing to do with the comparison. It is probably fair to compare conditions at one college with conditions at another college if the two schools have the same kind of students and if the schools teach the same kind of courses in about the same way. It is probably fair to compare the results of fluoridation in one small western city with the possible results of fluoridation in another western town in the same kind of location.

But if the people who are against fluoridation go on to compare the effects of swallowing fluoride with the effects of swallowing arsenic, the comparison becomes unfair because the differences do have something to do with the comparison. It is true that both fluoride and arsenic (and table salt and aspirin and a good many other things we regularly put into ourselves) are deadly poisons when we take them in large quantities. But it is also generally agreed that fluoride in small quantities in drinking water is good for teeth, while even very small quantities of arsenic do no one much good.

Let's examine another common kind of comparison. When the Democrats are in power, a Democrat says, "The President is the captain of the ship of state. To criticize him during a time of crisis is like starting a mutiny in mid-ocean on a storm-tossed ship." But in what ways is a country during a crisis like a ship working its way across a stormy sea? Is a crisis really very much like a stormy ocean? Is a president really much like a sea captain? And is a nation of two hundred million people really much like a single ship? If the differences are more important than the similarities, is it fair to say that criticism of the administration is the same as mutiny? The question that must always be asked is, "Are the things being compared really alike? And are the differences unimportant?"

This chapter has talked about several common errors in reasoning and, although it certainly isn't complete, it does provide some important ways to test persuasion. Anybody who wants to tell good reasons from bad must ask the right questions:

1. Are any actual reasons given or does the argument deal only in emotional language and glittering generalizations?
2. Do the examples make a generalization clearer or a situation more vivid?
3. Are the statistics based on a large enough number of representative cases? Are the statistics presented objectively and specifically?

4. Are the authorities speaking about their own fields? Do they have anything to gain from their testimony?
5. Are the predictions based on dependable generalizations or are they just wild guesses?
6. Have all the possible causes been considered?
7. Are the things being compared really alike?

These seven tests apply equally to your own attempts to persuade and to other people's attempts to persuade you. Use these tests on any information you are given. You will never be a competent reader until you have learned to question what you read. You will never be a competent writer until you have learned to question what you write. These tests for sound reasoning work. Apply them.

Key Words

Here are some of the important terms used in this chapter. Without referring back to the chapter, see whether you can answer these questions about them.

1. Explain the difference between responding *emotionally* to arguments and reacting *rationally* to them.

2. What is the difference between *slanted words* and *glittering generalities*? Do slanted words and glittering generalities encourage you to react emotionally or rationally? What steps can you take to make sure that your response is always rational?

3. What four questions should you ask to test a *survey*?

4. What two rules must you follow in using *authorities* fairly?

5. What are two good things that *examples* can do?

6. What kind of *predictions* are likely to be reliable? What kind are likely to be unreliable?

7. What do you need to ask before you can be sure that one thing has been *caused* by another?

8. How can you decide whether two things have been fairly *compared*?

9. What is wrong with *guilt by association*? What is wrong with *glory by association*?

10. Explain why *"everybody does it"* is not a good reason. Is *"we've always done it"* a good reason?

Vocabulary

Pick the answer that most closely fits the meaning of the word as it has been used in the chapter. Look up in your dictionary the meaning of all the words you miss.

1. When we *associate* one thing with another, we _____
   (a) connect them together in our minds
   (b) make them colleagues and confederates
   (c) make them assets
   (d) give them a degree

2. *Implication* means something _____
   (a) highly complex
   (b) hinted but not stated
   (c) folded over
   (d) made simple and open

3. A man who *endorses* something _____
   (a) writes an address on it
   (b) forwards it to the next address
   (c) says how good it is
   (d) says how bad it is

4. Material that is *durable* is _____
   (a) hard to put up with
   (b) easy to put up with
   (c) long-wearing
   (d) covered with a heavy nap

5. *Magnitude* means _____
   (a) ability to attract other metals
   (b) large size
   (c) magic
   (d) bright and shiny

6. If you practice good *etiquette*, you   _____
   (a) like good foods
   (b) raise beautiful vegetables
   (c) perform a complicated dance step
   (d) don't eat your peas with your knife

7. *Atheists* are people who   _____
   (a) deny the existence of God
   (b) live only in Russia
   (c) do not believe in government
   (d) grow horns on their heads

8. A *Freudian* is   _____
   (a) a psychoanalyst
   (b) a scaredy-cat
   (c) a man who hates his mother
   (d) a Buddhist of a special sect

9. If you join a *conspiracy*, you   _____
   (a) get to wear a fraternity pin
   (b) have to pass a physical examination
   (c) plot secretly to overthrow something
   (d) sign up for the army

10. A *device* is   _____
    (a) one of the numbers used in division
    (b) a well-meant suggestion as to how you should
        behave
    (c) a scheme to accomplish something
    (d) something that is worn out and run down

11. *Legitimate* means   _____
    (a) lawful, permissible
    (b) born out of wedlock
    (c) large, clumsy
    (d) late to arrive

12. A person who is *emaciated* is   _____
    (a) probably a heavy eater
    (b) marked with scars on his face
    (c) engaged to be married
    (d) very gaunt and thin

13. A man who gives *testimony*, makes   _____
    (a) a declaration to establish a fact
    (b) a contribution to help the poor

(c) a payment to his divorced wife
(d) an attempt to escape the police

14. *Bland* means   ———
    (a) level
    (b) pointed
    (c) soothing
    (d) spicy

15. If something is *minute*, it is   ———
    (a) in a considerable hurry
    (b) extremely small
    (c) extremely timely
    (d) sixty seconds wide

16. *Significant* means   ———
    (a) having to do with billboards
    (b) properly signed and endorsed
    (c) important and meaningful
    (d) too small to notice

17. A *mutiny* is   ———
    (a) a person who has lost the power of speech
    (b) a revolt against authority
    (c) a testimonial praising an officer
    (d) a change in inherited characteristics

18. If someone says you are *competent*, he means you are   ———
    (a) unable to hold a job
    (b) a rival of his in sports
    (c) a companion or comrade
    (d) capable and well-qualified

Exercises

Exercise 1. Look at these advertisements. What associations make them attractive? How many purr words do you find? Be prepared to discuss the ads in class.

1. Comes the dawn of a new day for your complexion! The most effective way to outwit time this side of Shangri-la! It's Du Barry's discovery—Creme Paradox—a beauty sleep cream as sheer and luxurious to slip on as chiffon. Because of its exclusive ingredients, N. O. R., just the slightest touch does more than any old-fashioned heavy cream to help your skin retain youth-sustaining moisture—the vital essence of a smooth, unlined skin. Yes, the paradox is—so little does so much. With Creme Paradox . . . you can wake up tomorrow morning looking younger than you do today. Creme Paradox by Du Barry. (copyright 1962, DuBarry)

2. This is a pale Gamin. Take it south for the winter. With its lovely, delicate complexion and shapely form, this Gamin impresses the crowd at chic resorts. And who can resist its temptingly barer look, cut down all around for more sun exposure. $20, at Andrew Geller stores, where it's always fair weather. GAMINS (trademark). (*The New Yorker,* Dec. 21, 1963.)

    Without a picture of a pair of shoes, would you know what this ad was talking about?

3. Give us that rare man in whom civilization poses no threat to virility. The one who is, in short, a gentleman. If you know such a man and would like to do him a good turn, we have just the thing. In the unmistakably masculine tradition of our original shop at 30 Duke St., London S. W. 1, we continue to offer these and other Gentlemen's Imperatives by Alfred Dunhill. (an ad for after-shave lotion and cologne, in *The New Yorker,* Dec. 14, 1963)

4. Cool and refreshing as a mountain stream! Next time it's a hundred and four in the shade, try our Mint Collins. Take one part lime juice, four parts Old Keg Rum, and a sprig of fresh garden mint. Fill a tall pale green goblet with crushed ice—pour your Collins in—and you'll not miss the mountains. Actually, any old glass will do. It isn't the green goblet that does it—it's the Old Keg Rum.

5. May the holy star of Bethlehem shine over your house this Christmas season. May peace and goodwill fill your hearts, and may the joys of Christmas follow you into a happy New Year. The Quick and Easy Home Loan Company.

6. Isn't it good to be an American? Isn't it nice to know that the kid that delivers your paper can grow up to be President of the Bank? Or even of the country? Aren't you glad you can invest your money wherever you please, at the highest rate of interest you can find? Aren't you glad you're an American? The Quick and Easy Home Loan Company.

Exercise 2. Rewrite the ads in Exercise 1, avoiding all emotional words yet retaining all factual information. Don't worry if your version is *much* shorter than the original. Keep in mind that the purpose of this exercise is not to keep the product glamorous but to *stick to the facts actually given* in the ad. If you can distinguish fact from fairy tale in buying a pair of shoes, you can probably make the same distinction when you are buying a house, selecting a car, or voting on a constitutional amendment.

Exercise 3. Bring to class three examples of advertisements, editorials, or letters to the editor which try to persuade by association— using glamor, guilt, or glory. List all the slanted words and glittering generalities which appear in your samples.

Exercise 4. Examples are often useful in helping us understand the speaker's definition of some term he is using. If you believe the example is a fair one, mark it O.K. If you find the example does not fit your own meaning of the underlined term, substitute an example that makes clear what you do mean.

1. Rupert has a wonderful <u>sense of humor.</u> He laughed like crazy when old Mrs. Hobble slipped on a banana peel last week and broke her leg.

2. My father has no <u>sense of humor.</u> I told him all the elephant jokes I knew, but he didn't laugh once.

3. My father doesn't believe in <u>democracy.</u> Both my brother and I voted that Dad should buy a new Jaguar, but he bought a used Ford instead.

4. Tansy is a very <u>poor speller.</u> For instance, she couldn't spell either "miscegenation" or "cyclothymia" without looking them up.

5. My uncle has a lot of <u>un-American</u> ideas. He doesn't like hot dogs and apple pie.

6. I can't stand Mary, she's so <u>disloyal.</u> She said she didn't like my hair when I dyed it orange.

_____

_____

_____

7. My mother is a <u>cheapskate.</u> When we wanted T-bone steaks for dinner, she bought <u>hamburger</u> instead.

_____

_____

_____

8. Mrs. Creech likes <u>highly spiced foods.</u> For instance, she puts Tabasco sauce in her coffee and cayenne on her oatmeal.

_____

_____

_____

9. Old Tom Arbuthnot has <u>taken to drink.</u> He drank a glass of sauterne with his Christmas dinner.

_____

_____

_____

10. You can often choose between two punctuation marks, both of them <u>acceptable.</u> For instance, the remark "I'm fine; how are you?" can be written either with a semicolon or with a period: "I'm fine. How are you?"

_____

11. Twins are not always <u>compatible</u>. Audrey, for instance, enjoys rock-and-roll and likes her hamburger rare. Her twin sister Tawdry won't listen to any music except hymns and is a strict vegetarian.

Exercise 5. For the following generalizations, provide examples that make the generalization more vivid.

1. Children of divorced parents are often poorly adjusted.

2. African plane crash kills eighty.

3. College education makes better-adjusted individuals.

4. Driver-training courses increase driving safety.

_____

_____

_____

5. Algernon Creech is stupid.

_____

_____

_____

6. Rupert Creech is quite brilliant.

_____

_____

_____

7. Fluoride taken in small quantities has a beneficial effect.

_____

_____

_____

8. Children of working mothers are frequently neglected.

_____

_____

_____

9. Children of working mothers develop self-reliance.

_____

10. Cynical men often mislead the innocent young.

Exercise 6. (a) Are these statistics reliable? If not, why not? Examine both the statement and the statistics to see whether the statistics, even though they may be reliable by themselves, actually do support the statement. (b) If they don't, explain why.

1. Take Darwin's Monkey Oil.

   Four out of five doctors interviewed recommended Darwin's Monkey Oil as a cure for longevity.

2. Vote for slot machines!

   A recent poll shows that more than half of the citizens of Cat's Elbow Junction favor legalized gambling.

3. Be sure to see that the baby gets his whooping-cough shots.

   The county health report shows that there were thirty-nine cases of whooping-cough in Yahoo County in 1959, all of them contracted by children of preschool age. Three cases were fatal.

_____

_____

_____

4. Stanley Steamers are better cars than Locomobiles.

   I asked twenty people who drive Stanley Steamers which they thought was the better car, and eighteen of them preferred Stanley Steamers.

_____

_____

_____

5. It's apparent that most Americans dislike spinach.

   I know because the local bean-growers made a survey.

_____

_____

_____

6. Beards are going out of style.

   Only thirty-three and a third per cent of the members of my family are bearded.

_____

_____

_____

7. More students go to college now than went ten years ago.

   According to the 1964 *Information Please Almanac,* the U.S. Office of Education reports that for every 1000 students in the fifth grade in 1944, 234 entered college in 1952. For every 1000 students in the fifth grade in 1954, 336 entered college in 1962.

---

8. The percentage of students attending college has increased enormously.

   The U.S. Office of Education figures for 1962 show that only 336 out of 1000 students went to college, or almost exactly one third, whereas in my 1963 graduating class almost exactly two thirds (66 out of 100 graduates) went to college.

---

9. Marriages are on the increase.

   Sixty-six and two thirds per cent of my family got married last year.

---

10. Glitter and Glow toothpaste reduces cavities.

    Sixty-six and two thirds per cent of those tested reported fewer cavities after using Glitter and Glow for a year.

---

11. Our family is abnormally large.

    There are four of us, but the U.S. Census Bureau says the average American family in 1962 consists of only 3.67 people.

_____

_____

_____

12. Evening papers are more popular than morning papers.

My brother and I both deliver papers. He delivers the *Morning Cuckoo* and I peddle the *Night Owl.* One day, after we got into an argument about whether morning or evening papers were more popular, we decided to make a survey. Eighty-nine per cent of his customers preferred morning papers; ninety-five per cent of mine said evening papers were more satisfactory.

_____

_____

_____

13. I won't live as long as my twin sister.

According to the January 1964 issue of *Science Digest,* in an article called "How Long You Have to Live," an eighteen-year-old white male will live 52.8 more years, but an eighteen-year-old white female will live 58.5 more years.

_____

_____

_____

14. Insurance salesmen guarantee peace of mind.

Peter Premium, who has been selling insurance for more than fifty years, recently conducted a survey that showed the average man who carries ten thousand dollars' worth of life insurance has more peace of mind than the average uninsured citizen.

_____

_____

15. Editorials in the *Daily Rag* reach only a few students.

    A questionnaire submitted to three hundred Raglan College students, selected at random, revealed that only a few of them read the editorials in the college paper.

    _____

    _____

    _____

Exercise 7. You've seen these generalizations before. Examine them again and decide what kind of proof would be needed to make the generalization acceptable.

1. Smoking is bad for the health.

    _____

    _____

    _____

2. Driving on ice is dangerous.

    _____

    _____

    _____

3. Competent drivers are as safe driving in icy weather as in any other kind of weather.

    _____

    _____

    _____

4. Music hath charms to soothe the savage breast.

_____

_____

_____

5. Children without brothers or sisters are usually spoiled.

_____

_____

_____

6. Getting your feet wet is likely to lead to pneumonia.

_____

_____

_____

7. State patrolmen are kind and considerate to motorists.

_____

_____

_____

8. State patrolmen are rude and inconsiderate.

_____

_____

9. Telephones are a great help and convenience.

_____

10. Telephones are a nuisance.

Exercise 8. State whether the following people are acceptable as authorities on these subjects. Give reasons for saying *yes* or *no*.

1. Mickey Mantle endorsing No-Cough cigarettes.

2. Mickey Mantle endorsing a baseball bat.

3. *Webster's Third New International Dictionary* on the most common pronunciation of *negligee.*

4. Your math teacher on a shortcut method of finding square root.

_____

_____

5. Your math teacher on disarmament.

_____

_____

_____

6. Mrs. Algernon Creech, who spent a week in Cairo last summer, on the economic problems of central Africa.

_____

_____

_____

7. Chief Thundercloud on how to cure a cold.

_____

_____

_____

8. Your family doctor on how to cure a cold.

_____

_____

_____

9. Egyptian Oil Company on the superior virtues of Egyptian oil.

_____

10. Sterling Moss on perfume.

11. Everybody knows wearing high heels is bad for posture.

12. John Glenn on how to lead a Girl Scout Troop.

13. John Glenn on the dangers of communism.

14. John Glenn on divorce problems.

_____

_____

15. Governor Wallace on states' rights.

_____

_____

_____

16. Chief Justice Earl Warren on states' rights.

_____

_____

_____

17. Chief Justice Earl Warren on the New Zealand climate.

_____

_____

_____

18. Martin Luther King on civil rights.

_____

_____

_____

19. The town's leading stockbroker on the advantages of owning stock.

_____

_____

_____

Exercise 9. What type of persuasion is used in the following statements? Explain why you find the support acceptable or unacceptable.

1. Don't vote for Alfy Arbuckle—his great-aunt's husband was a horse thief.

_____

_____

_____

2. Don't vote for Alfy Arbuckle; he's been divorced.

_____

_____

_____

3. Put your money in the Benjamin Franklin Savings and Loan Association.

_____

_____

_____

4. Don't hire that boy to mow the lawn; I saw him reading Karl Marx in the library yesterday.

_____

_____

_____

5. Oh, look! Here's *Webster's Complete Comprehensive Peanut-Size Vest Dictionary* for only fifteen cents.

_____

6. I'd be pretty careful about getting involved with Kenny Kettle; his wife used to go to communist parties.

7. That Steadfast Insurance Company must be pretty good; their billboards have the cutest babies on them, and the family in the picture looks so solid and happy.

8. I don't care if the American Civil Liberties Union does support the Bill of Rights—they defended some communists and fascists, didn't they, when the police tried to shut down a meeting?

9. All the girls who wash their faces with Shinyclean ride around in Cadillac convertibles with tall handsome men; you can see them on television every night.

10. In the name of Washington, Jefferson, Lincoln, and John Kennedy, those great Americans, I urge you to vote in favor of this progressive proposal to widen the highway in front of my business property.

_____

_____

_____

Exercise 10. Are the following predictions sound? Why or why not?

1. When I get out of college, I'm sure to get a high-paying job.

_____

_____

_____

2. My cousin, who had dinner with me last night, has come down with measles this morning, so I suppose I'll catch them pretty soon.

_____

_____

_____

3. The sun will rise tomorrow at 7:08 A.M.

_____

_____

_____

4. I'm late again. My wife will sure be mad at me.

_____

5. It won't take more than fifteen minutes to write this exercise.

_____

_____

_____

6. The earth will revolve on its axis exactly once in the next 365 days.

_____

_____

_____

7. The earth will complete its orbit around the sun in 365¼ days.

_____

_____

_____

8. It's cloudy tonight, so it will rain tomorrow.

_____

_____

_____

9. My son will certainly be pleased with the new bike I'm giving him for his birthday.

_____

_____

10. If you don't study, you will flunk out of college.

_____

_____

_____

Exercise 11. How sound are the following statements on cause and effect? If you find them unsound, what *other cause* might have produced the effect?

1. The best way to make it rain is to wash your car.

_____

_____

_____

2. Getting married sure improved Rupert's grades.

_____

_____

_____

3. Yesterday a black cat crossed my path, and today I slammed my thumb in the door. I wish I had knocked on wood or thrown salt over my shoulder.

_____

_____

_____

4. Professor Gargle gave Helen Troy an *A* because she is so good looking.

_____

_____

_____

5. Rupert caught cold because he got his feet wet.

_____

_____

6. He avoided pneumonia by soaking his feet in hot water.

_____

_____

_____

7. You can cure the hiccups by drinking water upside down from the far side of the glass.

_____

_____

_____

8. Helen Troy got an *A* in psychology because she got the highest grade in the final exam.

_____

_____

_____

9. Americans are losing their sense of independence because of the effect of television.

_____

_____

_____

10. Americans are becoming more and more like vegetables because of the effect of television.

_____

_____

_____

11. I'm not using Greasy Kid Stuff on my hair, so I'm sure to be a big hit with the girls.

_____

_____

_____

12. I do use Greasy Kid Stuff on my hair; no wonder the girls leave the room when I walk in.

_____

_____

_____

13. Regina drank a quart of orange juice every day since she was two months old; no wonder she's seven feet tall.

_____

_____

_____

14. Arnie drank a quart of pickle juice every day since he was two months old; no wonder he's only twenty-two inches tall.

_____

_____

_____

15. Eliminating mid-quarter exams certainly did lower the quality of scholarship at Heatherclump College.

_____

_____

_____

Exercise 12. Which of the following comparisons are fair and which are unfair? Give reasons for your answer.

1. If you think of the sun as an orange and the earth as a marble moving in an ellipse around it, you can get a fairly good notion of the earth's movements during the year.

_____

_____

2. Getting money from Uncle Ephraim is like taking candy from a baby.

_____

_____

3. Expecting me to cook biscuits on that antiquated electric stove is as unreasonable as expecting a cavewoman to turn out a batch of chocolate eclairs.

_____

_____

_____

4. A good deed in a wicked world is like a candle shining in the dark.

_____

_____

_____

5. I can't explain to Janet how to start the car any more than I can teach the cat calculus.

_____

_____

_____

6. The Lower Hill Primary School has been so successful with its campaign to collect galoshes for underprivileged children that we ought to attempt a similar campaign at Upper Hill Primary School.

_____

_____

_____

7. Professor Gumshoe is a bear in psychology, so I suppose Professor Gargle is, too. Both of them went to Whitman.

_____

_____

_____

8. We'd better re-elect Senator Hoaxshell, at least until the emergency is over. It won't do to change horses in midstream.

_____

_____

_____

9. There is no real difference between teachers and school-patrol boys. Both of them have to keep students in order. The schoolboys do it for free; why can't the teachers?

_____

_____

_____

10. If you wouldn't steal butter from a supermarket, why do you steal words from an encyclopedia?

_____

_____

_____

11. If you're old enough to fight, you're old enough to vote.

_____

_____

_____

Exercise 13. The following are attempts to persuade. (a) What *device* is being used to convince you? (b) Is it effective? Why?

1. Drink Coke. It's the most popular soft drink in the world.

_____

2. Nine out of ten doctors take aspirin. Buy Bayer aspirin.

3. Croft is the murderer. I saw him leave the house just before we found the body.

4. *God's Little Acre* is a literary classic. It has sold over two million copies.

5. Our school system is lousy. My kid's in the eighth grade and still can't read.

6. *Lady Chatterley's Lover* is not a work of art. The Postmaster General would not allow it to go through the mails.

_____

_____

7. Fords are no good. I had one once and it was at the mechanic's all the time.

_____

_____

_____

8. John is a rich man, and he says this stock is a good buy.

_____

_____

_____

9. Socialized medicine must not be good. The American Medical Association is opposed to it.

_____

_____

_____

10. Bufferin is a good preventive medicine. I take it before I go to bed and never have a morning headache.

_____

_____

_____

11. Paroling convicts is like letting tamed lions roam the streets. You never know when they will go bad again and raise havoc.

_____

12. The United Nations has had twenty years to establish world peace and hasn't done it yet. If we want world peace, we had better abolish the United Nations.

13. My great-grandfather, a doctor in Salem, Massachusetts, in 1832, said there was no preventive medicine for polio. I'm not going to bother with polio shots.

14. Education is an elevator to success. If you get off at the wrong floor, you will not arrive at your highest goal.

15. Be like Rupert Creech. Eat Wheaties.

16. Electricity is cleaner, safer, cheaper.

_____

_____

_____

Exercise 14. Here are four themes, all of them giving reasons to support a belief. One of the themes is fairly good, and one of them is quite bad. Analyze all four themes carefully, and then, on a separate sheet, answer these questions about each of them.

1. How well does the title fit the main idea? Can you think of a better title?
2. What is the main idea of the first paragraph? Is the purpose of the paper made clear in the first paragraph? How?
3. What is the main idea of the last paragraph? Is there enough difference in the wording of the first and last paragraphs? Could you have told which was the introduction and which was the conclusion if they had been turned around? How?
4. Does the paper use any specific examples? What is the purpose of the examples: to make a generalization clearer? To make a situation more vivid? Do the examples help to persuade you? Why?
5. Are any statistics used? What are they? Is the source of the statistics given and does it seem reliable? Explain why you do or do not think the statistics can be depended on.
6. Does the paper use authority? Explain why you think it is good or not good.
7. Are consequences suggested? Are you convinced by them? Why or why not?
8. Is there a comparison used? What is it? Is the comparison a fair one? Why or why not?
9. Does the paper use slanted language and glittering generalities? What are they?
10. Does the paper say one thing caused another? What? Are you convinced that the first thing really did cause the second? Why or why not?
11. Are the reasons arranged in sensible order? If they are not, how would you rearrange them to make the order better?
12. What grade would you give this paper? Explain your decision.

The Library

There is a necessity for a larger, more adequate study area in the library.

The fact that there are sixteen hundred students attending day school at Black Creek College and the fact that there is a seating capacity for approximately two hundred students in the library certainly does not show sensible correlation.

A student who wishes to study in the library often finds that there is not adequate seating. He must either resort to the Student Center or hope that there is a vacant classroom in Hilary Hall. If there isn't a vacant classroom, the Student Center is usually a last resort. Here it is almost entirely impossible to study. There are the familiar distractions such as friendly well-wishers and the typical student who is in the Center to socialize.

I feel that an addition to Black Creek's library would certainly be an asset to our school. More individual tables could be added with dividers which would rise from the center of the table. This would be a help to eliminate the excessive talking which is common in our library.

Also more study rooms would improve the present library conditions. If a person needs to discuss with a friend, he may then go to a study room where he would not distract others.

If our library were expanded, I am certain that more students would use it and discover that a library, when used correctly, can be an asset to a student's college career.

John Hag for School Board

No, I don't think so. At least I think there are, or must be, some people just as well qualified, or maybe better—although all people don't agree with me.

John Hag struts bad enough now, and his head is already so swollen with self-conceit that he never wears a hat. Besides, he smokes cigars, black smelly ones, and you know what kind of guys smoke cigars. In every movie I've ever seen, the bad guy always smoked at least one cigar, and most of the time they smoked them all through the show. If he looks like a bad guy, we don't want him running our schools. Voting for John Hag is the same as voting for Scarface Capone.

Everybody knows that a well-educated America is a free

America. And everybody knows that ignorance means slavery. So if you don't want slavery in America, vote against John Hag.

Besides that, he is also a terrible drunkard. My sister's cousin, who has had psychoanalysis, says that men like him are always drunkards, whether anybody knows it or not, and she should know. They do it in secret. But besides that, I saw him take a cup of punch during the dedication of the new courthouse—and you know what that means. Shortly after he had drunk the cup of punch—only one cup because he knew everybody was watching—he tripped on a workman's trowel and almost fell down. The punch must have made him drunk, because he stumbled after he drank it, not before.

Even experts agree that he should not be elected. Elmo Mogrow, famous all over the world for the rhododendrons he breeds, says he doesn't like the looks of John Hag.

No More Killing

I think we should pass a law against capital punishment. If the Bible says, "Thou shalt not kill," it means we ought not to kill people any time, for any reason at all. I think it is just as wrong for a large group of people to combine and call themselves a state and then hire somebody to kill a man as it is for one man to do it all by himself. It just means that a million people do something wrong, instead of just one.

If a man commits murder or treason against the government, then he has to be punished. But he doesn't have to be killed. Kidnapping is another thing that capital punishment is used for. However, murderers and spies can be put in prison to keep society safe from them.

People who are against abolishing capital punishment say that it is too expensive to keep feeding murderers for all the rest of their lives. But I think we ought not to decide what is right and wrong by figuring out how much it costs. If we are going to look at it that way, we might as well say that we ought to hang everybody who commits any crime because it would save so much money. Murderers don't eat any more than bank robbers, and we don't hang bank robbers just because it would save money.

Another reason for not having capital punishment is that sometimes juries make mistakes. If we find out after a man has been hanged that he wasn't guilty after all, then what can we do about it? And that happens a lot oftener than people think.

Another thing people say is that there will be a great many more murders if we let them live. But that isn't so, because statistics prove that in the states where they have abolished capital punishment there aren't any more murders than there used to be.

There are lots more reasons against capital punishment, but the main one is that it isn't right. Killing is always wrong.

Support the United Fund

Have you ever seen a little kid that was hungry? Not just after-school hungry, from playing too hard and his mother saying, "You can't have any more bread and peanut butter because it will spoil your supper," but *really* hungry. Hungry because the peanut butter jar has been empty for a long, long time and because he was hungry yesterday and the day before that and the day before that. The kind of kid you don't have to worry about spoiling his supper because whatever it is, he eats it, if he's lucky enough to get any.

Lakima County has a lot of kids that are always hungry. According to the Lakima County Welfare Department, there are 426 families who get Aid to Dependent Children. They get twenty dollars a month for each child, but that has to cover shoes and clothes and food and anything else they need. It doesn't leave much for after-school snacks, and if these kids are going to have any extras, the Children's Care Agency has to give it to them. The Children's Care Agency gets its money from the United Fund.

But that isn't the worst part. There are 78 more families, according to the Welfare Department, that don't get any welfare checks at all because they haven't lived in the state long enough. There are 185 children in those families. The grownups work in the berry harvest in the summer, but they wouldn't get anything to eat at all in the winter, when they can't get work, if the Food Basket Committee didn't help them. The Food Basket Committee gets its money from the United Fund. If people don't give generously to the United Fund, these kids won't be just hungry. They will be starving.

At Glengate School there is one little boy named Reggie that makes you feel bad just to look at him. Reggie is nine years old, and he needs glasses. He's very thin and little and rather dirty. He came here from California last summer, so he can't get glasses from the state. Reggie gets very bad grades at school because he can't see the blackboard. The Children's Care Agency would get him the glasses, but their money is all used up. They told Reggie's mother he could have the glasses if the United Fund Drive was successful this fall. They will get Reggie some shoes too, because his brother's outgrown ones hurt his feet. They will—if they get enough money.

United Fund goes to several other agencies, too, and they all do lots of good for everybody in Lakima County. Some money goes to the hospital and some to the orphanage and some to the Salvation Army. Some goes to the Boy Scouts and the Camp Fire Girls, and they give some fun to kids like Reggie and keep them from growing up to be bums. But if the United Fund didn't do anything else except take care of kids like Reggie through the winter, it would deserve to be supported. It's no use saying there aren't very many poor people around here. Anybody who thinks that should just go down to Glengate School and look at Reggie, and then think about those 184 other kids who aren't any better off than he is. If we don't help them, nobody will.

Exercise 15. Look again at the persuasive theme you wrote in connection with Chapter 7. How good were your reasons? Evaluate your own paper, using the set of questions given on pages 231-32. Then write another persuasive theme on the same subject if your reasons were not sound. If both you and your teacher think your original reasons were sound, choose another subject.

Exercise 16. Write a persuasive theme on something you believe in, using *three well-chosen examples* to back up your main point. (Avoid religious subjects; almost anything else will do.)

Exercise 17. Make a *survey* of the attitude of your fellow students on some problem of current interest. Write a paper using the results of your survey.

Exercise 18. Write a paper opposing some national policy. You probably are not an authority on national problems, so support your point of view by the opinions of *at least two qualified authorities*. Be sure to state their qualifications and give the source of your information.

Exercise 19. Write a paper of persuasion primarily supported by your *prediction* of consequences.

Exercise 20. Write a paper against some local proposal, *comparing* the proposal to some other similar attempt that has failed.

Exercise 21. Write a more ambitious paper—your teacher will tell you how long it should be—using as many of these persuasive devices as you can comfortably and honestly employ. Before you hand your paper in, check it against the set of questions given on page 266. If your answers do not satisfy you, rewrite the sections you do not like before you turn the paper in.

IX

Something About Summary

Your father has been lecturing you all evening. He has touched on all the times you have neglected your chores—the lawns you didn't mow, the dishes you didn't dry for your mother, the tire you didn't change (of course, you weren't home at the time), and the car you didn't polish. He has thoroughly covered the expenses involved in running a household—the insurance and the shoes, the cost of gasoline and the price of milk and hamburger, the mortgage and the mattresses. He has almost made you cry by his pitiful picture of the old folks at home, with nothing to entertain them except bridge and the color television, while the selfish young are gadding about, burning up gasoline and increasing the insurance premiums. He has been talking for almost two hours. When it's all over, and your sister asks you what your father said, you reply, "He said we can't take the car. He's going to a lodge meeting tonight." Chances are that's a fairly good summary. It may be brief, but it catches the main point.

Or you go to church on a fine bright day and gaze dreamily at the stained glass windows. Just as you're about to doze off, you hear the preacher say, "To sum it all up in the words of the Bible, it is more blessed to give than to receive." And you're grateful to him because he *has* summed it all up. He has provided you with a ready-made answer, so that when Grandpa raises his ear trumpet and demands to be told what the preacher said, you can shout back, "He said we should all give as much as we can to the missionary collection, because it is better to give than to get." Then you add, "Of course, that's just a summary."

All your life you have been making this kind of summary. You have been listening to other people talk, and, if you got the point of what they were saying, you could, without any strain at all, tell somebody else what had been said. As you told them, you shortened the original a lot or a little, repeating what seemed to you the highlights of the discussion. Such summarizing is simple, natural, and easy. And for ordinary situations this system works very well.

But you are bound to run into some situations in which your summaries must be more careful and more complete. If your science professor asks you to go to the library and find out what boll weevils are, a single sentence re-cap may not be enough to cover what you have read. If the professor pops a quiz the next day, you won't do very well if the only thing you write is, "Boll weevils are bad for cotton." What is good enough for Grandpa won't be good enough for Professor Fossil. The students who get the A's will be the students who write careful, accurate *summaries* of what they have read.

Suppose this is the account that you find in the library:

> BOLL WEEVIL is a small beetle that feeds inside the *bolls* (seed pods) of cotton plants. Native to Mexico, it crossed into Texas about 1890. Since then, it has spread into most cotton-growing areas of the United States. This insect causes damage to U.S. cotton crops of $200,000,000 or more each year.
>
> Brownish or black in color, the boll weevil is about ¼-inch long. It is one of a group called *snout beetles*, because of the long beaks or snouts with which they feed. The boll weevil's snout is about half as long as the rest of its body.
>
> In winter, adult boll weevils hide in trash in or near cotton fields. When buds appear on the cotton plants in spring, female boll weevils open them with their snouts. They lay eggs inside the buds, and the eggs soon hatch into wormlike grubs. The grubs feed inside the buds, usually causing them to fall off the plant. Continuing to feed, the grubs become adult boll weevils in about 2½ or 3 weeks. They then eat their way out of the buds and attack other buds. Later in the season, they attack the bolls, where the females deposit more eggs. The eggs become grubs, which eat the insides of the bolls. Several generations of boll weevils may be produced in a single season.
>
> Many different insecticides are used to control boll weevils. Large cotton fields are often sprayed with insecticides from airplanes.

The coming of the boll weevil to the United States caused great damage to cotton crops, yet it produced some good results, too. It forced many farmers to plant other crops, and to use some of their lands for raising cattle, hogs, and chickens. Many of the localities which raise a variety of crops are now more prosperous than when they raised nothing but cotton.[1]

Although this explanation of boll weevils is clear and simple, you probably will not be able to remember the details if all you do is read through it rapidly and then say to yourself, "There, I guess I finished *that* assignment." Instead, you must take some brief notes.

Your notes should begin with the *purpose* of what you have read: "explanation of boll weevil." They should include the *main idea*: "boll weevil a beetle that does great damage to cotton crop." They should include the *main subdivisions*: where it comes from, how much damage it causes, what it looks like, how it destroys cotton, how it is controlled, how it has changed farming. Since the most important thing is how it destroys cotton, your notes ought to be most detailed on this part. Perhaps they will look something like this:

Purpose: explanation of the boll weevil
Main idea: a beetle that does great damage to cotton crop
came from Mexico around 1890
$200,000,000 damage annually in U.S.
brownish or black, ¼″ long—beak or snout ½ length of body
female lays eggs first in buds, then in bolls later in season
eggs hatch into grubs, which feed on plants
grubs mature in 2½-3 weeks; several generations per season
controlled by insecticides sprayed from airplanes
good result: forced farmers to vary crops

Notice that these notes follow the order and keep about the same proportion as the original material. Following the same order makes for clarity, and keeping the same proportion helps you give the same emphasis to each point as the original source does. The notes, as given above, leave out only one thing you will need: information telling where you found your material, so you can give credit to your source. Here too you must be complete and accurate. Copy the author's name, the book title, the publisher, the date, and the pages you read. Since this is an encyclopedia article, no author is given, but when your material comes from a book that does give an author's name, you must give it too. For encyclopedia articles, give the volume number.

Now you are ready for the pop quiz. If Professor Fossil lets you use your

[1] "Boll Weevil," *The World Book Encyclopedia* (Chicago, 1965) II, 358.

notes, fine; if he doesn't, the mere process of writing them down will help you remember the most important points. Here is a summary that ought to lead to a good grade:

> The boll weevil is a type of beetle that does great damage to cotton. It came to the United States from Mexico around 1890, and now destroys $200 million worth of cotton annually. It is brownish or black in color, about ¼-inch long, with a long snout or beak which the female boll weevil uses to open the cotton buds. She lays her eggs first in the buds and then, later in the season, in the bolls (or seed pods) of the plants. The eggs hatch into grubs which feed on the plant and within two or three weeks grow into adult boll weevils. Thus, several generations are produced each season. The boll weevil can be controlled by insecticides sprayed from airplanes. Its one advantage is that it has forced farmers to raise a greater variety of crops. (This information was taken from *The World Book Encyclopedia*, Volume II.)

Your summary differs from the original in two important ways. It is less than half as long, and it uses your words, not the *World Book's*. The summary is shorter because it leaves out some of the information. It omits the kinds of livestock the farmers raised after the boll weevils had damaged the cotton, and it shortens the explanation of how the grubs eat. Although these details are interesting, they are not really necessary for your summary. And putting the ideas into your own words, instead of just copying the original, proves that you really understand what you have read.

The process that you used in this summary will work for any summary, although you may need to change it a little if you are summarizing a different kind of material. Both your notes and your summary should include these things:

1. the purpose of the original writing
2. the main idea
3. the main subdivisions
4. the author and title of what you are summarizing.

When you turn your notes into essay form, that is, when you put your notes into sentences, you should try to

5. keep the same order and about the same proportions as the original
6. use your own words.

The *World Book* article gave you five paragraphs on boll weevils which you shortened very nicely into one paragraph. However, some writing is so packed with information and so fully developed that single paragraphs may need to be summarized by themselves. This paragraph, explaining the kind of people who will enjoy being sociologists, is complete in itself:

> People who like to avoid shocking discoveries, who prefer to believe that society is just what they were taught in Sunday School, who like the safety of the rules and maxims of what Alfred Schuetz has called the "World-taken-for-granted," should stay away from sociology. People who feel no temptation before closed doors, who have no curiosity about human beings, who are content to admire scenery without wondering about the people who live in those houses on the other side of that river, should probably also stay away from sociology. They will find it unpleasant or, at any rate, unrewarding. People who are interested in human beings only if they can change, convert or reform them should also be warned, for they will find sociology much less useful than they hoped. And people whose interest is mainly in their own conceptual constructions will do just as well to turn to the study of little white mice. Sociology will be satisfying, in the long run, only to those who can think of nothing more entrancing than to watch men and to understand things human.[2]

Before you begin to summarize anything as short as this paragraph, read it all the way through. Perhaps there will be some words you don't know. (You were lucky in the piece about the boll weevil. It contained easier words than most of the things you will read for college work.) In this paragraph, there are three things you may need to look up. What is a *maxim*? What are *conceptual constructions*? What does *entrancing* mean?

Even after you have all the words under control, you may not be sure what the main idea sentence is. If you are not, jot down, point by point, what the author is saying. This paragraph provides some easy clues as to what the separate points are. Each time the author begins a sentence with "people," he is introducing another point. Glancing through the paragraph again, you can see that there are four such sentences, and that each one explains a kind of person who should stay away from sociology. Your notes, then, should look something like this:

[2] Peter L. Berger, *Invitation to Sociology: A Human Perspective* (New York: Doubleday & Company, Inc., 1963), p. 24.

Stay away if—
    take world for granted, easily shocked
    not curious about people
    want to reform people
    see things in terms of own theories

Once he has got rid of the people who will not like sociology, the author uses his last sentence to say who will like it. This idea, too, should go into your notes:

Will like if—
    find people fascinating and want to understand them.

The purpose of Berger's paragraph, then, is to explain, and the main idea is found in the last sentence. Sometimes summarizing not only makes material shorter and thus easier to remember, but it can also lead to a clearer understanding of the material itself. Now that you have found the purpose and can state the main idea clearly ("People who find other human beings fascinating and want to understand them are the only ones who will like sociology") you are ready to write your summary. Since the author kept his main idea for the end of the paragraph, you should too. Work from your notes, rather than from the paragraph itself, so that you will be sure to use your own words.

> Peter Berger says there are four kinds of people who should stay away from sociology: those who take the world for granted and are easily shocked by what other people do; those who aren't curious about other human beings; those who want to reform other people, and those who like to see the world in terms of their own theories. People who find other human beings fascinating and want to understand them are the only ones who really like sociology.

Your summary could be shortened even more, down to a single sentence:

> Sociology is satisfying only to people who are fascinated by humans and want to understand them.

However, the rest of the summary, by showing what kind of people won't like sociology, suggests lots of things about the people who will like it.

Sometimes the author makes it practically a cinch to take notes, as in this selection from an essay on what happens in college:

> *What happens to students in college?* The teaching institution is faced with an onslaught of freshmen who are impelled toward the campus for a great variety and complexity of reasons. What

happens to them there is something not even they can predict
or expect. They enter college as adolescents; when they leave
some four years later, with or without a degree, they are young
adults. Some of this is simple maturation, of course, but some
is also the direct result of their college experience. College
experience itself is partly the experience of learning, the acquisition of a certain amount of ordered knowledge. It is also a
combination of other forces not directly related to the classroom
and the library, forces whose impact is more diffused but no less
important. They are essentially part of the hurly-burly of campus life.

It is the students' first meeting, most likely, with a national
and perhaps international group of men and women of their
own age. Excepting those fortunate enough to have attended
a very superior and international prep school (and only a tiny
minority have), a high-schooler's contacts are likely to have
been restricted to other inhabitants of the same town, even of
the same neighborhood in a larger town. It is small wonder, then,
that living in a dormitory with and attending class with, say,
a Pakistani, an Italian, or a Norwegian, makes students over-
whelmingly aware of a difference of lives, opinions, values.

Even the shift in the kind of curriculum is upsetting. The students are used to having the day arranged for them from, say,
nine to three, high school fashion. They now find themselves
attending classes for only fifteen hours or so a week. The con-
centration in depth on a few subjects is a new idea to them.
The requisite self-discipline is often something they learn only
after painful experience.

Furthermore, college is the students' first encounter with live
intellectuals. They meet individual members of the faculty who
have written important books or completed important pieces of
research. The various intellectual fields become matters of personal experience. The students learn that work does not just
happen to get done. They find that the productive intellectual
is not a superman but an everyday figure. They will also make
the discovery that there are those who consider intellectual
pursuits reason enough for an entire life. Students are nearly
always surprised to find such pursuits valued so highly.

Students are surprised, too, at their first meeting with really
violent political opinion of all possible varieties. Their parents
and/or their friends may have held violent political preferences,
but it isn't until college that they see the full range of political
possibility. Through student organizations and student publi-

cations, they meet for the first time with Democrats *and* Republicans, with conservatives *and* radicals. They are urged to take sides, if not as voters, then at least as partisans.

It is in college, too, that the sharp, bitter sting of failure is first experienced to any appreciable extent. A good high school student may find himself only a passing college scholar. Inequalities become painfully obvious. It is perhaps a matter of capacities. Those who develop long legs could become runners; those with short legs could not. Some are born with excellent intellectual capacities; some are not. One student will make good grades without any effort; another will fail even though he sits up most of the night with his books. The recognition of native inequalities is often hard for students to accept.[3]

Notice that the selection begins with a question set in italics. The first paragraph gives a general answer to the question (the answer is the main idea) and the other paragraphs answer it in more detail. In other words, the last five paragraphs *develop* the general answer, putting each point into a separate paragraph. The author uses plenty of transition words (*even, furthermore, too*) to warn you that he is going to change the subject slightly. What he has done is classify the kinds of college experiences that help students grow up. Once you discover that the author is classifying, and find out what it is that he has classified, you are well on your way to understanding the article. In taking your notes you need only jot down the main idea of each of the supporting paragraphs; then you will be ready to write your summary.

Paragraph 1 (main idea): The many things that happen to students at college change the way they grow up.

Paragraph 2: For most students, college is their first chance to know other students from outside their own neighborhood or their own country.

Pargraph 3: College forces them to plan their own time and work hard on a few subjects.

Paragraph 4: College lets them get to know real intellectuals, who value intellectual things more than anything else.

Paragraph 5: In college, students meet people who hold really violent political opinions of all kinds.

[3] James K. Feibleman, "What Happens in College," *Saturday Review* (October 20, 1962), 75.

Paragraph 6: And some students discover that they can't do as well in college as some other students, no matter how hard they work.

The note-taking on this one was practically automatic. And because you have taken your notes in complete sentences, actually summarizing each paragraph as you worked, the writing of the summary will be nearly automatic, too. Begin by giving credit to the author:

James K. Feibleman, in an article called "What Happens in College," published in the *Saturday Review* in 1962, says that the experience of going to college helps students to grow up.

Then go on with the sentences you have already written, keeping them in the same order.

All three of the things you have summarized so far have clearly been explanations. The first one explained what a boll weevil is; the second one explained who will like sociology, mostly by explaining who will not, and the last one explained some of the ways college helps students become adults. These are all straightforward purposes, and they were all developed in a fairly straightforward way.

Much of what you read, however, will be mixed in its purpose, and a mixed purpose is harder to be sure about. For instance, what is the author up to in this paragraph?

Because, by virtue of his greater physical power, man has been able to determine the fate and development of woman, men and women have come to assume that it was natural for men to do so, and both have come to mistake their prejudice for the laws of nature. That men may bully women into a position of subservience is not a biological fact but a cultural one, a cultural misuse of a biological condition. That is a very different thing from saying that women are biologically determined to occupy a subservient position to the male, and that the male is biologically determined to keep the female in a subservient position. Female subservience is a culturally, *not* a biologically, produced condition.[4]

After you have read the paragraph carefully and looked up the words you don't know (*subservience* and *subservient*? *biological*? *cultural*?), you must try to figure out what the purpose of the paragraph is. Certainly Montagu is trying to show the difference between a biological condition

[4] Ashley Montagu, *The Natural Superiority of Women* (New York: The Macmillan Company, 1953), p. 46.

and a cultural condition, but is that his main purpose? Why does he want to show the difference? If you look back at the beginning of the paragraph, you will notice that the author uses the words *assume* and *mistake*. Apparently he thinks that what most people take for granted about the relationships between men and women is wrong. He is trying to get his readers to throw out their old ideas and agree with him, he is trying to *convince*. Once we have decided that he is using his explanation to convince us of something, we can ask ourselves what he is trying to convince us of. If we can agree that he is trying to convince us that women don't really have to be inferior to men, we have found the main idea.

The next step is to see how he develops his idea. He begins by agreeing that men are physically stronger than women. Then he points out the difference between a cultural condition (the habits men develop as they live in social groups) and a biological one (the abilities humans are born with). Notice that he uses words that will help you to think that men should not have treated women like that: *bully* once and *misuse* twice. Then he states his conviction in a single, direct sentence: "Female subservience is a culturally, *not* a biologically, produced condition." As you write your summary, you must get all these ideas in:

> Montagu begins by admitting that men are stronger than women. Then he points out that there is a difference between the habits and customs men have developed (cultural conditions) and the abilities they are born with (biological conditions). He says men have taken advantage of their strength to keep women in an inferior position. His main point is that man's success in keeping woman under his control is cultural, not biological.

This time your summary is almost as long as the original paragraph, but that can't be helped. Some material is hard to shorten without leaving out important points. Even though you haven't made it much shorter, you have put it into your own words and proved that you understand it. And probably, if you were summarizing a longer section of Montagu's book, you would not deal with this paragraph in so much detail. Probably you would use only the main idea and leave out the development.

Let's try one more:

> There are roughly three New Yorks. There is, first, the New York of the man or woman who was born here, who takes the city for granted and accepts its size and its turbulence as natural and inevitable. Second, there is the New York of the commuter— the city that is devoured by locusts each day and spat out each night. Third, there is the New York of the person who was born

somewhere else and came to New York in quest of something. Of these three trembling cities the greatest is the last—the city of final destination, the city that is a goal. It is this third city that accounts for New York's high-strung disposition, its poetical deportment, its dedication to the arts, and its incomparable achievements. Commuters give the city its tidal restlessness; natives give it solidity and continuity; but the settlers give it passion. And whether it is a farmer arriving from Italy to set up a small grocery store in a slum, or a young girl arriving from a small town in Mississippi to escape the indignity of being observed by her neighbors, or a boy arriving from the Corn Belt with a manuscript in his suitcase and a pain in his heart, it makes no difference: each embraces New York with the intense excitement of first love, each absorbs New York with the fresh eyes of an adventurer, each generates heat and light to dwarf the Consolidated Edison Company.[5]

This paragraph uses several words you may not know: *turbulence, inevitable, deportment, incomparable, indignity, generates.* But in spite of using more hard words than the other paragraphs, this one presents more vivid pictures. White makes us see some of the people who come to the city, the grocer from Italy, the girl from Mississippi, the boy from Iowa. He uses some unusual comparisons that make us think of familiar things in a fresh, new way. Everybody knows that commuters come and go, but when White says that they are like locusts who eat up the city in the morning and spit it out at night, we get a fresh vision of the crowds of people who pour in and out of the railroad stations and the highways. We are not used to thinking of a city as having a "high-strung disposition" or a "poetical deportment," but when White makes these comparisons, we think of the noise and movement of the streets, and we wonder whether looking up at the buildings and down the long streets may be a little like reading a poem. White makes us think of New York as though it were a person. His purpose is to describe New York, not its physical appearance, but its atmosphere. He wants his readers to feel about it the way he feels.

What he actually does, however, is to classify the people who live or work in New York into three groups. When he begins with what is probably the main idea sentence of the paragraph ("There are roughly three New Yorks"), he doesn't mean that there are three cities, or three geographical divisions within the city; he means that there are three different ways of thinking about New York, and that these ways depend on who is doing the thinking. The people who were born there see one

[5] E. B. White, *Here is New York* (New York: Harper & Row, 1949), pp. 17–18.

city; the commuters see another, and the people who come from far away, looking for something or hoping for something, see it in still a third way. We can say, then, that White describes the atmosphere of New York by giving examples and classifying.

Because so much of the meaning of this paragraph depends on the way White says it, you will be tempted to use White's words instead of your own. Undoubtedly White can say it better than you can, but you must use your own words anyway. If you write your summary by lifting a sentence here and there, you will come up with something like this:

> There are roughly three New Yorks. Of these three trembling cities the greatest is the last—the city that is a goal. Each embraces New York with the intense excitement of first love.

But this is not only a cheating method, it is confusing and misleading. It destroys the proportions of the original, and it leaves your reader wondering what on earth you are talking about. What are the three New Yorks? Why are they trembling? What is meant by calling a city a goal, not a place? And who are the "each" who embrace New York so excitedly? You have not kept the flavor of White's writing as you were trying to do; you have only spoiled his meaning.

Moreover, you have not acknowledged the source, either of the idea or of the actual words, as you did in the other summaries. You have forgotten to say "E. B. White says" or "according to White." And you have broken one of the main rules of writing: you have used more than three consecutive words belonging to another writer without putting quotation marks around them. Properly punctuated, this summary would be nothing but quotation marks; it would not be a summary at all. If your assignment was to summarize White's paragraph, your teacher will not be pleased with your copy job. He's trying to teach you summarizing, not penmanship or typing. Try again, and this time use your own words and include all three of White's divisions, even though you do lose some of the flavor of the writing:

> In an essay on New York, E. B. White says that there are three different ways of thinking about the city. The people who were born there take it for granted. Commuters come and go every day and give the city its restless feeling. But the people who come to New York from far away come because the city represents something wonderful to them, and they are the ones who find it exciting and love it most passionately.

Certainly this summary is not as good as White's version. In trying to be both accurate and honest, you have had to leave out White's carefully chosen words; and in shortening the paragraph, you have had to leave out the examples. You have kept the *idea* of the original, but you have lost much of the effect.

In summarizing the White paragraph, losing some of the effect is probably unavoidable. There is not much you can do about it. If you wrote as well as White, you'd be publishing, not taking freshman writing. However, you can do something about keeping the *tone* of the original. Although you use your own words when you summarize, you must try as hard as you can to use the same *kind* of words the original writer used. If the first writer used a lot of slang, you may use slang, too. If he was trying to be funny, you may try to capture his humor. But if he was using a specialized vocabulary, although you may simplify the language, you must not do violence to the intention or the overall effect.

For instance, don't summarize the Montagu paragraph by saying:

> Montagu says that just because guys have bigger biceps than dames have, they can beat 'em up if they want to. The guys whack the skirts around because. . . .

You may find your version funnier than the original, but Montagu was trying to be serious, and you must treat his ideas seriously. If you are summarizing a writer who talks about "an underprivileged child from a city slum," you must not talk about "this dead end kid," although you may say "this poor child." If the author mentions a "somewhat pompous mortician," you must not talk about a "stuffy body-snatcher," although you may say "the undertaker." You must avoid slanting in summaries just as carefully as you avoided it in reports. Honest summaries reflect the spirit, as well as the ideas, of the original writing.

Most of the material you will be asked to summarize in college will be explanations and arguments. However, you may sometimes have to summarize a third kind of writing purpose, telling what happened. Perhaps you will need to report on some world event for a class in contemporary problems. Perhaps you will have to summarize the plot of a short story or a novel for your literature class. If you do need to summarize what happened, here are a few pointers that may help.

Be sure that all the people you mention are identified. Don't just dump in a name you haven't mentioned before and assume that your reader can guess who it is. If you are summarizing a news event, be sure to include where it happened and when. If you are summarizing a story, don't repeat conversations or long descriptions. If you do, you'll waste too much time on them and have to skimp on events that may be more important to the story. Whether you are summarizing an actual event or an imaginary one, the battle of Bunker Hill or last week's riot at the post office, Ulysses' long journey home or Holden Caulfield's weekend in New York, don't spend a lot of space on one incident that you found especially interesting at the expense of another one just as long in the original. In other words, when you summarize what happened, it is especially important to keep the proportion right.

In keeping the proportions of fiction right, you will not have the same clues that helped guide you through explanations and arguments. Certainly there won't be main topic subdivisions in heavy type. And few stories begin as E. B. White began his paragraph on New York, "There are roughly three New Yorks," followed by three sections explaining what they are. Even such useful separators as "further," "second," "next," "another reason," may be missing. There will only be the story itself.

Neither will fiction openly state the main point. When you wrote about your own experiences, sometimes you didn't put the main point into your paper, although you had to keep very clear in your own mind what it was. In the same way, when you read an account of what happened to other people, either real or imaginary, you will have to figure out what the main point is. You will not put it in if you are writing a straight summary, because your job in summarizing is simply to shorten and say in your own words what the first writer said. But keeping the main point in mind as you write will help you decide what to put in the summary and what to leave out, just as it helped you decide what to include when you were writing about what happened to you.

For instance, if you were summarizing the story of Little Red Riding Hood and the Wolf, it might help you to remember that the point of the story is that little girls who don't mind their mothers will get into trouble. Another point, perhaps, is that little girls ought not to talk to strangers, no matter how much sweet-talking the strangers do. If you think minding mother is the main point of the story, you will not want to leave out the mother's warning as she ties the strings on the little red bonnet and sends her daughter out into the big woods. If you think the main point is not talking to strangers, you will want to emphasize the way the wolf flattered the naïve little girl. Naturally, nobody this side of kindergarten is going to ask you to summarize a nursery story. It is used here for an illustration only because everybody has read the story, and because it is so simple that the relation between summary and point can be easily seen. What is true for summarizing a nursery story is true for summarizing a longer tale, although the point may not be quite so easy to find.

If you have read Orwell's *Animal Farm,* you know that the main point, or one of them, is that people who seize power often forget their promises and become even worse tyrants than the people they overthrew. If you are summarizing *Animal Farm,* you will want to keep that idea in mind. Remembering it will remind you to include what the pigs were like before they got rid of the farmers, and what they were like afterwards. But you will not include the idea in the actual summary, any more than you will include the comment that the pigs remind you of the Nazis or the Communists. If you are asked to summarize *and comment* on what you have read, then certainly you will put in what you thought the point was, and what the pigs reminded you of.

If you are asked to comment on what you have read, you are being asked for more than a summary. You are being asked for a *review.* Whenever you are asked to report on outside reading, be sure to find out what your professor wants, a summary or a review. The difference is important. *Summaries,* like reports, *keep opinion out. Reviews put opinion in.*

When you have read an article whose purpose is to explain or to convince, you may be asked just to summarize it. Or you may be asked to comment on it. If you are asked to comment, say what you think of the article as clearly as you can. If you are asked to summarize, make sure you stick to summarizing. The teacher who asked for a summary of Montagu will not be pleased if you come up with something like this:

> This fool thinks women are just as good as men. He says it's only cultural chance that makes men in charge of things. But I'm a woman and I know that's nonsense. My boy friend can do everything better than I can. He gets better grades, and that doesn't take strength. Montagu must be crazy.

If you write like that, you're not summarizing, you're arguing. On the other hand, if you have been asked for a *review,* it's all right to point out that you think Montagu is wrong, although perhaps you should do it a little more politely.

The main problem in reviews is to separate *what you think* from *what the author says.* You must keep this separation so clear that your reader can always tell which part is summary and which part is your opinion.

There are two ways to keep your comments separate from your summary. The easiest way is to write the summary first, just as you would any other summary. After you have finished your summary, say what you think about it, referring back to points in the summary to support what you mean. A more polished way to do it is to give one section of summary and then discuss it; give another piece of summary and then discuss that one. Doing it this second way will take a little more work. You must be especially careful to keep the parts straight. Every time you go back to summary, say something to remind your reader: "Googlestump also says . . ." "Another point Googlestump mentions is . . .," etc.

For instance, here is a selection from a book called *The Miracle of Language*, assigned as the subject for a student review:

The End and Means of Meaning

How is it possible that two people who may never have seen each other before, or who may not even live on the same continent, or be alive in the same century have immediate, similar, and complicated ideas in the presence of a sound? Especially is this event amazing when we consider that there are hundreds of thousands of these sounds with millions of meanings and still more millions of implications so delicate that they cannot be defined. Somehow millions of people have agreed, at least roughly, as to the meaning of the word *wrist* and the other countless words in the language, and this in spite of the fact that the human animal is so varied and contentious that seldom will two human beings agree about anything, whether the subject be religion, politics, or what will "go" with that hat.

Of course when the word *wrist* is spoken by one person and heard by another, little communication has as yet taken place. The single word raises almost as many questions as it answers. Is the speaker thinking that his wrist is arthritic, or that certain brush strokes can best be made with the wrist? These questions can be partially answered by adding a few more words, but in spite of anything he can do the speaker is likely to remain to a degree ambiguous. He cannot be precise because the syllable he is uttering has no precise meaning.

Thus "the miracle of the desart" is far enough from the divine to exhibit a human flaw. Exact communication is impossible among men. Gertrude Stein may have felt that "a rose is a rose is a rose," but our speaker, if he considers the matter carefully, must know that a wrist is not necessarily a wrist. It may be some bones hung together by ligaments. It may be the skin outside these bones. It may be the point which marks the end of the sleeve. If the speaker is a tailor, *wrist* may be a command to hem a glove. But even granted that both speaker and hearer agree that *wrist* is here associated with the bones, flesh, and skin at the juncture of the human hand and arm, they may still associate highly varied feelings with this part of the body. The speaker may have big, bony wrists, and have hated them all her life. The hearer may have been forced out of an Olympic skiing contest when he fell and broke a wrist. There is no one thing which *wrist* calls up in exactly the same form to everyone; there are not even areas of meaning which are the same for everybody. Meanings exist only in minds, and minds result from beings and experiences; no two of them are alike, nor are the meanings they contain. Still, granted that meaning is not and never can be exact, there remains a body of agreement as to the association to be connected with certain sounds which is staggering to contemplate.

But we have only begun, for we started with the simplest sort of example of spoken language. A word like *no* can mean *no, damn it,* or *yes,* or dozens of things between and among these meanings, depending upon the way in which the word is pronounced and the sounds modulated. The uttering and grasping of words, furthermore, become immeasurably complicated as soon as a speaker starts running them together into sentences. But for the moment let us complicate the situation only slightly by making the speaker also a writer, and let him make a few marks on any sort of object. These marks can now take the place of sound and can call up the concepts associated with *wrist* wherever they go. They can continue calling up these concepts long after the man who made them is dead; they can do so for hundreds, even thousands, of years. Clay cones and slabs of stone, scratched with marks which were long undecipherable, could still produce something like their original meaning when their language was rediscovered, although no living man had known how to speak or write or think the language for thousands of years.

Man, then, can be defined, if one wishes, as a languagized mammal. A cow can communicate in a cowlike way by bawling and dogs can express themselves to a degree by looking soulfully from one end while wagging the other, but man is probably more significantly distinguished from his fellow creatures by his complicated means of communication than by any other difference. In short, man as we know him could not exist without language and until there was language. Civilization could not exist until there was written language, because without written language no generation could bequeath to succeeding generations anything but its simpler findings. Culture could not be widespread until there was printed language.

In the beginning was the word. Or, if in the beginning was the arboreal ape, with the word and an opposable thumb he scrambled down from the trees and found his way out of the woods.[6]

Here is a review of Laird's essay:

The End and Means of Meaning

Laird says that it is amazing that millions of people who don't even know each other can get "immediate, similar, and complicated ideas" when they hear the same sound. He illustrates what he means by using the word "wrist," and he goes on to say that if "wrist" is said by itself, not everybody will get exactly the same idea as everyone else when he hears the sound, although they will all get the same general idea. Some people will think of a part of the body, but a tailor might think of a glove. And part of what people will think will be influenced by what has happened to their own wrists.

What Laird says is interesting because it makes you stop and think about words. It is easy to think of words as being things instead of just sounds. After I read Laird, I sat and said some words very slowly, listening to myself make the sounds. I said "rist" and "wist" and "rit" and "ris." After awhile I couldn't remember which sounds were words and which weren't. But when my brother came in, he said, "What are you mumbling about? The only thing I can make any sense out of is *wrist*. Did you sprain it or something?" I could see what Laird meant. It was amazing that my brother could sort the word out of all the sounds I was making.

Laird says it is just as amazing that people can make marks on stone or paper and other people can get the same ideas from them thousands of years afterward. I wasn't so surprised by what he said about writing, although I can see how much information would be lost if nobody could read or write. Once or twice I've wanted to leave somebody a note when I didn't have pencil and paper. I should think the cavemen would have been awfully frustrated.

Laird ends by defining man as a "languagized mammal." He thinks the main difference between men and animals is that men have a complicated means of communication.

I found the essay very interesting because I had never thought

[6] Charlton Laird, *The Miracle of Language* (New York: The World Publishing Company, 1953), pp. 7–9.

much about language before. I can't remember not being able
to talk and so I just took talking for granted. But now I can see
what Laird means by calling it a miracle.

The student who wrote this review has carefully separated his summary from his comment. It's clear that paragraph one is summary and
paragraph two is comment. Paragraph three is a mixture. It begins as
summary, but the last three sentences are the student's opinion. We can
tell the two apart easily enough because the student has used the phrases
"Laird says . . .," "I wasn't surprised . . .," "I can see . . .," and "I should
think. . . ." When he returns to the summary in paragraph four, he begins
with "Laird ends . . ." and starts his own conclusion by saying "I
found. . . ." The overuse of these phrases can be tiresome, and they may
seem a rather obvious way of separating summary and comment. But
they work, and until you can think of some other way that is just as
clear-cut, you must use them.

Notice also the quotation marks the student has used. He has carefully
followed the rule that more than three consecutive words, copied
exactly, must be put in quotation marks. The phrase "immediate, similar,
and complicated ideas" belongs to Laird, and the student has not tried
to copy it without acknowledging it. His other use of quotation marks
covers only two words—"languagized mammal." Here the student has
realized that the phrase was so unusual that it too was private property.
He has taken no chances; he has acknowledged his debt.

Do you think the student's summary is complete and accurate? You
can check the success of the summary part by asking yourself the usual
questions:

(1) Has the student found the purpose of Laird's essay?
He has done fairly well. Laird was explaining what a remarkable and
complex thing a word is, and the student's report deals mainly with the
idea that language actually is a miracle.

(2) Has he stated the main idea clearly?
"The main difference between men and animals is that men have a complicated means of communication" comes pretty close.

(3) Has he included all the main subdivisions?
Yes. If you go back through the Laird essay paragraph by paragraph,
you can see that the idea of each paragraph has been at least mentioned
in the student's summary.

(4) Has he followed the same order as the original?
Laird begins with a single word, goes on to talk about the limitations of
exact meaning, mentions writing, and ends with a definition of man.
The student does the same thing.

(5) Has he kept the same proportions as the original?

More or less, although he may have given less space to the limitations of meaning than to the other sections of the essay.

(6) Has he restated the material in his own words?

Using quotation marks took care of that one.

(7) Has he given a complete acknowledgement of the source of his material?

We've already mentioned how careful he was to keep saying "Laird says," but, of course, he must do more than that. He must tell us where Laird says it (in what book and on what page); when he said it (date of the book); and who printed it for him (name of the publisher).

What about the comment part of the student's review? This question is harder to answer, since the comment is supposed to be the student's own opinion. This student has not said anything very startling or original, but he has thought about what he has read and tried to report his thoughts honestly. He has stuck to the subject, and sticking to the subject proves that he understood Laird's article.

Actually, this student has shown three things: he has shown that he understood the article; he has shown that he can keep his comments separate from his summary; and he has shown that he can summarize. (For a fuller discussion of how to write reviews, see the section on writing a book review, in the appendix.)

All the things summarized so far have been very short, sometimes a paragraph, sometimes a page or two. Space has kept us from showing you how to summarize a twelve page article or a full length book. And although the general principles are much the same, the way you go about it is a little different. If what you are summarizing is fairly short, you can read it all the way through and then go back to take notes on it. If what you are summarizing is long, you may want to take notes as you go. If your material is divided into sections, treat each section separately, deciding what the purpose is, finding the main point, and noting the important subdivisions. In textbooks, the sub-topics will often be printed in heavy type to help you out, and this heavy type will often be a strong hint as to what the author intends the point to be.

The longer the thing you are summarizing, the more you will have to condense. If you are summarizing an entire book, it is especially important to get the proportions right. Work on one chapter at a time, but be sure to work on all the chapters. You may be tempted to do a thorough job on the first few chapters and then skimp on the last half. After all, you will be pretty tired when you get to chapter six. But if you have taken it section by section, making brief notes on each section as you finished reading it, you may be able to resist the temptation. Remember that the most important ideas often come at the end; you won't want to leave those out.

Good summarizing is a very important writing skill. It comes in handy in a lot of the writing you will do. If you need to explain something you don't already understand, what do you do? You find a book and look it up. And when you have found the explanation, you summarize the information, remembering, of course, to give credit to the source.

If you need to tell what happened when you weren't around, either because you weren't born yet or because you didn't happen to be on the spot at the time, what do you do? Look it up, in a history book, a newspaper, or a magazine. When you have found someone else's account of the battle you didn't fight in, or the earthquake you didn't run from, you summarize the account and acknowledge your source.

If you want to support your argument by what some authority says, what do you do? At the risk of sounding monotonous, we'll say it again: look it up, of course. And summarize it. And acknowledge it.

College will give you many chances to improve your skill in summarizing. And good summarizing will do a great deal to improve your college work. Summarizing can help you remember what you have read. As you answer test questions, good summarizing can convince your teacher that you understand what you have read and can relate it to the rest of the course. If you are asked to report on outside reading, summarizing the material intelligently will make the difference between a bad paper and a good one, a bad grade and a good one.

Key Words

Here are some of the important terms used in this chapter. Without referring back to the chapter, see whether you can answer these questions about them.

1. Why is it necessary to recognize a writer's *purpose* before you begin to summarize?

2. Why should you want to keep the *order* of the original?

3. Why should you want to include all the *subdivisions*?

4. What is the difference between *taking notes* and writing a *summary*?

5. How can *transition words* help you in planning a summary?

6. What is meant by keeping the *tone* of the original?

7. What are some of the ways that summaries of **reports** and **fiction** differ from summaries of other kinds of writing?

8. What things are the same whether you are summarizing a **paragraph** or a **book**? What do you do differently when you summarize a **book**?

9. Explain the difference between **summaries** and **reviews**. What is the main thing to keep in mind in writing reviews?

Vocabulary

Check the answer that most closely fits the meaning of the word as it has been used in the chapter. Look up in your dictionary the meaning of all the words you miss.

1. If you are **gadding** about, you are _____
   (a) playing golf with a two under par
   (b) swearing mildly
   (c) moving around, looking for amusement
   (d) tickling other people with a gad

2. If an arrow hits its mark **unerringly**, it _____
   (a) wavers as it flies through the air
   (b) flies surely and exactly to the target
   (c) finally gets there after several mistakes
   (d) travels in a vacuum

3. If an editor is **emitting** profanity, he is _____
   (a) cutting it out of his manuscripts
   (b) letting it stay in his manuscripts
   (c) correcting the spelling
   (d) sending forth a stream of swear words

4. A **maxim** is _____
   (a) a large bottle of champagne
   (b) a European military officer
   (c) a neatly expressed statement of general truth
   (d) a good-natured Scotsman

5. An **entrancing** child is one who is _____
   (a) trying to put the cat into a trap
   (b) digging a trench through his sandbox
   (c) delightful to see and delightful to know

(d) so spoiled that he leaves the beholder in a dazed
   condition

6. If a doctor talks about the **onslaught** of a disease, he means _____
   (a) the violence with which the disease begins
   (b) the seriousness with which it continues
   (c) the speed with which the patient gets over it
   (d) the likelihood that the patient will die

7. If you feel **impelled** to do something, _____
   (a) you think your ability to do it has been damaged
   (b) you are doing it just because it would be fun
   (c) you do it in your sleep
   (d) you feel forced or compelled to do it

8. **Maturation** means _____
   (a) a fancy word for matching
   (b) reaching full normal development
   (c) arrested development
   (d) remaining in an immature state

9. People with an instinct for **acquisition** like to _____
   (a) collect things
   (b) dissect things
   (c) gossip about things
   (d) damage things

10. If something is **diffused**, it is _____
    (a) mixed up and hard to understand
    (b) spread or scattered widely
    (c) concentrated and isolated
    (d) without an electrical connection

11. If something is **requisite**, it _____
    (a) must be done before something else
    (b) must be done after something else
    (c) is finely and precisely made
    (d) is needed or required

12. A **partisan** is one who _____
    (a) believes strongly in another person or cause
    (b) is skilled in some industrial art
    (c) is partly skilled in some industrial art
    (d) is skilled in some part of an industrial art

13. If you have an **appreciable** amount of something, you have _____
    (a) an amount that increases every day

(b) an amount that gets less and less every day
(c) as much of it as you are interested in
(d) enough that the quantity can be measured

14. A person who is *subservient* is _____
    (a) a servant of servants
    (b) a servant on submarines
    (c) in an inferior position
    (d) a miner

15. A *cultural* difference is _____
    (a) a disagreement about classical music
    (b) a liking for operas and art museums
    (c) a difference in the ideas and customs of two groups of people
    (d) a difference in the methods and results of two rose-growers

16. *Turbulence* means _____
    (a) disorder and commotion
    (b) vivid colors and bright lights
    (c) thick potato soup
    (d) very wet

17. A result that is *inevitable* is _____
    (a) never before equalled
    (b) very uneven
    (c) certain to happen
    (d) very unfair

18. The line "He has *devoured* the infant child" means he has _____
    (a) washed its face
    (b) performed an operation on it
    (c) eaten it
    (d) spit it back up

19. To go on a *quest* means to _____
    (a) take an overnight camping trip
    (b) go in search of something
    (c) head out west
    (d) stay overnight at a friend's house

20. *Deportment* means _____
    (a) being sent out of the country
    (b) not very important
    (c) a group of offices
    (d) behavior

21. An *incomparable* book is _____
    (a) beyond compare
    (b) incomplete
    (c) easily compared with other books
    (d) about writing compositions

22. If a piece of writing has **continuity**, it _____
    (a) is always published in sections
    (b) is always concerned with telling what happened
    (c) always reads as though it were a connected whole
    (d) always reads as though some connection had been left
        out

23. If you are offered an **indignity**, you should _____
    (a) take it and eat it
    (b) feel insulted
    (c) say, "No, I can't afford it"
    (d) say, "Thank you very much"

24. **Generates** means _____
    (a) produces
    (b) gets worse
    (c) gets better
    (d) goes away

25. If you call one of your friends **naïve**, you mean that he is _____
    (a) incapable of learning
    (b) trusting and not very sophisticated
    (c) bad tempered
    (d) very nice looking and sweet tempered

26. **Contentious** means _____
    (a) relaxed and well-fed
    (b) nervous and sickly
    (c) quick to quarrel
    (d) easy to get along with

27. An **ambiguous** statement is _____
    (a) one that can be taken two ways
    (b) equally at home on land or water
    (c) designed to promote the writer's ambitions
    (d) written by either the left or the right hand

28. **Juncture** means _____
    (a) old stuff nobody wants
    (b) a shop which sells such stuff

(c) a point where things are joined

(d) a Chinese boat

29. If you *modulate* your voice, you   ————
    (a) speak higher or lower, louder or softer
    (b) spend all your time screaming
    (c) speak so softly no one can hear you
    (d) never change the pitch

30. Writing that is *undecipherable*   ————
    (a) shows that the writer couldn't make up his mind
    (b) cannot be read
    (c) cannot be photographed
    (d) has not been paid for

31. To *bequeath* something means to   ————
    (a) trade it for something else
    (b) sell it for a profit
    (c) sell it at a loss
    (d) leave it to somebody after your death

32. *Arboreal* means   ————
    (a) happening on Arbor Day
    (b) happening in a harbor
    (c) living in trees
    (d) a lot of hard work

Exercises

Exercise 1. For each of these paragraphs,

1. Find the author's purpose: giving directions; explaining; telling what happened (a report); telling what happened (personal narrative); convincing; summarizing.

2. If you can, find the main idea sentence, underline it, and then restate it in your own words; if you cannot find a single sentence that expresses the main idea, say in your own words what you think it is.

3. Explain how the main idea is developed (examples, statistics, comparison, classification, definition, authority, etc.). Remember that the author may use a combination of methods.

4. Summarize the paragraph, making your version about half as long as the original, more or less.

1. With the collapse of the Confederacy, civil government and administration all but disappeared throughout the South. There was no money for the support of government and no authority which could assess or collect taxes. The postal service was paralyzed and it was fully two years before a normal service was restored. There were no courts, no judges, no sheriffs, no police officers with any authority, and vandalism went unrestrained except by public opinion or by lynch law. (S. E. Morison and H. S. Commager, *The Growth of the American Republic*, New York: Oxford University Press, 1942, II, p. 13)

Purpose_____

Main idea in your words _____

_____

_____

_____

Method of developing main idea _____

_____

Your summary _____

_____

_____

_____

_____

_____

2. Psychoanalysts . . . give special emphasis to unconscious motivation. Even slips of the tongue, forgetting of appointments, and other simple acts of everyday life are traced to motives of which the individual may not be aware at the moment. Thus, the bored hostess, after an insufferable evening, said, not what she intended (but what she meant): "Well, good-bye, I'm so sorry you came." Likewise, the deb at a dance, much interested in a certain young gentleman, intended to ask him when he was going to dance with her, but instead asked, "When are you going to marry me?" There is no good reason for supposing that all such lapses are unconsciously motivated—some may be purely accidental—but there is no doubt that many have such motivation. (Norman Munn, _Psychology: The Fundamentals of Human Adjustment_, Boston: Houghton Mifflin Company, 1946, p. 236)

Purpose_____

Main idea in your words _____

_____

_____

_____

Method of developing main idea _____

_____

Your summary _____

_____

_____

_____

_____

_____

_____

_____

3. When word-association tests were tried on people, the first thoughts that came to the surface of their minds in reference to prunes were such thoughts as "old maid," "dried-up." In his studies of the place the word prune had in the English language he came upon such phrases as "old prune face" and "dried-up old prune." When his investigators conducted their depth interviews they found that prunes were thought of as a symbol of decrepitude and devitalization. Others thought of prunes in terms of parental authority. They remembered that as children they were often directed to eat prunes because they "ought to" or because "prunes are good for you." Prunes were associated with boardinghouses where they were served by parsimonious landladies, with stingy, ungiving people, with joyless puritans. The black murky color of prunes as commonly served was commented upon unpleasantly. The color black was considered somehow symbolically sinister, and in at least one case the poor prune was associated with witches. (Vance Packard, *The Hidden Persuaders*, New York: David McKay Company, 1957, p. 137)

Purpose_____

Main idea in your words _____

_____

_____

_____

Method of developing main idea _____

_____

Your summary _____

_____

_____

_____

_____

_____

_____

_____

_____

_____

4. Mathematics is a science in its own right, but one which touches the outside world only insofar as it is used as a tool in the other sciences. Terrifying as the subject often seems to the uninitiated, it is indispensable to progress in physics and chemistry and astronomy. With symbols and equations a scientist can express concisely ideas which would require many pages of careful writing to explain in ordinary language. When his ideas are thus expressed in simple mathematical form, new relationships and new channels of investigation often suggest themselves which would be lost in verbiage if mathematics were not used. To simplify, to clarify, to coordinate, to predict—in all sciences mathematics serves these several purposes. (Konrad Bates Krauskopf, *Fundamentals of Physical Science*, 2nd ed., New York: McGraw-Hill Book Co., 1948, p. 47)

Purpose_____

Main idea in your words _____

_____

_____

_____

Method of developing main idea _____

Your summary _____

_____

_____

_____

_____

_____

_____

_____

5. As a general rule we wish politicians would leave God out of it. We don't mean to be irreverent, but refer to the "I'm-more-devout-than-you" plot. Senator Goldwater has used it recently; he deplores the Democratic platform's silence on school prayers, in what he describes as its "utter disregard for God." By inference he condemns all dissenters.

Mr. Johnson, in turn, is a fast man with a Biblical text. He also allows himself a mawkish sentimentality that is hard to take. ("He is the only man," observed columnist Peter Lisagor recently, "who can pick political lint out of the pockets of poverty.")

We aren't going to judge either candidate on this basis. Any moral afflatus going round in this campaign hasn't touched us. ("TRB from Washington," *The New Republic*, Oct. 24, 1964, p. 2)

Purpose_____

Main idea in your words _____

_____

_____

_____

Method of developing main idea _____

_____

Your summary _____

_____

_____

_____

_____

_____

_____

_____

6. Nothing is more essential to the process of intelligent, profitable reading than a sensitivity to connotation. Only when we possess such sensitivity can we understand both what the author means, which may be pretty plain, and what he wants to suggest, which may actually be far more important than the superficial meaning. The difference between reading a book or story or essay or poem for surface meaning and reading it for implication is the difference between listening to the New York Philharmonic Symphony Orchestra on a battered old radio and listening to it on a high-fidelity stereophonic record player. Only the latter brings out the nuances that are often more significant than the more obvious, and therefore more easily comprehended, meaning. (Richard D. Altick, *Preface to Critical Reading*, 4th edition, New York: Holt, Rinehart and Winston, 1960, p. 4)

Purpose_____

Main idea in your words _____

_____

_____

Method of developing main idea _____

_____

Your summary _____

_____

_____

_____

_____

_____

_____

7. . . . that a Beatle-bitten teen-ager let his hair grow into a shoulder-length bob, that the hair-do outraged the school system, that the school system kicked him out until he got his hair cut to its rather than to his own taste, that the school system's decision outraged the boy's father, that the outraged father took the case to court, and that the court ordered the school system to take the boy back, hair and all. A clear victory for what Charles Dickens called "fancy" and a rebuke to all the gradgrinds of the School of Hard Facts.

I should, in fact, like to believe that the court has reaffirmed the simple principle that a citizen's hair is his own to wear as he pleases. I must, to be sure, confess to some grudge in this, a grudge against all those army types from second lieutenant to colonel who spent years of their lives and mine, presumably in the service of the country, but actually in waiting for any hair of my head to grow longer than five-sixteenths of an inch. Thereupon they would leap upon me with a glee known only to commissioned stupidity and ask—always in that same tone—"You going out to buy a violin, soldier?" My part of the dialogue, always as sprightly as theirs, alas, consisted of four short sentences, of which only the first could actually be spoken aloud: "No, sir. Cannot play violin, sir. Wish I could, sir. May I request transfer to music school, sir?" After which, having been forced to swallow the best of my conversational effort, I

would be told to "Get yourself a haircut and start looking like a soldier."
(John Ciardi, "Manner of Speaking," *Saturday Review*, Dec. 12, 1964,
p. 15)

Purpose_____

Main idea in your words _____

_____

_____

_____

Method of developing main idea _____

_____

Your summary _____

_____

_____

_____

_____

_____

_____

_____

_____

_____

_____

_____

8. Beethoven's success, however, was marred by the greatest misfortune that could possibly befall a musician—deafness. The disease had made itself manifest as early as 1799, and in a most moving document, a letter to his brothers written in 1802, Beethoven pathetically described his own despair at the life of isolation that lay before him. By 1814 the deafness had become so complete that he was prevented from making any further appearances as a soloist. At the first performance of the great Ninth Symphony in 1824, the composer, who sat on the stage, had to be turned around so that he might see the tumultuous applause that the second movement had brought forth. (Martin Bernstein, *An Introduction to Music*, 2nd ed., New York: Prentice-Hall, 1951, pp. 177-8)

Purpose_____

Main idea in your words _____

_____

_____

_____

Method of developing main idea _____

_____

Your summary _____

_____

_____

_____

_____

_____

---

9. For your candlemaking you will need wax, wicking, coloring material (children's wax crayons work well), several 1- or 2-pound coffee tins, a collection of molds, some cheesecloth, and whatever aromatic leaves you have growing near you. Hobby shops sometimes carry candle-wax and wicking. Be sure to buy both hard and soft wax and mix them half and half. Candles made entirely of soft wax will melt in a warm room and bend out of shape. . . .

First melt wax and coloring material in a coffee can placed in a pan of simmering water. (You can judge the color by dipping up some wax in a deep spoon and cooling it.) While the wax is melting, cut the leaves in small pieces and tie loosely into a bag of cheesecloth. For a 2-pound coffee tin three-quarters full, you will need about two handfuls of leaves. Push the leaves below the surface of the wax and let the mixture stand 10 minutes while you prepare molds. (*Sunset*, Dec. 1964, p. 96)

Purpose_____

Main idea in your words _____

_____

_____

_____

Method of developing main idea _____

_____

Your summary _____

_____

_____

_____

_____

_____

_____

_____

_____

_____

_____

Exercise 2. For each of these longer articles, taken from a Sunday paper, follow the same steps you used in Exercise 1: (1) find the writer's purpose; (2) find the main idea sentence, underline it, and restate it in your own words; (3) explain how the main idea is developed; (4) summarize the article in a single paragraph. Do this exercise on a separate sheet.

1. *Your Garden Will Never Be Superior To Your Soil*

Gardeners are sometimes inclined to slight soil preparation, some because they have been misled into thinking that throwing a mulch over the soil eliminates the need for digging, others for different reasons.

Yet, the fact remains that the most flourishing gardens in this country are grown on the best-prepared, best-fed soils.

Unlike woodland soils, garden and crop areas are called upon to produce abundantly year after year. This tends to compact many soils through a depletion of the humus. Also, the soil nutrients are used up.

This means that they must be loosened periodically, the valuable humus content restored and the nutrients replenished. We do this in the home garden by digging it up at the beginning of each season, after first applying a 1 to 2-inch layer of compost, peat, or some other humus material over the soil.

For this use a good, strong spading fork and go down the full depth of the tines. Lift out the piece, turn it over and break it up by striking it with the fork, if necessary. This will also tend to incorporate the humus at the same time.

In days gone by, this was also considered the time to apply one's fertilizer but it tends to put the fertilizer down too deeply where the young plants can't reach it during their early stages of growth.

Instead, apply one-third on top of the soil before digging and one-third on top of the soil after digging. Then rake this into the top 2 or 3 inches with a good, strong steel rake.

The remainder is applied when you hoe out the rows to make the seed drills—just make them deeper than necessary, place the fertilizer in the bottom, mix it in lightly and pull an inch of soil back over this before planting to keep the fertilizer safely away from the seeds. For this many gardeners like to use a triangular hoe, often called a Warren Hoe.

In very light soils where leaching (draining down through) is a problem some gardeners are also successful with covering large seeds with soil and putting the remaining fertilizer above.

The important part is to keep the fertilizer away from the seed so that the tender young rootlets will not be burned.

If the garden is small and the soil shallow, it pays to double dig. That means to take out the top layer of soil about a shovel-blade deep and put it aside on a piece of canvas or anything else that makes cleaning up easy.

Then the soil underneath is dug up with a fork, 2 to 3 inches of humus and some good vegetable fertilizer (2 to 3 lbs. per 10 by 10 feet) are thoroughly mixed in before returning the top layer which is similarly enriched.

Of course, if you run into rocks, roots or any other obstructions in your digging, they should be removed. For this a good, strong pick or pick-mattock is best. Don't run the risk of springing the tines on your fork.

It may represent a little work, but if you prepare your soil as outlined here, you will be well rewarded later. (*The Sunday Oregonian*, April 11, 1965)

2. USAF Gets Word; Eyesores To Go

WASHINGTON—Green leaves versus scrap metal is the new watchword, and the Air Force has got the message.

With Mrs. Johnson's committee for a more beautiful capital recently organized and presidential concern for a more sightly land clearly outlined, the first hopeful sign towards the junking of junkyards has appeared. It comes as the result of a letter written to the first lady by a Dayton, Ohio, businessman.

"I have been reading about how much you dislike the eyesore of the used car junkyards across this great nation of ours and I sincerely agree with you," he wrote.

"Mrs. Johnson, wrecked auto graveyards are bad enough, but wrecked airplane graveyards also scar our view around Dayton.

"When traveling northeast out of Dayton on Route 69 towards Route 40, all motorists are greeted with an eyeful of the Wright Patterson Air Force Base airplane graveyard.

'How About Hint?'

"How about dropping a hint to those responsible?" he concluded.

Mrs. Johnson immediately brought the letter to the attention of Secretary of Defense Robert McNamara, who alerted Secretary of the Air Force Eugene M. Zuckert, a Pentagon spokesman said.

The Pentagon found that the area in question—some seven acres of open land about a quarter-mile from the state highway, had been used for the past 10 years for base crash-fire training.

There, old airplanes whose flying days were over, stripped of their retrievable aluminum, were being set on fire to train crews in the business of putting them out and rescuing dummy people.

Almost every base has such a place where the fire department trains for crash rescue. Five old hulks were found to be in residence.

So the Air Force has now made plans to move the site to a new area, 500 yards to the south, which is screened from the highway by a thick grove of trees. (*The Sunday Oregonian*, April 11, 1965)

3. *"See America Now!"*

President Johnson has issued this urgent message to all Americans: "Today our encouragement must be directed to travel in the United States, both by our own citizens and by our friends abroad. I ask the tourist industry to strengthen and broaden the appeal of American vacations to foreign and domestic travelers, and I will support its efforts through the 'See the U.S.A.' program."

THIS WEEK Magazine is proud to join the President's drive. For many years we have promoted America as "the world's greatest travel bargain." We do so again with a brand-new concept in travel aids—a unique new *Vacation Planner and Road Atlas* with many distinctive features. In it you will find thousands of reasons why you should see North America first.

Says World-Traveler Lowell Thomas:

"I've spent a good part of my life chasing travel adventure everywhere, and after almost satisfying my wanderlust from the Antarctic to the Orient, I've come to this conclusion:

"All the travel excitement that anyone could want is in North America. Anyone who can't reach the tingling pinnacle of high adventure in this country and its neighbors couldn't reach it anywhere."

Speaking of the new Road Atlas, Mr. Thomas says: "It is the handiest, most complete guide of its kind that I've ever seen. It will give you everything you need to know on where to go, how to get there and what to do. It is perfect for planning any trip. Always keep it in your car for constant reference." (*This Week Magazine*, April 11, 1965)

Exercise 3. On a separate sheet, make a careful summary of this selection from a statement made by a federal judge. Before you begin, make sure you understand what the judge says; look up all the words you don't already know. After you have written your summary, write a *review* of the judge's comments, being sure to separate your opinions from his.

Judge Jerome Frank

. . .

To date there exist, I think, no thorough-going studies by competent persons which justify the conclusion that normal adults' reading or seeing of the "obscene" probably induces anti-social conduct. Such competent studies as have been made do conclude that so complex and numerous are the causes of sexual vice that it is impossible to assert with any assurance that "obscenity" represents a ponderable causal factor in sexually deviant adult behavior. "Although the whole subject of obscenity censorship hinges upon the unproved assumption that 'obscene' literature is a significant factor in causing sexual deviation from the community standard, no report can be found of a single effort at genuine research to test this assumption by singling out as a factor for study the effect of sex literature upon sexual behavior." [social psychologist Leo Alport] . . . Macaulay, replying to advocates of the suppression of obscene books, said: "We find it difficult to believe that in a world so full of temptations as this, any gentleman, whose life would have been virtuous if he had not read Aristophanes and Juvenal, will be made vicious by reading them." Echoing Macaulay, "Jimmy" Walker remarked that he had never heard of a woman seduced by a book. . . .

Most federal courts . . . now hold that the test of obscenity is the effect on the "mind" of the average normal adult, that effect being determined by the "average conscience of the time," the current "sense of what is right"; and that the statute does not intend "to reduce our treatment of sex to the standard of the child's library in the supposed interest of a salacious few." . . .

However, there is much pressure for legislation, designed to prevent juvenile delinquency, which will single out children, i.e., will prohibit the sale to young persons of "obscenity" or other designated matter. . . . (From U.S. Court of Appeals opinion in *United States* v. *Roth*, 237 F. 2nd Series, 2nd Circuit, 1956.)

Exercise 4. Summarize an article that discusses your major. If you are planning to be a nurse, use an article on something about nursing. If you are majoring in data processing or diesel technology, use an article on computers or diesel engines.

Exercise 5. Write a review of the article you summarized in Exercise 4, combining your summary with your comments. In your comments, discuss the article in the light of what your courses have taught you. For instance, if you are taking nursing, you might comment on whether the writer gives a fair account of hospital work as you know it. If you are taking data processing, ask yourself whether the article covers the problems of programming as you understand them. In other words, use your comments to compare your experience with what the author says.

X

A Note to the Student Who Has Used This Book

Much of the writing you will be asked to do, in school and afterwards, will seem more specialized than the writing covered here. In one sense it will be, for some kinds of writing have special directions you must follow. (See Appendix for the special requirements of book reports, term papers, and application letters.) But in another sense, all the writing you will ever have to do has the same requirements as the writing you have been doing in this class. All writing—book reports, answers to essay tests, term papers, letters to the editor, speeches read at political rallies or P. T. A. meetings, application letters—must be clear, orderly, and logical. None is any more than an extension of the problems of a well-written half page.

Whether you are answering an essay question or writing a report of the decoration committee for the Birdcatchers' Ball, if it is worth writing, it is worth your best efforts. Don't ruin the effect of your paper by carelessness. If you punctuate and spell in the normal way, you will make a better impression on the teacher who reads your work, on the prospective boss who receives your application letter, on the readers of your letter to the editor. After all, many of these people are well educated and likely to be just as fussy about what is "correct" as your English teacher ever thought of being. Some of them are fussier because they are not in the habit, as English teachers are, of looking beyond the illiteracies for the carefully thought-out idea that redeems them. Try for both correctness and sense. But remember, all the commas in the handbook and all the correctly spelled words in the dictionary will not make up for the lack of an idea, or for a garbled, silly, meaningless paper.

You are not likely to be writing papers that are garbled, silly, or meaningless if you are still with us at this point in the course. You have learned to decide what you want to say and to say it sensibly.

Still you have not learned everything there is to know about skillful writing. Your style may be less elaborate than Faulkner's, less dramatic than Hemingway's. It may not even have occurred to you that you have a style. Perhaps when you began this book, you did not even have an awareness of style in others. But every time you made your meaning clear by finding the words to express exactly what you meant, every time you experimented with the order that expressed it best, you were both refining your ideas and developing your style. As you have discovered, ideas and expression, like reading and writing, work together. As your expression became more precise, your thinking cleared up.

If your style is not a many-splendored thing, don't worry. Hoaxshell has a fancy style, but it often conceals a shoddy thought. You know how much harder it is to communicate in plain English, clearly expressing honest ideas, than it is to hide behind grand style which is all form and no content—a big balloon has lots of air but no weight. You may well say to the ad writers and the Hoaxshells, as we have been saying to you, "Don't try to gussy it up. Instead, put the same amount of work on it and give us plain English, please."

Appendix I

Writing a
Book Review

What's a Book Review For?

Schools with their teachers, desks, blackboards, and bells may not be necessary to education, but books are. Plays, histories, novels, poems, biographies, can all contribute to your enjoyment and understanding of life. The need for reading is clear, but the need for reporting on what you have read is harder to see.

First of all, you have to prove to your teacher that you have read the book. (Just as you would not try to pass off a phony review of a book you have not read, don't try to run in an old report that you wrote in high school, whether or not you read the book or wrote the report yourself. The idiot who bragged about submitting the same book report on *Call of the Wild* six times got only a *C* the last time. Had he read six different books, the new knowledge he would have acquired might have raised his grade. *Call of the Wild*, while a good book of its kind, is hardly worth six reworkings.) The process of writing lets you prove something to yourself, too. Writing is a way of learning and a way of helping you remember what you have learned. Some people can look at all the words in a book and still have only a vague notion of what the book was about.

Too often reading is passive, even lazy. But when you know you must write something about the book, your reading becomes active, not passive. You watch for ideas and developments just as a hawk watches for rabbits and sparrows. And if you are accurate and alert, you profit from your reading as much as the hawk does from his hunting. And you both experience something of the same kind of satisfaction. But instead of rabbits and sparrows, you are full of thoughts about the book. Writing a book review forces you to order your thoughts and thus helps you to make the book a part of you.

Choosing a Book

Reading ought to be enjoyable. The world is full of books. Bookstores and libraries offer you a wide choice. But to find the book that will interest you, you must spend some time browsing. You browse when you look at the outsides of books, touch them, and read a little here and there. Take your time. You will find most college librarians and bookstore managers will do everything they can to help you.

But you can help yourself, too. The first step in browsing is to look at the cover of the book. Publishers spend a lot of money on book covers, sometimes producing artistic designs and sometimes producing dirty pictures. A look at the cover will not always give you an accurate notion of the book. Often the cover contains a blurb. The blurb is more useful than the picture, but blurbs are advertisements and are primarily intended to sell the book. You need not believe the writer is the greatest thing since Shakespeare, or that his ideas have set the world shuddering on its axis. But simply knowing who the author is may help you decide whether you want to read the book. Perhaps you have heard something about him or read some other book he has written.

The best way to find out what a book is about is to open it, just as you would open the hood of a car you were thinking of buying. Just as you would take a trial run in a car, take a trial run through the book. Read the table of contents. Read the first page and read here and there in the middle. You can tell by the sound of the engine whether a car is a good risk. In the same way, you can tell fairly quickly whether a book is a good risk for you. Buy books, and a lot of them—they're cheaper than cars—but you don't need to spend your book money foolishly.

Contents of the Book Review

The first paragraph of your book review should state clearly the full name of the author; the exact title of the book, underlined to indicate italics; the publisher; and the date the book was first published.

Your review should tell something of what the book is about. It should either tell a very condensed version of the story (a summary) or list the main points the author emphasizes (a summary), whichever seems more suitable. This summary section of your book review, however, should *never* be more than a third of the whole. The other two thirds will be your comments on what you have read, and should cover most of these points:

Something about the author. If the book is a novel, what is the author's reputation among people qualified to judge fiction? If you don't know, look in encyclopedias or *Twentieth Century Authors* in your college library. If the book is a report or an evaluation of something, is there anything in the author's background that makes him an authority on this subject?

Don't give biographical details that have no bearing on the book you have read. Does it really matter what the author's mother's maiden name was, that his father was a missionary, that he kept pet snakes and went to school in Pago-Pago? What does this have to do with how clearly he writes or the soundness of his reasoning? The author's hobbies have as little to do with his argument against atomic war as ex-president Truman's opinion of modern art has to do with the current value of paintings. No matter how juicy his biography turns out to be, keep it out unless it directly relates to the book you are reviewing.

Something about purpose and main idea. The purpose of novels and short stories is to tell what happened. The term *fiction* means "made up or invented"; that is, fiction tells what happens to imaginary characters in an imaginary place. Since the writer has created his characters and his events, instead of being obliged to report what did happen to actual people in a real world, the kind of people he has created and the way they react to what happens to them are important to our understanding of the book.

The fiction writer uses his main purpose, telling what happened in this imaginary world, for another purpose, to show us, rather than tell us, how he looks at life and what he thinks it means. Fiction seldom explains, argues, or reports objectively. But even fiction which seems intended only to entertain is based on some observation the author has made or some conviction he holds. It is your job, as a reader, to discover what this observation or conviction is; when you have found it, you will have found the main idea—or one of the main ideas—that underlie the story or the novel.

Writers of good fiction always keep their main ideas clearly in mind. When Sinclair Lewis wanted to dramatize the cloddishness of a middle-class businessman, he made Babbitt convincingly human and even a somewhat likable man. But Lewis did not let us lose sight of his message: that Babbitt is a clod and that his life is meaningless. In writing a review of *Babbitt,* don't just say, "Mr. Lewis wrote this book to show what it was like to live in Zenith in the 1920's." That won't do. You must make clear what Lewis's convictions were. And then you must refer to the things in the book that will back up your interpretation.

You can use your previous knowledge and experience to evaluate what you read. Although the characters and events in fiction are imaginary, fiction succeeds only if the author can make us believe in the people he has created and in the things that happen to them. One way of judging fiction is to test its reality. Are the characters like people you have read about or have known? Does the author describe places so you can see them? Are the events believable? You should remember, though, that some characters, places, and incidents will be unfamiliar to you. Some books may even seem revolting. But you should not condemn a book only because its characters and events disgust you or because they are outside your own experience. Instead, try to discover the author's reasons for using such characters and events.

And not all books attempt to be true to life. *Animal Farm* has animals for characters, but George Orwell knows that pigs don't talk. *Lord of the Flies* takes place on a desert island after an atomic war, but William Golding knows that there is no such island and there has been no such war. *A Connecticut Yankee in King Arthur's Court* has a man travel through time and space, but Mark Twain, although he knows about science and history, deliberately ignores scientific and historical facts. In fantasies, as in any fiction, you must do the same three things: discover the author's aim in writing as he does; decide whether he accomplishes this aim; and decide whether it is an aim worth accomplishing.

The aim of fiction is to show you life as the author sees it, by presenting either a "real" picture, a fantasy, or a blend of both. The purposes of nonfiction vary. Some nonfiction books tell you how to do something, some explain something, some tell you what happened in the actual world, and some try to convince you. You should ask the same questions about those books as you asked of your own papers.

Something about style. One way of judging style is to ask yourself whether there is anything really unusual about the way the author expresses himself. It is probably not worthwhile commenting about the length of his sentences or the length of his paragraphs unless they are unusually short or unusually long—three-word sentences in one-sentence paragraphs, for instance. But if the author's tone is light and humorous, or deadly solemn, or tense and excited, perhaps you should make some comment on the tone. If you do comment, support your comment by quoting a typical example.

Other questions that may lead to useful comments on style are: Is the method of telling the story or presenting the facts noticeably different from the method used in other books *of the same type* you have read? (Don't compare a book of one kind to a book of another kind. Do compare biographies with biographies, westerns with westerns, etc.) What is the difference? If there is some difference, do you think it made the book more or less effective? Why?

Something about what you gained from reading this book. If the book is a novel, has your understanding of people outside your own experience been increased? How? If the book is nonfiction, what has been added to your stock of information? Have any of your ideas been changed? What ideas? In what way?

Something about whether you liked it. Would you recommend this book to your friends? What do you think they would get out of it? If you would not recommend it, say why.

Here, as in all parts of your review, you must do more than make bare statements of opinion. Don't just say, "This author writes well." Rather, show *why* you think he writes well. You can support your reasons by quoting directly from the book and explaining why you chose that quotation, or by explaining how the author made you see things his way and saying why the method was good. In all the comments you make, *be definite*. Refer to specific things in the book to support your comments. Whether you liked or disliked the book, whether or not you would recommend it, are unimportant unless you can show the reasons for your opinion.

Form of the Book Review

There is no special length for a book review, but usually it will take at least four or five hundred words to cover what must be said. Sometimes you will need to write more than that.

Book reviews, like any other paper, must be in ink or typewritten, double spaced, and written on one side of the paper only.

And like summaries, book reviews must carefully acknowledge the source of any ideas or comments that do not belong to you. In sorting out your ideas, it is perfectly all right to read other people's opinions of the book. You may even use some of their comments, enclosed in quotation marks if you copy more than three consecutive words, or properly acknowledged if you borrow just the idea, not the exact words.

Reviews of Magazine Articles

Reviews of magazine articles have the same basic requirements as book reviews, although they may be shorter. In mentioning what article you have read, put the title of the article in quotations, put the name of the magazine in italics (underline it), and give the date and volume number of the magazine.

Appendix II

Writing a Term Paper

The main difference between a term paper and any other college writing assignment is length. Term papers are certainly expected to be longer than ordinary papers. But there is no need to fall into a state of hysterical paralysis just because your teacher says you must write a term paper—or a reference paper or a research paper or even a thesis—and casually adds, "Make it about twenty-five hundred words long." Resist the temptation to count quickly on your fingers (twenty-five hundred words is about ten typed pages) and then faint dead away. ("Term paper," "reference paper," "research paper," and "thesis" are all names for the same thing, and so is "dissertation." The difference again is length. A dissertation is to a thesis as a thesis is to a reference paper. And a thesis is to a reference paper as a reference paper is to an ordinary theme. In other words, the dissertation is the longest of all. But you don't have to worry about that for a while.)

You'll be all right if you remember that you are almost never expected to produce ten pages out of your own unassisted head. Long-paper assignments take it for granted that you will get some of your material from magazine articles and books. What you must furnish out of your own unassisted head is the main idea for the paper and the plan for using the material. So far a term paper is no different from any other paper, is it? And if the main idea is clearly stated and the plan sound and logical, the paper will be no harder to write, although it may take you a bit longer.

The only special problems that arise in term papers are similar to the problems in writing reviews. You must keep other people's ideas, opinions, facts, or figures clearly separate from your own comments. The published (or typed) ideas, opinions, facts, figures, and *words* of other people belong to them just as much as their cars, their money, and their wives belong to them, and the moral problem involved in stealing words, statistics, and ideas is exactly the same problem involved in stealing another man's car or his wife. If you would not help yourself to someone else's money, don't help yourself to what he has written.

The moral question involved is the same, but the approved method of borrowing written material is different, and much simpler, than borrowing money. For one thing, you don't have to pay words back. All you have to do, when you use other people's ideas and information, is to acknowledge your debt.

There are two standard ways of giving the original writer credit for his material. The first method, footnoting, is used for specific borrowing. Whenever you use statistics collected by someone else or a piece of information or an example that is not common knowledge, or the exact words of someone else, or even your own very slightly changed version of his words, you must give the original writer the credit. You give the credit in a footnote. The test for common knowledge is not whether *you* already knew it, but whether someone fairly familiar with your subject would have known it. That Abraham Lincoln was born in a log cabin, was president of the United States during the Civil War, and, when he was young, may have walked many miles to return a penny, is common knowledge. What Carl Sandburg (a Lincoln expert) says about Lincoln's personal sorrows during the war years is not common knowledge, and if you use Sandburg's information, you must give Sandburg credit.

The second method is a bibliography. A bibliography is simply a list of all the sources you used in getting ready to write your paper. It should contain not only the sources you footnoted from, but the sources you got your general ideas from, too.

There are several acceptable ways of arranging footnotes and bibliographies. It is a good idea to find out what form your teacher wants you to use. If he has no preference, get a standard style manual and do what it tells you to do. Good footnotes and bibliographies are just a matter of following directions, carefully and consistently. There is no more excuse for doing footnotes wrong than there is for writing "to" when you mean "too." Your college library owns several different style manuals, and your college bookstore undoubtedly sells the one recommended by the

English department on your campus. Style manuals are usually inexpensive; we know at least one college that still sells them at cost—ten cents.

The style manual will give you other information, too: what goes on a title page, how wide the margins should be, how to indent and single space your long quotations. You may think your instructor won't pay much attention to such details. But if your paper follows the standard rules and is neat, your teacher may be impressed enough to raise your grade a notch or two.

Appendix III

Writing an Application Letter

From your point of view, your application letter means "I want a job with this company." But from the employer's point of view, the letter means "The writer of this letter is (or is not) able to do a good job for my company." Since the success of your letter depends on pleasing the man who reads the letter, you had better write it from his point of view.

Trying to butter up the man who reads the letter is probably just as much a waste of time as trying to butter up your professor to raise your grade. It may help a little, but not much, to imagine what would impress you, if you were the boss. Because you can't guess what kind of personalized approach would impress a man you don't know, the surest way is to follow a standard plan.

Keep the letter short, usually not more than four or five paragraphs. Include in it (1) how you heard about the vacancy; (2) the most important of your reasons for thinking you are suited for the job; (3) a word or two about your reasons for thinking the job would suit you; (4) any other definite information you have been asked to give; and (5) the best way to get in touch with you and, if the job is within traveling range, an offer to come in for an interview.

If you are answering an advertisement, you might begin by saying, "I saw your advertisement for an assistant fish counter in the *Battlefield Bugle* of March 4, 1966, and I would like to apply for the job." Or if you heard about the vacancy from a friend, start with, "Senator Hoaxshell of Mossy Stone told me that you are looking for an assistant fish counter, and I would like to apply for the job."

If you have had any experience in fish counting, that experience is certainly your best recommendation. Mention it next, and say exactly when, how long, and for whom you worked: "During the summer of 1964, I worked for two months as a fish counter at Bonneville Dam, and Mr. Oscar Salmon, who was in charge of the project there, is willing to recommend my work." If, as is more likely, you have never counted any fish, be honest about your lack of experience: "Although I have never worked as a fish counter, I have taken a year of zoology and two terms of mathematics at Raglan College, where I will graduate in June. I am very interested in wildlife conservation and wrote my term paper for zoology on the spawning habits of northwest salmon." Don't say any of this unless it is so. But most people have something in their backgrounds that could be related to fish counting, if it is nothing more than an ability to count to a thousand without using their fingers, and the patience to do it. If you can't think of anything in your background, keep searching the help-wanted ads until you find a job you are qualified for and then apply for that one.

The reason for saying why the job would suit you is not that the employer cares much about what will make you happy, other than a normal good-natured interest in the welfare of his fellow man, but because the employer knows that unless you are fairly happy in your work, you will not be a very good worker and will probably not stay very long. Don't say you plan to make fish counting your lifetime profession (unless you really don't have any other plans for the next forty years), but do emphasize the parts of the job you think you would like. Say, "I like working outdoors and enjoy any work that calls for methodical attention to detail."

A request to "state salary expected" appears frequently in job advertisements. Expected salary is awkward to discuss in a letter. You may ruin your chance at the job if you ask for too much. But if you ask for too little, you risk getting hired for less than the employer might have been willing to pay. You can't ignore the specific request, but you might sidestep it by saying, "I would expect to be paid at the usual rates for assistant fish counters."

As for how the employer can get in touch with you, be sure to give both an address and a phone number. If you are away at school from eight to five every day, say, "I can be reached at CLumsy 8-6092 any evening after five o'clock." The comment that you will be glad to come in for an interview whenever it is convenient for the company makes a good closing line.

Your application letter should be accompanied by a personal data sheet, giving a complete account of (1) all the personal details employers are curious about; (2) your education; (3) your working experience; and (4) at least three references. All of this information could be included in the letter, of course, and some of it has been, but it looks better in the form of a chart. Besides, if you keep a copy for your own records, you will have all the information at hand when you want to apply for another job and thus you will save yourself the trouble of gathering it again.

Personal details should include age, height and weight, sex (if your name leaves this question in any doubt), whether you are married or single, and how many children you have, if any.

Your educational record should begin with the school you attended last and work backward toward grade school. Give the name of the school, the city and state where it is, the years you attended, and, for high school and college, the date of your graduation.

Under job experience, again begin with the present and work backward. Give the name of the person or company you worked for; the address; the name of your immediate superior, if it is different from the name of your employer; a description of the kind of work you did; the dates of your employment; and your reason for leaving. Ordinarily, your educational record and your job record, taken together, should account for all your time from the age of six. If there are any large gaps, they may lead a prospective employer to wild speculations about what you were doing in that unexplained year or two. Better satisfy his curiosity, even if you can do no better than "September 1960–March 1961—unemployed." Unless your record of full-time employment is fairly long, it is better to include all the jobs you have ever had—paper routes, baby-sitting, even lawn-mowing. Though these jobs may seem very unimportant and quite different from the job you are applying for, the habits of responsibility and self-control demanded by any regular work may be just what will sway the employer in your favor.

Your three references should include at least one person you have worked for, and they may all three be previous employers, if you have worked for that many people. If you are short of previous employers who will speak well of you, include a teacher who knows you well. It is all right to include one character reference, but he should never be a relative, and he ought not to be such a close friend that he would be obviously prejudiced in your favor. Never give anyone as a reference until you have asked his permission. For one thing, asking permission is an ordinary act of politeness, and for another, you should not take the chance of naming someone who might be unwilling to speak well of you.

PERSONAL DETAILS

Name: Rupert Creech

Address: 80 Dusty Street
  Bury-Your-Dead, Wyoming

Phone: 909 963-7004

Age: 20

Born: April 1, 1945, Boston,
  Massachusetts

Nationality: United States citizen

Height: 5 feet, 2 inches

Weight: 273 pounds

Marital status: unmarried

EDUCATION

Raglan College, Bushytail,
  Oregon   1964-65

Bury-Your-Dead Consolidated
  High School, Bury-Your-Dead,
  Wyoming   1960-64, graduated, 1964

Underhill Primary School,
  Bury-Your-Dead, Wyoming   1951-60

JOB EXPERIENCE

Liberty Theater, Bury-Your-
  Dead, Wyoming: Mr. Hiram
  N. Firam, manager.
  Duties: sweeping out the
  theater; taking tickets;
  filling candy machine   summer, 1964

Senator Orville Hoaxshell,
  14 Summit Street, Lasso,
  Wyoming.
  Duties: lawn-mowing and
  basement-cleaning once a
  week after school   1962-64

REFERENCES

Mr. Hiram N. Firam
Liberty Theater
Bury-Your-Dead, Wyoming

Senator Orville Hoaxshell
14 Summit Street
Lasso, Wyoming

Professor Barry Fossil
Raglan College
Bushytail, Oregon

On page 239 is a sample personal data sheet. Yours should look something like it.

By now you have learned to proofread and correct everything you write, but it is particularly important to do a careful job on an application letter. The care with which you write your letter may be the employer's best indication of the care with which you will do your job. A sloppy, misspelled letter (even though the job itself may not even require you to spell "fish") will prejudice the employer against you and may keep him from lifting the receiver to call your number.

Other simple things that may affect his decision are the neatness of your typing, the acceptable form of your letter, and your ability to balance between boastfulness on the one hand and an apologetic overmodesty on the other. Some ads ask you to reply in your own handwriting—another possible index of care and character. Whether you type or write, always sign, rather than type, your signature. Don't worry about beginning your sentences with "I." After all, you are telling about yourself, and the straightforward approach is better than the awkwardness of walking halfway around the block to avoid what would, anyway, be natural in plain, honest English.

Appendix IV

Comprehension Questions

Comprehension: Chapter I

Answer this multiple choice quiz according to what is said in the chapter, whether or not it agrees with your own opinion. Sometimes there is more than one right answer; if so, use the letters for all the right answers. Sometimes the right answer may not be given; if no right answer is given, write it in your own words.

1. The study of English, though worthy of study by itself, is primarily (a) an end in itself (b) useful for more advanced English study (c) a tool subject (d) a punishment inflicted by cruel college authorities.

2. Understanding of English can come through other classes because (a) history and psychology teachers often lecture on English (b) history and psychology are important subjects by themselves (c) the other classes are taught in English (d) you will learn about your own writing from reading other writing carefully.

3. If you read well, you will probably (a) write well (b) write poorly because you would rather read (c) be elected to a student office (d) have to read aloud to your class.

4. Reading and writing are different because in writing you must (a) find your own ideas (b) choose the best words (c) develop a sensible order (d) work out examples (e) put your ideas into the proper form (f) revise your work.

5. Although there are many different things to consider in writing, the most important is (a) the proper form (b) correct spelling (c) conventional punctuation (d) clarity (e) writing in ink, double spaced, and on only one side of the paper.

6. When writing a paper, the best thing is to (a) follow directions (b) make up your own assignment (c) make up your own assignment only if you can think of a more interesting one (d) make up your own assignment only if you can think of a better one.

7. The problems of revising are (a) different from the problems of writing (b) the same as the problems of writing (c) aided by dictionaries (d) aided by handbooks (e) just a matter of correctly and exactly copying the first draft.

8. Following directions means (a) doing the right kind of assignment (b) getting a paper of approximately the right length (c) having the paper in the correct form (d) turning the paper in on time.

9. If your spelling and punctuation are shaky, a good way of making your paper more acceptable (and thus improving your chance for a better grade) is to (a) decorate your paper with art work, either your own drawings or clippings from magazines (b) use colored paper (c) perfume the paper with lilac water (d) put the paper in an expensive folder (e) fasten it together with earrings instead of paper clips.

10. Conventional usage means (a) using the same spelling as the educated people in your community (b) using the same punctuation as the educated people in your community (c) choosing the same kinds of words as the educated people in your community (d) judging people by their usage.

Comprehension: Chapter II

Answer this multiple choice quiz according to what is said in the chapter, whether or not it agrees with your own opinion. Sometimes there is more than one right answer; if so, use the letters for all the right answers. Sometimes the right answer may not be given; if no right answer is given, write it in your own words.

1. Before you begin to write anything, you (a) write an application for membership in the Writers' Guild (b) write a letter to the editor (c) diagram your main idea sentence (d) ask yourself "Why am I writing this anyway?" (e) ask yourself "Is there any way I can get somebody else to write this?"

2. Among the people who write for fun are (a) Homer (b) Shakespeare (c) Dickens (d) most professional writers (e) Dorothy Parker (f) all college freshmen (g) teachers.

3. Nobody can write effectively unless he (a) writes for the pleasure of it (b) has a definite aim in mind (c) understands his purpose clearly (d) keeps his purpose firmly in mind all the time he is writing.

4. Four common purposes that occur over and over again in all writing are (a) begging for money (b) telling why the bridge fell down (c) telling why frogs make good mousers (d) making grocery lists.

5. Explanatory writing is writing that (a) classifies (b) compares (c) analyzes (d) gives excuses.

6. Reports (a) are always oral (b) do not tell you how to do anything (c) do not try to change your opinion (d) tell what happened.

7. Convincing writing persuades the reader (a) to do something (b) not to do something (c) to believe something (d) to doubt something.

8. The four basic purposes of writing (a) always occur separately (b) are always mixed (c) sometimes are used in the same piece of writing (d) should be carefully avoided by beginning students.

9. After you know where you are headed, you (a) relax and stop worrying (b) distinguish between a topic and a main idea (c) make a definite statement that cannot be misunderstood (d) put your paper into the typewriter and get yourself a cup of coffee.

10. A main idea is (a) usually a complete sentence (b) distinguishable from a topic because it makes a definite statement (c) always present when you say, "I am going to write about something." (d) unnecessary if you are writing persuasion.

Comprehension: Chapter III

Answer this multiple choice quiz according to what is said in the chapter, whether or not it agrees with your own opinion. Sometimes there is more than one right answer; if so, use the letters for all the right answers. Sometimes the right answer may not be given; if no right answer is given, write it in your own words.

1. To write a good paper giving directions, you must (a) thoroughly understand the thing you are giving directions about (b) write a clear main idea sentence (c) list the steps in the right order (d) hold the plan in the right hand while demonstrating with your left (e) try very hard to be entertaining.

2. A paper giving directions must include (a) pen and ink sketches illustrating each step (b) a list of all equipment needed to do the job (c) a joke to catch the reader's attention (d) an introductory paragraph.

3. The purpose of an introduction to a paper of directions is (a) to make a short paper longer (b) to tell the reader what the subject is (c) to give your name, class section number, and teacher (d) to introduce you to your reader (e) to catch your reader's attention with a joke (f) to serve as a contract between the writer and the readers.

4. The purpose of a conclusion is (a) to make a paper seem longer (b) to include everything you forgot in the body of the paper (c) to introduce a new idea (d) to repeat the material in the introduction (e) to fill out the page.

5. The best way to inspire confidence in your reader is to say, every now and then, (a) it seems to me (b) I'm not an authority, but I think that . . . (c) in my opinion (d) it is my belief that. . . .

6. A transition is (a) part of an automobile (b) something you put on some broken legs (c) a period of time between historical events (d) a sudden and abrupt change of weather (e) a city streetcar system.

7. Addressing the reader directly is (a) justified in papers giving directions (b) known as "second person" writing (c) the best method to use in any writing (d) characterized by the use of "you" when speaking to the reader (e) continued throughout the paper if used at the beginning.

8. Becoming pronoun conscious means (a) making clear what each pronoun stands for (b) avoiding the use of all pronouns (c) making sure you have plenty of different kinds in each sentence (d) using the pronoun "one" whenever possible because it sounds so dignified.

9. After you have written your paper, you should (a) hand it in at once (b) put it away for a day or two and then reread it (c) read it aloud (d) change anything that needs changing.

10. During the final check on your paper you should ask yourself (a) if you have done everything your first paragraph promised (b) if your last paragraph fits with your first paragraph (c) if you included all the necessary steps in logical order (d) if the meaning of each sentence is clear and unmistakable (e) if you have used enough transitions (f) if your conclusion makes your paper sound finished.

Comprehension: Chapter IV

Answer this multiple choice quiz according to what is said in the chapter, whether or not it agrees with your own opinion. Sometimes there is more than one right answer; if so, use the letters for all the right answers. Sometimes the right answer may not be given; if no right answer is given, write it in your own words.

1. The purpose of a paper of explanation is to (a) explain how to do something (b) explain what happened (c) explain which of two things you like the best.

2. A good definition (a) must be complete (b) must apply to the thing you are defining and nothing else (c) should never be more than three or four words long (d) often must say what something is *not*, as well as what something is.

3. General and specific (a) mean roughly the same (b) are relative terms (c) are absolute terms (d) are transitional words.

4. A generalization (a) should always be avoided (b) is better than a specific statement (c) always refers to one particular thing (d) makes a statement about a group of things (e) should be backed up by specific instances.

5. A good comparison (a) tells how things are different (b) tells how things are alike (c) tells which of two things is better (d) tells which of two things is worse.

6. You are classifying things when you (a) give directions on how to do something (b) explain in detail what you mean by a word (c) explain how two things are different (d) tell what happened.

7. Explaining a whole thing by examining it piece by piece is called (a) giving directions (b) persuasion (c) comparison (d) analysis (e) contrast (f) telling what happened.

8. Writing out the main idea of your paper may help you to (a) stick to the point (b) limit your subject (c) avoid using opinion words (d) go to sleep.

9. Writing out the points you mean to cover may help you to (a) get along with your wife (b) get along with your grandmother (c) get along with your mother (d) get along with your mother-in-law (e) get along with your work.

Comprehension: Chapter V

Answer this multiple choice quiz according to what is said in the chapter, whether or not it agrees with your own opinion. Sometimes there is more than one right answer; if so, use the letters for all the right answers. Sometimes the right answer may not be given; if no right answer is given, write it in your own words.

1. Reports should contain (a) lots of opinion (b) lots of description (c) anything that will add color (d) lots of explanation (e) lots of directions.

2. Chronological order means (a) order of importance (b) order in time (c) order of unimportance (d) random order.

3. The main idea sentence of a report can be used to (a) make the reader laugh (b) gauge which details are too trivial to be included (c) capture your reader's attention (d) say when an event took place (e) say where an event took place.

4. Reports should be (a) orderly (b) precise (c) to the subject (d) complete (e) accurate (f) objective.

5. In deciding which details should be included in a report, the writer may want to ask (a) are the details related to the event being reported? (b) can the event be understood without them? (c) are they interesting? (d) are they humorous?

6. "Don't use a word unless you are absolutely sure of its meaning" means (a) you should only use words that would be clear to a fifth grader (b) you should avoid using words just for their fine sound (c) you should use words which fit your meaning accurately and precisely (d) you should consult your dictionary about the precise meaning of words.

7. Factual statements (a) contain material which can be checked (b) contain only a little opinion (c) contain only one or two subjective words (d) contain only a few subjective words (e) are always true.

8. "Greater," "smaller," "better," "worse" are (a) subjective words (b) objective words (c) judgment words (d) opinion words (e) interpretation.

9. Many bitter arguments are caused by (a) failure to define terms (b) overuse of factual material (c) too many objective statements (d) too many objectionable statements.

10. Objectivity is characterized by (a) absence of slant (b) neutral terms (c) factual statements (d) absence of opinion words.

11. Using words which reflect your opinion on what has happened is called (a) objective writing (b) subjective writing (c) factual writing (d) slanting.

12. Subjectivity is characterized by (a) more subjects than verbs (b) a tendency to see everything from a personal point of view (c) opinion words (d) a condition of slavery.

13. The term "writing a report" might be applied to (a) the minutes of a meeting (b) an accident form (c) a love letter (d) the write-up of a laboratory experiment (e) a poem.

Comprehension: Chapter VI

Answer this multiple choice quiz according to what is said in the chapter, whether or not it agrees with your own opinion. Sometimes there is more than one right answer; if so, use the letters for all the right answers. Sometimes the right answer may not be given; if no right answer is given, write it in your own words.

1. The first sample theme in this chapter was bad because it (a) made no point (b) was subjective (c) used personal experience (d) was too long (e) was about hunting.

2. If you want to write tales of personal experience, you should (a) make sure they have a point (b) throw them away (c) mail them off to your own true love (d) keep them objective.

3. The main idea sentence for a theme of personal experience (a) is not important (b) is never considered by the writer (c) should fit the sample pattern (d) should avoid a "so what" response.

4. Making a point in personal experience themes means (a) the meaning grows out of the events described (b) the meaning will carry over into other experiences (c) being sure that the theme explains how to do something (d) being sure that the theme never gets personal.

5. One way to add interest to a theme of personal experience is to use (a) specific detail (b) drawings (c) maps (d) generalizations without details.

6. If you use lots of details (a) you do not need to be selective (b) the interest will take care of itself (c) keep them objective (d) discard them all (e) keep the related ones (f) discard the unrelated ones.

7. The main idea sentence for a theme of personal experience (a) may not appear at all (b) must appear in the first paragraph (c) must appear in the last paragraph (d) is exactly like any other main idea sentence.

8. Natural-sounding language (a) sounds conversational (b) sounds pedantic (c) is stilted (d) is exactly the same as conversation (e) is 90 per cent slang.

9. To make your writing sound natural (a) use as many slang expressions as you can think of (b) write exactly the same way that you talk (c) omit your main idea sentence (d) be pedantic.

10. Personal experiences (a) must always be isolated from other kinds of writing (b) must never be used (c) can be usefully blended with other kinds of writing (d) must be kept objective.

Comprehension: Chapter VII

Answer this multiple choice quiz according to what is said in the chapter, whether or not it agrees with your own opinion. Sometimes there is more than one right answer; if so, use the letters for all the right answers. Sometimes the right answer may not be given; if no right answer is given, write it in your own words.

1. Persuasive writing (a) is relatively rare in the world today (b) is never found in explanations and reports (c) should not be found in explanations and reports (d) should never be attempted by students.

2. Some common examples of persuasion can be found (a) in advertisements (b) on billboards (c) over the radio (d) over the television (e) in newspapers (f) in the world almanac.

3. Some people who use persuasion are (a) small children (b) students (c) teachers (d) public relations men (e) politicians (f) preachers.

4. An implied contract between the writer and the reader should appear in (a) the title of the paper (b) the last paragraph (c) the second supporting reason (d) the last supporting reason (e) a notarized agreement attached to the paper.

5. A good way to arouse the reader's interest is to (a) keep him guessing about the point of the paper (b) use a lot of words he doesn't know (c) keep your most fascinating information for the last paragraph (d) write the title in red ink.

6. The best way of getting other people to see it your way is to (a) use a lot of exclamation marks (b) underline key words (c) pound the table with your shoe (d) outshout the opposition.

7. The supporting reasons in a persuasive theme may be effectively arranged by (a) scattering them haphazardly (b) listing them in order of importance (c) arranging them chronologically (d) tacking them to the wall and throwing darts at them.

8. Reasons may commonly be supported by (a) giving directions (b) giving examples (c) giving statistics (d) citing authorities (e) predicting consequences.

9. The introduction to a paper of persuasion (a) should always be written before the rest of the paper is begun (b) ought to arouse the reader's interest (c) should bear a clear relation to the conclusion (d) may contain such words as "should" and "should not" (e) should be underlined.

10. A paper of argument (a) should be free of opinion words (b) often deals with the arguments of the other side (c) should contain supported reasons (d) should contain exaggeration and melodrama.

Comprehension: Chapter VIII

Answer this multiple choice quiz according to what is said in the chapter, whether or not it agrees with your own opinion. Sometimes there is more than one right answer; if so, use the letters for all the right answers. Sometimes the right answer may not be given; if no right answer is given, write it in your own words.

1. Glamor by association is (a) a device to get you to associate socially with glamorous people (b) an unfair persuasive technique (c) frequently found in advertisements (d) based on the reader's ability to respond to sugared words.

2. Good and evil (a) are terms understood by everyone (b) are terms everyone agrees to (c) are terms everyone responds to emotionally (d) are vague terms that need more specific definition.

3. Senator Hoaxshell was guilty of evasion when he (a) talked about communism instead of answering the question about Medicare (b) dodged a tomato thrown at him by an irate voter (c) urged invasion of Cuba (d) said that senior citizens should have the natural dignity of paying their own way.

4. Adequate examples must be (a) representative (b) relevant (c) helpful in making a meaning clearer (d) helpful in making the reader see something more vividly.

5. Subjective words (a) can never be explained by example (b) are always sugar coated (c) depend on guilt by association (d) can never be used as the object of a verb.

6. Making a survey is (a) un-American (b) the American way of establishing facts (c) sometimes useful in providing statistical facts (d) always a foolproof way of supporting reasons.

7. An adequate sample (a) should include a fair cross section (b) should be selected at random (c) should contain enough instances (d) should be free of bias.

8. Effective persuasion always (a) interprets its statistics (b) employs the word "typical" (c) prefers "many" or "few" to exact figures (d) distorts figures.

9. Winston Churchill is an acceptable authority on (a) politics (b) American movie stars (c) modern art (d) facial tissue.

10. Guilt by association is (a) a smear technique (b) sometimes a sound method of supporting reasons (c) based on the truth that birds of a feather flock together (d) based on the belief that because some people are alike in one respect, they must think alike in all respects.

11. Good reasons for not studying would be (a) nobody else studies, why should I? (b) nobody ever has studied for that course, why should I start now? (c) everybody else gets by without studying, why shouldn't I? (d) all changes are bad, so I had better not change horses in the middle of a stream.

12. Predictions are fairly safe if they (a) deal with dependable generalizations (b) are limited to the physical world (c) deal with the behavior of people (d) are limited to situations that are new and complex.

13. In analyzing cause and effect relationships, you should remember that (a) if one thing comes after another, the first one always causes the second (b) if one thing comes after another, the first one never causes the second (c) most events have only one true cause (d) most events have several causes (e) nobody can ever tell what caused anything.

14. In fair comparisons (a) the things being compared must be alike in significant ways (b) the differences must be unimportant (c) the statistics must not misuse authority (d) the things being compared must be identical.

15. The habit of asking suitable questions (a) will drive your listeners mad (b) will improve your writing (c) will improve your reading (d) will improve your ability to believe everything (e) will make you skeptical of everything.

Comprehension: Chapter IX

Answer this multiple choice quiz according to what is said in the chapter, whether or not it agrees with your own opinion. Sometimes there is more than one right answer; if so, use the letters for all the right answers. Sometimes the right answer may not be given; if no right answer is given, write it in your own words.

1. To make a good summary, you should (a) follow about six steps (b) follow about fourteen steps (c) take a sentence here and a sentence there (d) be sure to make a random sampling.

2. Writing a good summary (a) takes practice and hard work (b) is so simple even a baby could do it (c) requires the writer to use his own personal experiences (d) is rare and unimportant, and thus is the last chapter in this book.

3. In the samples which the book summarized, the first step was always to (a) look up any strange words (b) start with the main idea sentence (c) use quote marks (d) copy whole sentences from the original.

4. After you are sure you understand the paragraph, the next thing to look for is the (a) purpose (b) main idea sentence (c) tone (d) proportion.

5. Once you have discovered the purpose, the next thing is the (a) tone (b) main idea sentence (c) purpose (d) proportion.

6. Using your own words means (a) it is OK to quote the author if you omit the quote marks (b) you should liven up the original language as much as you can (c) the tone of the original must be kept (d) more than three consecutive words of the original must be kept in quote marks (e) more than three consecutive sentences of the original must be in quote marks.

7. Taking a sentence here and there from the original is (a) misleading (b) dishonest (c) a good way of summarizing, so long as the sentences are chosen at random (d) better than putting the same sentences into your own words.

8. When you summarize somebody else's material, you must (a) acknowledge the source (b) give the original author's name (c) give the name of the book or magazine from which the material was taken (d) give the date of the author's birth.

9. Proportion means (a) height and weight (b) distribution of weight and height (c) figure or shape of girls (d) amount of emphasis put on each point.

10. If you are summarizing a piece of writing that tells what happened (a) don't just dump in names you haven't mentioned before (b) don't repeat conversations (c) don't repeat long descriptions (d) don't worry about keeping the proportions (e) do copy the main idea sentence exactly as it appears in the original.

11. If you are summarizing a report of something that actually happened (a) tell where it happened (b) tell when it happened (c) include your own comments (d) identify the people involved (e) keep the proportions right (f) acknowledge your source.

12. Summary and review (a) are exactly the same (b) are exactly opposite (c) can be used interchangeably (d) both use summary, but review also comments on the material reviewed.

13. The comments in a review (a) must stick to the subject (b) can be anything that the writer wants them to be (c) should be removed (d) should be in quote marks (e) must be kept separate from the summary.

14. A carefully written review shows that the writer (a) is completely objective (b) understood what he has summarized (c) keeps his comments separated from the material he summarizes (d) understands how to summarize.

NOTES

NOTES

NOTES

NOTES

NOTES

NOTES